Why Do I Need a Teacher When I've Got Google?

Why Do I Need A Teacher When I've Got Google? is just one of the challenging, controversial and thought-provoking questions Ian Gilbert poses in his long-awaited follow-up to the classic *Essential Motivation in the Classroom*.

Questioning the unquestionable, this book will make you re-consider everything you thought you knew about teaching and learning, such as:

- Are you simply preparing the next generation of unemployed accountants?
- What do you do for the 'sweetcorn kids' who come out of the education system in pretty much the same state as when they went in?
- What's the real point of school?
- Exams – so whose bright idea was that?
- Why 'EQ' is fast becoming the new 'IQ'
- What will your school policy be on brain-enhancing technologies?

With his customary combination of hard-hitting truths, practical classroom ideas and irreverent sense of humour, Ian Gilbert takes the reader on a breathless rollercoaster ride through burning issues of the twenty-first century, considering everything from the threats facing the world and the challenge of the BRIC economies to the link between eugenics and the 11+.

As wide-ranging and exhaustively-researched as it is entertaining and accessible, this book is designed to challenge teachers and inform them – as well as encourage them – as they strive to design a twenty-first century learning experience that really does bring the best out of *all* young people. After all, the future of the world may just depend on it.

Ian Gilbert is an educational innovator, award-winning writer, entrepreneur and inspirational speaker, delivering training to schools and colleges in the UK and Europe for the 'Independent Thinking' organization, which he founded in 1994.

A breath of fresh air and hope for the future of learning!

Ian Gilbert exposes the impossible paradox of meeting the learning needs for the 21st century with the continuation of a factory-model paradigm of schooling from the 19th and 20th centuries. This divergent-thinking book is a must read for all who want real, sustainable and effective reform for learning for this century; it should be embedded in the syllabi of colleges of education and education graduate studies worldwide.

Dr Earle Warnica, Professor of Education at the
American University of Ras Al Khaimah, United Arab Emirates

This book is a stunner. Writing in an entertaining, page turning style, Ian Gilbert engages the reader with some powerful ideas about learning and teaching. He draws on a wealth of reading and research to support his arguments. From looking at the history of damaging notions of intelligence as narrow and fixed, he inspires us to consider the role of the teacher not as the fount of knowledge but as someone who helps children to learn. We can't do without inspirational teachers, even though we have Google.

Sara Bubb, Senior Lecturer at the Institute of Education, London

From economics, to climate change, to technology, [this book] explores the way the world shifts and questions whether the schooling world merely stands still. Spiced with examples to make adults think ... and to question their own experience and practice, it is sweetened with suggestions and techniques to bring out the flavour of true learning.

Above all the book achieves that trick of leaving a nagging doubt about the current world, whilst offering enough optimism to make it worth doing things differently.

Mick Waters, Professor of Education and
President of the Curriculum Foundation

This book does what it says on the tin: it won't make you teach better but it will help you be a better teacher. In his inimitable style, laced with humour and wisdom, Ian Gilbert makes neuroscience reachable, digestible and, above all, applicable to classroom practice. By a clever synthesis of the past, present and future, he proposes a new moral purpose for education – to play a central role in the creation of a society in which you would want your own grandchildren to live. It will become compulsory reading. I couldn't put it down.

Sir John Jones, Presenter, Writer and Educational Consultant

If there is one book recommended for all school staffs' reading lists this year, this has to be the one!

Dr Lesley P. Stagg,
Accreditation Officer for the Council of International Schools

Why Do I Need a Teacher When I've Got Google?

The essential guide to the big issues for every twenty-first century teacher

Ian Gilbert

Routledge
Taylor & Francis Group

LONDON AND NEW YORK

This edition published 2011
by Routledge
2 Park Square, Milton Park, Abingdon, Oxon OX14 4RN

Simultaneously published in the USA and Canada
by Routledge
270 Madison Avenue, New York, NY 10016

Routledge is an imprint of the Taylor & Francis Group, an informa business

Typeset in Galliard by
Taylor & Francis Books
Printed and bound in Great Britain by
TJ International Ltd, Padstow, Cornwall

British Library Cataloguing in Publication Data
A catalogue record for this book is available from the British Library

Library of Congress Cataloging in Publication Data
Gilbert, Ian, 1965–
Why do I need a teacher when I've got Google? : the essential guide
to the big issues for every 21st century teacher / Ian Gilbert.
    p. cm.
1. Teaching. 2. Education–Aims and objectives. 3. Current events. I.
Title.
    LB1025.3.G443 2011
    371.102–dc22
                            2010005917

ISBN 978-0-415-46831-2 (hbk)
ISBN 978-0-415-46833-6 (pbk)
ISBN 978-0-203-84608-7 (ebk)

To my parents – for being there through it all. Thank you.

Contents

Acknowledgements   ix
Independent Thinking Ltd   x
Preface   xi

Introduction   1

1 Save the world   3

2 The future's coming   9

3 The great educational lie   16

4 So, go on then, why do I need a teacher when I've got Google? 21

5 AQA v AQA   25

6 Your EQ will take you further than your IQ   31

7 Nothing is more dangerous than an idea when it's the only idea
   you've got   42

8 It's the brain, stupid   46

9 Neuromyths debunked!   50

10 Your hands in their brains   57

11 Talk to the hand coz the nucleus accumbens ain't listening 63

12 Is that an iron bar through your frontal lobes or are you just
    pleased to see me?   70

13 Don't make 'em mad, make 'em think?   75

14 Teacher's little helper   81

15 The 'f-word'   84

16 It might be touchy-feely but it's still the most important thing
    you do   91

17 What's the real point of school?   99

18 An accidental school system   103

19 Exams – so whose bright idea was that!?   112

20 Educated is not enough   117

21 Is yours a teaching school or a learning school?   120

22 Things that get in the way of the learning that are nothing to do
    with the teaching   127

23 What do you use when you don't know what to do?   134

24 A short word on thinking about thinking   143

25 Remember to succeed   148

26 How are you smart?   158

27 Muchos pocos hacen un mucho   164

28 Your classroom is not just an environment in which you can
    show how clever you are   168

29 Teach less, learn more   172

30 Enthusiasm and the sort of 7 per cent rule   181

31 Everyone remembers …   187

    Postface   194
    Notes   195
    Bibliography   205

Acknowledgements

To all of my friends and colleagues at Independent Thinking Ltd, especially Julie Tribe for keeping things afloat when I was elsewhere and Andrew Curran who knew when to call and what to say, to Alison and the team at Routledge for being so understanding, to everyone at Crown House for all their support, to all the wonderful teachers and school leaders, the children, advisors and governors I have met over the many years through Independent Thinking, to all the people who have taken even one of my ideas and used it to make a difference and, most importantly, to my children who have watched me walk out of the door so often to do this job, a big heartfelt thank you. Even if I could have done it without you all there would have been no point.

Independent Thinking Ltd

In 1994 I established Independent Thinking Ltd to 'enrich children's lives by changing the way they think – and so to change the world'.

This loose affiliation of practising educational mavericks and reactionaries has grown into one of the UK's most innovative and effective educational organizations, working across the UK with hundreds of thousands of teachers, children, parents and school leaders as well as in many countries across the world.

As a result, my life has been enriched by some quite extraordinary people – colleagues and now friends whom I am proud to have with me under the Independent Thinking banner. I freely draw on their inspiring work and understandings in this book, especially Dr Andrew Curran, paediatric neuroscientist and consultant at Alder Hey Children's Hospital in Liverpool.

For more information about Independent Thinking Ltd and the growing range of Associates, resources, courses and books we offer please go to www.independentthinking.co.uk.

Preface

The seven-lesson schoolteacher

These are the things you pay me to teach. Make of them what you will.

1. Confusion
2. Class Position
3. Indifference
4. Emotional Dependency
5. Intellectual Dependency
6. Provisional Self esteem
7. One Can't Hide.

(Gatto 1992)

Introduction

This book is not designed to help you teach better. But it is intended to help you become a better teacher.

It consists of a series of discrete chapters addressing what I consider to be some of the most important questions and controversies, insights and innovations in the world of education today. The sort of things that all teachers should know about but, for all sorts of reasons, so few do. You can read it cover to cover if you like or you can dip into it and learn about, reflect on, assimilate, experiment with or even reject what I am suggesting. It's not a series of 'cut out and do' exercises, rather it is designed to make you think. And then do.

Unlike my first book, *Essential Motivation in the Classroom*, I have tried to include wherever possible references and, appropriately, website links, for you to follow up what I am saying. Over the years I have adhered to what *QI* creators John Lloyd and John Mitchinson call their three rules of discovery,[1] 'Accept you know nothing; if it's worth writing down it's worth writing down clearly; embrace humour'. Unfortunately I sometimes failed with rule two. So, if I'm missing any references I apologize. But then, in the spirit of the book, you go and find them![2]

To make life easier and save your typing finger, I have also put up a page on the Independent Thinking website with all of the links on there. This way all you need to do is to 'click through' to get to the original source of what I am describing. Simply go to www.independentthinking. co.uk/googlebook.

What's more, deliberately controversially, I have used *Wikipedia* very often to source and verify information. After all, despite what many teachers claim, research by the journal *Nature* found that not only did *Wikipedia* stack up well in a direct head-to head analysis with *Encyclopaedia Britannica*,[3] but also that this latter, traditional source of knowledge, was not infallible when it came to erroneous 'facts'. If anything I subsequently quote here you know or find to be untrue, then you can not only let me know on ian@independentthinking.co.uk but you can also log onto *Wikipedia* and change it yourself immediately. You can't do that with the *Encyclopaedia Britannica*.

Like the brain science I so often draw on, especially the insights of Independent Thinking Associate and paediatric neurologist Dr Andrew Curran of Alder Hay Children's Hospital, none of what I am writing here is rocket science. Nor is it startlingly new in the big scheme of things. It is, like all creativity, a new combination, and I hope you will find plenty here to feed your professional desire to do what you do even better than before, combined with a sense of urgency that time is running out. If you are a good teacher then I'm not saying you're doing a bad job, but sometimes I am saying you are doing the *wrong* job, that the very nature of what traditional 'teaching' is all about may be antithetical to what is needed when it comes to twenty-first century learning. Every child that we let slip through our fingers is one child too many and every opportunity we miss to teach children to think and learn for themselves is one opportunity wasted.

The challenges facing the world are huge and the answers lie in your hands. A report from *The Economist*,[4] commenting on the PISA tests I come back to in chapter 31 points out that two of the most significant ways proven to raise educational standards are to devolve power to schools and to empower headteachers to be able to make decisions about spending and staffing. 'More important than either, though,' the article continues, 'are high-quality teachers.' In another article, this time in *Fortune* magazine[5] (and notice how interested in education the world of business and commerce is), it is pointed out we will be paid what we are worth in the new global economy. If anyone anywhere else can do the same job, for less, they'll get the work. The only way to compete, the article points out, 'is by getting an education that's world-class and *constantly improving*'. The italics are mine, by the way. The world needs you to be great at what you do. And then better. 'Satisfactory' is not good enough; 'outstanding' barely so.

I hope this book will help you be great, challenge you to be better, and inspire you to be the best you can be. I've done my bit. Now it's over to you. The future of the world could just depend on it.

Chapter 1

Save the world

The future of the world is in your hands. I know that might seem a bit steep considering you've got that year ten coursework to sort out and the lesson observation on that nervous looking NQT but that's the way it is I'm afraid. You chose to be a teacher, you mould young minds on a daily basis and those minds have got to grow up and save the world.

There's a line that keeps going round my head ever since I first came across it from Albert Einstein. It gets to the very heart of what education should be about, but what schooling sometimes isn't. He said:

> We can't solve the problems by using the same kind of thinking we used when we created them.

We'll play Doomsday Bingo in a minute to see how many of TEOTWAWKI (The End Of The World As We Know It) scenarios you can identify, but take a minute to reflect on Einstein's words. How much of what goes on in schools is the development of children's own thinking – 'education' – and how much of it is training them to think our thoughts – the 'schooling' that John Taylor Gatto refers to in the preface to this book? There's a case for both, but the argument against doing just the latter and at the expense of the former has gone from a low murmur amongst marginalized teachers, to a more powerful and concerted call to arms.

If the Einstein argument doesn't sway it for you then try another thinker, Darwin. He didn't use the term 'evolution' until the sixth edition of *On the Origin of Species*, although it had been around a while. The term he used was 'descent with modification' (Jones 1999). As the world changes, slowly and subtly over time, the living things in that world need to change, slowly and subtly over time, to survive. If they don't then, like the camels of North America, they die. It's the same for thinking. If children leave school only thinking our thoughts then not very much is going to change. If they learn to adapt their thinking and evolve the general body of what's thought, we've got a chance.

There are two notable James Martins that I know of in the UK today. In 2005, the one who isn't a chef endowed Oxford University with the James Martin 21st Century School, the goal of which is 'to formulate new concepts, policies and technologies that will make the future a better place to be'. James Martin is, among other things, a Pulitzer-prize nominee for his 1977 book *The Wired Society: A Challenge for Tomorrow*, and a technology guru who has been ranked fourth in the list of 'most influential people in technology today' world rankings. In his 2006 book, *The Meaning of the 21st Century*, he identifies 14 significant problems facing the world, problems from which there may be no turning back. So, without unnecessarily trivializing the end of the world, I would like to take this opportunity to challenge you to a quick game of Doomsday Bingo. You have a couple of minutes to try and come up with as many reasons that you can think of as to why humanity may be currently staring down the barrel of its own gun. See if you can hit Martin's total of 14 (in my experience most players don't manage more than five or six, tops). Off you go ...

OK, so how many did you get? If you had cataclysmic asteroid impact that doesn't count because we didn't cause that and there's not a great deal we can do to stop it anyway, Bruce Willis notwithstanding.

Here is Martin's list to compare with yours (and in case you choose to simply pooh-pooh the list like some of the teachers I have shown it to, I have backed up Martin's claims with some of the best research Google has got to offer):

1 Catastrophic global climate change

An easy one here, unless you are a member of the former Bush administration. Did you know, though, that Internet data centres are predicted to have a larger carbon footprint than aviation by 2020?[1] Or that a city like London has an eco-footprint 12 times its surface area? Or that China has plans to build 400 cities the size of Bristol over the next ten to twenty years?[2] And did you know that 0.2 per cent of the oceans' energy could satisfy the entire world's demand for electric power?[3]

2 Unstoppable pandemic of new infectious disease

We were worried about bird flu in Chinese swans but then we were caught out by swine flu in Mexican pigs. At the time of writing, they have just discovered two turkeys with the H1N1 virus in Chile.[4] So, birds with swine flu! As William Karesh, vice-president of the Wildlife Conservation Society, who studies the spread of animal diseases, told the BBC, 'The only constant is that the situation keeps changing'. So, watch this space and, in the meantime, carry on sneezing into your own armpit as per government instructions.

3 Destitute nations slipping into a deepening trap of extreme poverty

You live in one of the poorest nations in the world and it would appear you have two choices – sit on the beach in Harardere whilst your family starves or grab a high-speed inflatable boat and a whole arsenal of firearms and go get yourself a supertanker and a yearly revenue of $150 million.[5] You choose.

4 Unstoppable global migrations of people

The key word here is 'unstoppable'. We're not talking about an influx of plumbers from the former Soviet bloc. According to UNHCR, the UN's refugee agency, the number of uprooted people in June 2009 was standing at 42 million worldwide. And then there was the trouble in Sri Lanka, and the Swat Valley in Pakistan, and the floods in the Philippines, and the tsunami in the South Pacific Islands, and the earthquake in Indonesia … .

5 Weapons of mass destruction becoming inexpensive

These are real WMDs, not pretend ones.

6 Growth of shanty-cities with extreme violence and poverty

Where do I start? Take Brazil. A recent study found that 5,000 people aged between 12 and 18 are killed in Brazil's cities and towns each year, most of whom are poor and uneducated black males.[6] The forecast is that figure will stand at 33,000 by 2012. Or India. This is from a report by the Asian Development Bank party funded by the British government:

> With more than half the world's population projected to be living in urban centers by 2020, the dream of a better quality of life is being undermined by an increasing menace—urban violence. Surveys and poverty assessments show that urban violence has risen by 3%–5% per year over the last 20 years—and the degree of violence has intensified. This violence ranges from street crime, such as muggings, robberies, and carjackings; to kidnappings, murder, drug-related violence, and organized crime conducted by gangs; to assaults, sexual violence, and personal abuse. Asia experiences lower rates of violence than other regions. But

it is home to an explosive growth in urbanization, which brings a
threat of more violence.

(www.adb.org/Documents/Periodicals/ADB_Review/2003/
vol35_6/violence_poor.asp)

7   Mass recruitment for suicide terrorism

From the book, *The Making of a Terrorist: Recruitment, Training, and
Root Causes* by James J. F. Forest, a three-volume set with over 50 contributors
from around the world:

> While conventional wisdom prior to 9/11 would have many of us
> believe that terrorists and potential terrorist recruits reside in some
> remote location, today it is much better understood that recruitment for
> terrorism can take place anywhere, from big cities like London, Hamburg
> and New York to the picturesque town of Cour d'Alene, Idaho or the
> tranquil villages of Kamikushiki and Tomizawa, near Mount Fuji, Japan.
>
> (Forest 2005)

8   Nuclear/biological terrorism

This is 'Recommendation 1' from the *World at Risk: The Report of the
Commission on the Prevention of WMD Proliferation and Terrorism*, a
report submitted to George W Bush on 2 December 2008.

> The United States should undertake a series of mutually reinforcing
> domestic measures to prevent bioterrorism: (1) conduct a compre-
> hensive review of the domestic program to secure dangerous patho-
> gens, (2) develop a national strategy for advancing bioforensic
> capabilities, (3) tighten government oversight of high-containment
> laboratories, (4) promote a culture of security awareness in the life sciences
> community, and (5) enhance the nation's capabilities for rapid response to
> prevent biological attacks from inflicting mass casualties.
>
> (www.scribd.com/doc/8574914/World-at-Risk-The-Report-of-the-
> Commission-on-the-Prevention-of-WMD-Proliferation-and-
> Terrorism-Full-Report)

9   Religious war between Muslims and Christians

Only a few months before his controversial *Nobel Peace Price* win in
October 2009, President Obama was still being accused of planting seeds
of 'revenge and hatred' amongst Muslims, by Bin Laden.

10 Exposure from extreme science to new dangers

This from a 2001 online BBC report[7]: 'Earlier this year, scientists in Australia were working on a genetically-based contraceptive to control the country's mouse plague. But, in the process, they accidentally created an unusually deadly strain of mousepox, which is related to the human smallpox virus.' Oops!

11 Rivers and aquifers drying up

A report in *The Economist* in April 2009[8] stated that the Rio Grande, the Colorado and the Yellow River no longer reached the sea and that, with farmers using three-quarters of the world's water, we need to find an extra 60 per cent more to feed the predicted two billion extra mouths by 2030. Bear in mind that China has 15 per cent of the world's population but just 5 per cent of the world's water. A 1999 report from Earthwatch identified the depletion of aquifers as one of the main three reasons why the death rate was rising in sub-Saharan Africa and the Indian sub-continent (the others were HIV epidemics and shrinking cropland area per person). It went on to state that in India, 'water tables [are] falling annually over much of the country by between one and three metres'. And this in a country whose population will eclipse that of China in 2045. (In fact, by 2016, the United Nations predicts India will have a larger population than Europe (Russia included), Australia, New Zealand, Japan, Canada and the United States *combined*.) And in 2009, the controversial Venezuelan Hugo Chavez president exhorted his countrymen and women to spend less time in the shower each day. 'Some people stay in the shower singing for at least 30 minutes. Three minutes is more than enough,' rallied Mr Chavez. 'One minute to get wet, another to put the soap on and the third to take it off. Any more time than this is a waste.'[9] Of note is the fact that, according to a scientist on Radio 4's *In Business*, 'We have no technological limitation to purifying to the highest degree all of the world's oceans.'[10]

12 Mass famine in ill-organized countries

According to a report in *The Guardian* in 2007:

Some 40% of the world's agricultural land is seriously degraded. Among the worst affected regions are Central America, where 75% of land is infertile, Africa, where a fifth of soil is degraded, and Asia, where 11% is unsuitable for farming.
(www.guardian.co.uk/environment/2007/aug/31/climatechange.food)

13 Destruction of life in the oceans

Heard about the Great Pacific Garbage Patch?[11] It's a soup of non-degradable suspended particles of plastic waste spinning endlessly in the North Pacific Gyre. How much is there? Oh, about 100 million tons. How big is it? According to one estimate, 'maybe twice the size of the continental United States'. It will never go away … .

14 Possibility of world war with nuclear and biological weapons

Einstein again – 'I know not with what weapons World War III will be fought, but World War IV will be fought with sticks and stones.'

So, there you have it. Feel better now? Let's say you choose to reject all of them but one (and Martin's particular front-runner is number 10) it doesn't really matter. TEOTWAWKI is TEOTWAWKI and we only have one world.

The good news is every single one of these 'mega problems' as Martin calls them is solvable. Human beings are infinitely resourceful. We've been through all sorts of rubbish in the past and pulled through. The thing is, it's not you, me or James Martin who are going to solve the problems. After all, we created them. It's going to be the children whose coursework you were going to mark before you picked up this book; it's going to be that bottom set year seven maths group you so dread teaching on a Thursday afternoon; it could even be – and this is where the pressure really is on you and your colleagues – that girl you are just about to permanently exclude for not following the school rules. These are the people that James Martin refers to as the 'transition generation'. They are the ones who are going to get us out of this mess. But they can only do that if we, as teachers, equip them with what they need to achieve this. That's not just knowledge but the skills, attributes, passion and commitment to make a difference, all of which need to be combined with the ability to think, not our thoughts, but new ones of their own.

The Director of Stanford University's Ventures Program, Tina Seelig, teaches her students of entrepreneurship to approach such problems with relish. 'Every big problem is a big opportunity,' she says, adding, 'No-one will pay you to solve a non-problem.'[12] What, then, are you doing in your day-to-day job to ensure that you are equipping the future saviours of the world with what they need to complete that task successfully, bearing in mind that, as Einstein said, the mess isn't going to be sorted by using the same thinking that created the mess in the first place?

Chapter 2

The future's coming

Next time you get the chance, open up Google and type in 'Goldman Sachs Global Economic Paper No: 99'. Economics may be the 'dismal science' as Thomas Carlyle called it, but don't let this paper's unassuming title fool you. I'm not sure what was covered by the 98 papers preceding it or any they have published since, but this one paper caused a very big stir and coined a name that has become a 'household word' in business, shorthand for 'things are changing!'

The report from 2003 subtitled 'Dreaming with BRICs: The Path to 2050'[1] described how, based on the bank's research into trends and forecasts, the future lay not with the original G6 countries but with the burgeoning economies of Brazil, Russia, India and China – the BRICs economies. The Goldman Sachs predictions – and remember, economics isn't fortune telling – can be summed up as follows:

- China to be larger than everyone but the US by 2016
- India to be larger than Japan by 2032
- BRICs economies to be larger than the G6 by 2039
- China to be larger than the US by 2041.

In other words, the post-Imperial, post-World Wars model of who's in charge of the world is changing. It's changing fast and it's changing now, before our very eyes. If they were open.

Take India. When I was entering the job market towards the end of the 1980s, there was a great deal of pressure on us all to be Japanese. No business meeting was complete without some reference to 'kaizen' (interestingly, the supposed antidote to the Industrial Method – see chapter 17), 'kanban' or even 'gembutsu' on a good day. And where was India? Nowhere. But Japan was about to enter its 'lost decade' as economists call it and we see India, in the following decade and a half, taking over what was left of British Steel, buying out Jaguar-Land Rover, sending rockets around the moon and Calcutta-born businessman Lakshmi Mittal topping the *Sunday Times Rich List*[2] in 2009 (with a Russian at number two, interestingly) even though his net worth was down by more than 60 per cent, a 'loss' of an estimated £16.9 billion.[3] In the words of Peter Day on BBC Radio 4's *In Business*, 'India – a place where people come to see the future'.[4]

That's a far cry from being the call centre capital of the world. And anyway, in case you haven't noticed, that Indian call centre thing? That's so last year. As India moves quickly up the pecking order it is passing the call centre mantle to countries in Africa, as major international conferences like *Contact Centres World Africa*[5] in Johannesburg testify. And don't just put China down as a nation of manufacturers who can 'copy everything but your mother' as their saying goes. According to consultants Deloitte, China is 'emerging as the global centre of management innovation'.[6]

Or what about that point in India where business, technology and education converge? Take the story of Infosys, India's second(!) biggest software company, as reported in *Fortune* magazine. In 2005, it expanded its workforce by 15,000 or a rate of 40 people a day. Of the jobs that were on offer, 1.3 million people applied but only 1 per cent was hired. (By comparison, the magazine describes how Harvard in the US accepts 9 per cent of all its applicants.) In 2009, *Fortune* magazine listed Infosys among its top 100 fastest-growing companies.[7]

Talking of higher education, bear in mind, too, that in 2008 China turned out 6.1 million graduates, almost a six-fold increase on its 2000 figure.[8] By 2011, that figure is estimated to be 7.6 million. And in case you feel that maybe we're safe over here from such competition because of the language thing, bear in mind that, in the cities at least, Chinese children start learning English at reception age and can only be entered for a doctorate, *regardless of the subject*, if they are fluent. Not to mention the fact that the government has recruited more than 10,000 volunteers to spread the Chinese language across the world too. In the words of one Chinese official quoted in *Three Billion New Capitalists: The Great Shift of Wealth and Power to the East*, 'We've had a couple of hundred bad years but now we're back' (Prestowitz 2006).

I'm not sharing with you such facts to shake you up but to wake you up. You have to produce world-class people and you have to start now.

Another publication that had a similar effect to the BRICs report was a book by three-time Pulitzer Prize winning journalist, Thomas Friedman. There are countless management/business/popular economics-type books published every year, as a visit to any airport bookshop will prove, but somewhere between the cheese-moving, fish-throwing black swans, you will find a book that really did set the world talking. *The World is Flat* did just that.

Friedman realized that, whilst he had been reporting on strife in the Middle East as a journalist for several years, something fundamental had changed in the world. Somehow, because of a series of unconnected global events such as the fall of the Berlin Wall, advances in technology and the Silicon Valley bubble leading to massive investment in fibre-optic cables, the playing field had been levelled. Suddenly, whether you were a multinational company from Tokyo or a 14-year-old boy in New Delhi or a housewife in Nevada, you had access to the same flat space. The rules had changed and now everyone could play.

As Friedman says, 'When I was growing up, my parents used to tell me, "Finish your dinner. People in China and India are starving." I tell my daughters, "Finish your homework. People in India and China are starving for your job."' (Friedman 2005).

Another point Friedman puts across is the insight that some jobs are what he describes as 'fungible'. This is a term relating to commodities that, although different, are alike enough in nature as to be interchangeable. As far as the flat world is concerned, a fungible job is one that can be digitized and transferred anywhere else in the world. For example, why should I continue to pay my accountant, who's very good and very quali-fied and lives comfortably in the middle of England, £40 an hour when I can pay someone in China £4 an hour to do pretty much the same job, namely moving digits about on a spreadsheet? And even if I think to myself benevolently, well, he's a nice enough chap, I'll hang on to him, then I end up paying over the odds for a basic service. Which is not good business for me. And ultimately him.

With this scenario in mind, I worry that, with our focus in education on grades, the successful schools being the ones with, ergo, the top grades, what we are doing is preparing the next generation of unemployed accountants. They're very good, very qualified, but, hey, who needs 'em?

Some jobs, on the other hand, are 'anchored'. You have to be there to do them. Nursing is a good example. To be a nurse you may have to apply a dressing to a wound which means you have to be physically present to do it. But in terms of analysing, diagnosing, prescribing, all that is 'fungi-ble' and can be digitized and sent to the best 'wound expert' in, say Sin-gapore, who can then tell the nurse what to do. The nurse's job, then, is OK. The doctor's job is up for grabs. What's more, in the UK we are facing a shortage of nurses and, according to one report, have 3,200 consultants too many.[9]

Friedman cites, as an example of the sorts of competition his daughters – and your students – will face, the 'Zippies', as originally depicted in Indian magazine *Outlook*. Zippies are the first generation of commercially global Indian citizens and are described in the magazine as:

A young city or suburban resident, between 15 and 25 years of age, with a zip in the stride. Belongs to generation Z. Can be male or female, studying or working. Oozes attitude, ambition and aspiration. Cool, confident and creative. Seeks challenges, loves risks and shuns fears.

The new flat world means the young people in your classrooms are about to come across Zippies and others like them head-to-head as they compete for the jobs and opportunities that are out there. How will they fare? Friedman quotes Bill Gates when he says, 'We are going to tap into the energy and talent of five times as many people as we did before.' That's great if you are an employer. A global pool of talent five times bigger than anything we have ever had before. But if you are an employee, that's five times the competition. Your children are going into direct competition with the best of the best of the rest of the world. And remember, they are not 'entitled' to the jobs and opportunities that are out there. Nor are you and I. We have to merit them. Indeed, as Friedman points out elsewhere:

The entitlement we need to get rid of is our sense of entitlement.[10]

Notice the Zippie attributes that are described there (as opposed to the qualifications). Ambitious, aspirational, confident, creative, risk taking, brave. Find out who your enterprise coordinator is at school and show them the list and they won't be surprised. We are very much in the realm of entrepreneurship here, (something someone once described as 'Jumping off a cliff and building an aeroplane on the way down'). Chris Lewis, author of the study on successful entrepreneurs entitled *The Unemployables*, suggests that the following is what is needed to succeed in business:

- Positivity
- Bravery
- Determination
- Self belief
- Creativity
- Sheer energy.

(Lewis 1994)

To what extent do you deliberately build the development of such attributes into your lessons? I first came across Lewis's work in a magazine article several years ago entitled *Unqualified Success*. It was highlighting six wealthy and successful entrepreneurs who, between them, had just three O-levels. Actually only one of them had all three, David Crossland who created *Airtours*. The rest of them, people like publisher Felix Dennis and John Madejski of football stadium fame, had none. Elsewhere Madejski has said, 'Education is important, but if you're a lateral thinker and have common sense, there's no reason why you shouldn't get on.'[11] With the OECD[12] in 2008 identifying that only 45 per cent of our children who leave schools without five A–Cs at the age of 16 are in employment a year later, maybe that is all the more reason to ensure our children develop such attributes. If they leave without the qualifications to get them a job, we sure as hell need to make sure they leave school with something that will. I don't think it is a coincidence that 20 per cent of UK entrepreneurs and 35 per cent in the US are dyslexic, compared with just 1 per cent across general managers.[13] But, in our tail-wags-the-dog, upside-down, if you can't measure it can't be important, educational world, developing these attributes can be easily overlooked because, as Lewis points out:

These are difficult skills to set exams for.

Or are they? Innovations such as the RSA's Competency Curriculum[14] and the focus on PLTS[15] – Personal, Learning and Thinking Skills – may not be everybody's cup of tea, especially if you are a teacher who is focused on teaching subjects rather than children, but they are a long-overdue and much-needed acceptance of the fact that your personal skills and qualities – your attitude – will take you further than your qualifications, and neither is as good as both together. After all, qualified *with* attitude is an unstoppable, but often rare, combination. (Or as one executive head-hunter contributing to Radio 4's *In Business* once said, 'People with great skills but no attitude are nerds not leaders'.)

In a world where the big organizations are being challenged on equal *terms* by small upstarts working out of garages, bedrooms and college dormitories, are we doing enough in the UK to encourage entrepreneurship? And at the sort of scale we are seeing in India and China? Again, a view from *The Economist*:

The opening up of China and India is releasing millions of new entrepreneurs onto the world market. Many of them have already shown themselves able not just to translate Western ideas into local idioms but also to drive technological advance of their own. The world has only just begun to feel their effects.

(*The Economist*, 12/03/09)

The BRICs economies research was published before all the recent economic unpleasantness, but there is a strong argument that all that mess actually serves the BRICs well, especially if China gets back the US$776.4 billion America owes it.[16] Indeed, these four countries held their own summit in 2009 and, according to *The Economist*, they are 'recovering fast and starting to think the recession may mark another milestone in a worldwide shift of economic power away from the West'. After years of being at the top table, maybe, just maybe, things are starting to change with, ironically, the greedy Western practices that brought about the latest recession being the seeds of a longer-term undoing:

> Almost 60% of all the increase in world output that occurred in 2000–2008 happened in developing countries, half of it took place in the BRICs alone.
>
> (*The Economist*, 20/06/09)

So, what does all this mean for you as a teacher and that set three science class whose lesson you should be preparing? It means that the children you are (1) teaching science and (2) preparing to make their way in the world are going into direct competition with amazing, wonderful, highly motivated, highly skilled, technologically savvy people from anywhere in the world, and if you don't equip them to be world class people who else will? Furthermore, if you fail, the country fails because if the money goes elsewhere, who's going to pay your salary? In his 1994 book the *Tom Peters Seminar*, one of the world's leading business gurus made the claim that, in the brain-based economy, 'education is economics and economics is education' (Peters 1994).

Now, this is the point where you tell me about your targets and the pressures on you from your school leaders, from the local authority, from the Department, from the government to get kids through the exam hoop and I agree with you. There is a tremendous amount of pressure on you. But the government has got hold of the wrong end of the stick and should be prodded with it. More more-qualified people does not a thriving economy make. Unemployed accountants will receive the same Jobseeker's Allowance as an unemployed car worker. A qualified population where everyone has been to something calling itself a university and everyone is 'above average' (the target for schools it seems) makes for good statistics and is certainly better than the reverse. But it guarantees nothing. Why? Because qualifications alone aren't enough, as we will see in the next chapter on 'The Great Educational Lie'. Your job isn't to school your children. Your job is to educate them. Friedman says, 'Being adaptable in a flat world, knowing how to "learn how to learn" will be one of the most important assets any worker can have.' To what extent are you contributing to this? There are many who have passed through our teacher hands who are schooled but uneducated and very many more who are neither. And neither option is enough for us to go into battle in the twenty-first century with the rest of the world.

At the foot of the BRICs report, its authors pose one question, 'Are you ready?'

Well, are you?

Chapter 3

'The Great Educational Lie'

In a conference room in London in 2004 the great American business guru Tom Peters addressed 500 of the UK's top business leaders, the future employers of your students (people like Woolworths, MFI, Northern Rock, Whittards, Principles, you know the sort ...). But I don't think they listened. One of his messages was this one:

> Never hire the people with exceptionally high grades at university and secondary school.
>
> (*Tom Peters, Live in London*, Red Audio)

His argument revolves around a basic syllogism that I develop further in chapter 7:

> To do well at school means you play by the rules.
> To succeed in business you need to break the rules.

Ergo

> If all your employees did well in school, your business is doomed.

Tom Peters's message is reassuring for me as it resonated with what I had been trying to get across to the educational world for a long time, something I call 'The Great Educational Lie'.

We tell our children, 'Do well at school and you'll get a good job', but there's a twist in the logic there that just doesn't hold water. I have met too many young people who simply expect to be 'given' a good job just because they've done well at school. We've all met people who are qualified but haven't a clue. 'Big hat, no cattle', as they say. And then when they fail that first job interview they are devastated. 'How could this happen, I did everything I was told to do and I'm a straight A student?!'

What's more, just because you *get* a good job doesn't mean you get to *keep* the good job, especially if you're not up to scratch. We've, also, all met people who are as qualified as they are incompetent. When was the last time you heard the personnel department discussing a dubious employee and reassuring themselves, 'She's costing the company thousands but you should see her key stage two SAT results'?

Of course, having great qualifications can open up many great jobs in the same way that having no qualifications can lead to a life of poverty and underachievement. But there is not a direct causal link, at least not in the West. There are people with great qualifications and no jobs, or lousy jobs, and there are many, many examples of people with no qualifications and great jobs. In other words, qualifications alone are not the maker or breaker of careers. We're back to attitude and a whole range of other skills like emotional intelligence, communication and creativity.

And if you decide you would rather not take the word of some American business guru, then how about this from David Frost, the head of the *British Chamber of Commerce* speaking in August 2007:

> Employers want someone who does the job and if necessary they will train them to do a particular task and give them one to one training ... Qualifications actually come pretty low down the agenda.

Yet, in schools, we still perpetuate 'The Great Educational Lie' – do well at school and you'll get a good job.

Remember, nobody is saying here don't bother getting qualified. There's a great line from Bill Gates I share with young people, 'Get the best education you can and keep on learning' and that's relevant whether you're 7, 17, 27 or 57. Another thing I do is get them to write the word 'learning' on their paper and then ask them to put their finger over the 'l'. 'What have you got?' I ask them. ('Ning!' came back the reply once. Pesky kids with mittens ... .)

An article in *The Economist* in 2006 entitled 'The Battle for Talent' stated that, 'The bottom line is you can buy almost ten Indian brains for the price of one American one'[1] and this is something supported by a story in *Fortune* magazine that same year. The biggest threat from outsourcing wasn't to factory workers but 'those college-educated desk workers' who were looking 'more outsourceable by the day'. After all, as the article points out, you can't outsource truck driving. In 2004, graduate earnings had dipped by 5.2 per cent whereas the pay packets of high school graduates had risen by 1.6 per cent. Again, the article wasn't encouraging people not to get an education, but it was a shot across the bows of those perpetrating 'The Great Educational Lie':

> Higher education still confers an enormous economic advantage. Just
> not as enormous as it used to be!
>
> (*Fortune*, 20/3/06)

Several years ago I interviewed James Dyson and posed the following
question to him. You have two students in front of you about to leave
school – one has stacks of qualifications, all A grades, and the other, Mr
Dyson, has none. (Interestingly in schools we talk about young people
who leave the education system 'with nothing', when what we mean is
they leave with 'no qualifications'. If you have over a decade of failure in
the same system, you don't leave with nothing do you? Have a think
about what is in the 'emotional suitcase' if you will of the children who
leave our care with no qualifications. I suggest that what they leave with is
no qualifications and a whole crate full of baggage about how bad they
are. Which isn't 'nothing'. 'Nothing' would be us in education, who
oversaw that decade, getting off lightly.) Anyway, Mr Dyson, what would
be your response? To the students with the grades he said he would say,
'You've shown you've got a brain, now go away and use it.' In other
words, you've shown there's something there, now the work really starts.

Before I tell you what he said he would say to those with no qualifications
let us look at another, more hidden, more pernicious conclusion to be
drawn if we choose to promote 'The Great Educational Lie'. If you can
only get a good job by doing well at school then, because I haven't done
well at school, it is clear that I will *never* have a good job. How many
people leave your school at the age of 16, about to set off on life's path,
less than a quarter into their one chance on this planet, but already feel
they are doomed to a life of failure, lack and subservience? How many
people have you met who see themselves as thick or stupid or incapable of
achieving anything of any worth because 'I didn't do very well at school'?
What is your message to the young people, the 'sweetcorn kids', who have
gone through the entire system and come out pretty much in the same
state as when they went in? Serves you right? You should have listened? I
can't help you now! Or maybe you can tell them what Mr Dyson would
tell them if he were there: 'It doesn't matter.'

Now, again, before you throw out your dual cyclone, he's not advocating
widespread academic failure. The James Dyson Foundation website[2]
encourages people to apply to them for jobs 'if you are a graduate'. But
he's also a realist and a pragmatist who knows, from his own experience at
school apart from anything else, that school is a narrow little academic
tunnel and there is a far bigger picture out there once you get out of
school if only you can hang onto your self-worth and your sense of ambition
as you go through it.

School, in other words, is just a phase you're going through.

Just before Christmas 2007, I was approached by the then exciting and vibrant QCA to explore the issue of 'Commitment to Learning', looking at motivation towards and perceptions of learning in key stage three children around the country. Through a wide range of media from online surveys to face-to-face *WIIFM?Cam* (What's In It For Me?) interviews in a number of schools around the UK we identified three major factors that seemed to contribute to poor motivation, disengagement and disaffection in the year eight students, one of which related directly to this idea of 'The Great Educational Lie':

> Our research showed that students felt that education was important for their futures (nearly 70% according to the online questionnaire) but what this meant was that learning 'stuff' was important if you needed that same 'stuff' in whichever job you were going to do when you were older: 'You need to do well in Food Tech if you're going to be a chef'. (With the corollary 'If I don't want to be a chef I can just mess around in Food Tech'.)
>
> (Gilbert 2008)

Another girl on one of our filmed interviews pointed out that she didn't need geography because 'I'm not going to be a, er, geography person'.[3]

In other words, by propagating 'The Great Educational Lie' and by doing so in an environment, such as school, where knowledge is demarked by department area boundaries, we have made a rod for own backs when it comes to trying to motivate children to learn a subject for which they can't see the point. (And I was a French teacher in Northampton so I know about these things. 'Why do we have to learn French, Mr Gilbert?' to which you give the set reply, 'Because you live in Northampton. And you never know ... !')

What's more, research on students with low self-esteem shows that they suffer most when they perceive there to be a big gap between how important they know schoolwork to be and how bad at it they feel they are. In the book *Social Motivation: Understanding Children's School Adjustment*, the authors point out that:

> One can reduce such a discrepancy by either increasing one's competence or by discounting the importance of the domain.
>
> (Juvonen and Wentze 1996)

In other words, students will simply claim that a particular subject is unimportant if they are under the impression, misguided or otherwise, that its mastery is beyond them.

What did we recommend to QCA as a result of our findings in the classroom?

> Grasping the opportunity to move away from the hegemony of content to a focus on skills and competences will contribute to increased commitment to learning if done well. 'Whatever the *subject* I'm in, I'm developing skills and attitudes that will help me get a better job. Therefore, all lessons are important' would be an important shift.

We're not advocating content-free lessons. The key will be to learn the content in a way that also develops the skills, attitudes and competences, something that the traditional chalk and talk lesson can't do.

In *Time* magazine in 2006, Bill Gates said, 'We don't just pick employees for the brains, but for their energy.'[4] Are you helping children develop the sort of energy that Bill Gates is referring to? And what, exactly, is your job? To teach history? Or to teach children history? Or is it to allow children to develop the skills and all-important attitude they will need to succeed as adults as *well as* pass their exams with flying colours?

Chapter 4

So, go on then, why do I need a teacher when I've got Google?

In the good old days, knowledge was fixed. It was there, written up in big books and it didn't really change very much. Various scholars over the years tried to record all human knowledge; and it was kept locked up in libraries and passed down through the ages, being translated as it went. Take the ninth century *Bait al-Hikma* or *House of Wisdom* to be found in Baghdad which, at that time, was the richest, most civilized city on the planet. Here scholars from around the world worked together across many disciplines from philosophy to mathematics, zoology to astrology, translating the works of the Ancients, especially the Persians and, ultimately, the Greeks. This they combined with their own thinking to produce, amongst other things, the book *Kitab al-Jabr* from which we derive the word, algebra (Lyons 2009).

But, like the great library of Alexandria around a thousand years before it, knowledge is power and the destruction of someone else's knowledge proves you are more powerful than they are. When the Mongols invaded Baghdad in 1258, it was said, depending on which source you read, the Tigris either ran red with the blood of the murdered scholars or black with ink from the books thrown into the river.

Fast forward to the early roots of the current education system and you find that the teacher's job is to take the fixed body of knowledge and pass it on. (The word 'teach' comes from the old Gothic word meaning 'token',[1] although 'teacher' didn't emerge until around 1300 to denote the person teaching. Before it meant 'index finger'. And while we're in etymological mode, I find it curious to note that the word 'pedagogue' used to relate to the slave who escorted Roman children to school.[2])

The teachers were the educated ones, who had been to university, and whose job it was to drip feed the knowledge back into the community for whom the teacher was pretty much the only source of such knowledge.

But then two interesting and related things happened to knowledge. Like an egg in a microwave, it exploded and went everywhere.

What's the most populous country on earth? Currently, as we have seen, China with 1,338,612,968 citizens.[3] But let me rephrase the question. What is the most populous *community* on earth? The answer, by a virtual mile, is the Internet with, as of 2009, 1,668,870,408 citizens.[4] That's a growth of over 360 per cent in less than a decade and means nearly a quarter of the world's population is online now. As you might expect, Africa scores lowest on the penetration rate with just 6.7 per cent of its population part of the Internet population, although, that said, it's still a growth of nearly 1,360 per cent on the figures at the turn of the twenty-first century. Interestingly, the highest growth over that time is in the Middle East, returning nearly 1,650 per cent growth in Internet users (Arabic recently knocking Russia out of the Net's top ten most widely used languages).[5]

And which region is top in terms of sheer weight of numbers of users? Asia, with over 700 million users.

Governmental censorship notwithstanding, any one of those users can share knowledge with the other 1,668,870,407 at any time and instantly. And as the knowledge changes, as it surely will, the Internet and its community will update it instantly. Google 'fellow' Amit Singhal recently said, 'Information is being created at a pace I have never seen before and in this environment, seconds matter.'[6] As an example, it is said that the sequencing of the HIV genome took 15 years. The sequencing of the SARS virus genome took 31 days. According to the UK government's *Digital Britain* report,[7] 494 exabytes were sent around the word on 15 June 2006. That's 494,000,000,000,000,000,000 bytes and bear in mind that one exabyte[8] is the equivalent of 50,000 years of DVD quality video. In 2008, 210 billion emails were sent and, although 78 per cent of them were spam, that's still a great deal of information moving about the world at practically instant speeds. In fact, it has been said that even if all but 1 per cent of what's on the web is rubbish, the scale of the thing is such that it would still take you more than a lifetime to read it. Compare that with the *Encyclopaedia Britannica*, first published between 1768 and 1771 (note how long it took to publish three volumes), and whose size:

> has remained roughly constant over the past 70 years, with about 40 million words on half a million topics.
>
>   (http://en.wikipedia.org/wiki/Encyclopædia_Britannica)

How do I know this? Wikipedia, in a scholarly and properly researched entry, where the source of this fact is attributed, if you follow the link to footnote seven, to the 15th edition of the *New Encyclopaedia Britannica*. Whatever your views on the academic merits or otherwise of Wikipedia, it stands as a shining example of the democratization of knowledge. 'To give every single person free access to the sum of all human knowledge', is Wikipedia's founder Jimmy Wales's mission for it, yet it does more than that. It allows you to contribute to it. It gives your knowledge a voice. It releases the inner expert. You know about something. You can add your voice and share that knowledge with anyone anywhere and instantly, regardless of who you are. As the saying goes, 'On the Internet, no-one knows you're a dog.' In the early days of Wikipedia, I met a geography teacher who was getting his class to contribute to the entry on their hometown. When one of the facts was challenged by the Wiki moderators and thrown out there was uproar until they were able to convince the Wikipedia people of the validity of their claim. Can you imagine anything like that happening even ten years ago?

In fact, such are the ramifications of the Wiki way (the word 'wiki', by the way, coming from the Hawaiian language and meaning 'quick') that in January 2009 the head of *Encyclopaedia Britannica* announced plans for accepting additions and edits from the general public on their online version of the encyclopaedia.

But let me take you back to Africa where a growing but still statistically small number of the population is linked into the World Wide Web. But let's look this time, not at PCs, but at mobile phones. According to a 2009 report from the International Telecommunications Union, an agency of the United Nations, more than half the people on the planet pay to use a mobile phone, with the biggest growth in new subscriptions being in Africa. On this continent, whereas only 4 per cent used mobile phones in 2002, by 2007 the number had risen to 28 per cent.[9] The phones are not solely for chatting on either. One of the most popular applications for mobile phones is the safe transfer of money across very risky countries by 'uploading' the cash before you leave and then 'downloading' it when you arrive. In fact, the term 'mobile phone' is already as much of an anachronistic misnomer as 'carphone' or 'Saturday night TV entertainment'.

And what are mobile phones doing, as any self-respecting 15-year-old will tell you? Merging with computers into 'smartphones' that do practically all that a PC can do as well as take pictures and slip into your pocket when the deputy is spotted coming down the corridor. In fact, your new 'personal digital device' such as the iPhone is not always a phone at all. 'It can be a spirit level, a bowling ball, a budget balancer or a breathalyser. The device in your pocket is not a phone any more. It is anything you want it to be', according to *New Scientist* in 2009. The article also describes how, 'In 10–15 years, app-enabled phones will be the number one channel through which we receive information.'[10] What are the implications of that in your classroom and in your school? For years, teachers have been the primary source of information in the classroom, backed up by textbooks that have been jealously guarded and kept locked in a cupboard or guarded by Conan the Librarian. But now, within a few years, the primary source will be a piece of technology children put in their pockets.

So, all the knowledge in the world instantly searchable, updated daily and linking over half the people on the planet in one giant and user-friendly network, accessible from my bedroom, on the bus, in the field, up a mountain or at sea, from a 'sexy' device I can slip in my pocket. Google isn't simply a way of accessing information; it is, in Richard Branson's words, 'an invention of change'.

So, you tell me. Why do I need a teacher when I've got Google?

The answer to that question depends, to be brutally frank, on how good a teacher you are.

The role of the twenty-first century teacher, I am suggesting, is to help young people know where to find the knowledge, to know what to do with it when they get it, to know 'good' knowledge from 'bad' knowledge, to know how to use it, to apply it, to synthesize it, to be creative with it, to add to it even, to know which bits to use and when and how to use them and to know how to remember key parts of it. Add to that your powerful role in helping them develop their communication skills, their creativity, their curiosity, their ability to work well as a team, their confidence and self-esteem, their sense of what is wrong and what is right, their ability to deal with adversity, their understanding of their role as a citizen of the world – in other words all the things computers can't do yet – then you have a powerful role for the twenty-first century teacher.

If the end of the twentieth century saw the democratisation of knowledge, then the role of the twenty-first century teacher is quite simple – to preside over the democratisation of learning.

That's why I need a teacher when I've got Google and Wikipedia and O2 and an iPhone and an iPad ... .

Chapter 5

AQA v AQA

Stepping outside a conference centre in the north of England a little while ago I was struck by one of life's little ironies and it made me smile.

I was walking past the offices, according to a large sign in the car park, of AQA, the Assessment and Qualifications Alliance.[1] This organization is the largest of the UK's three exam boards, responsible for nearly half of all GCSEs and A-levels in the country. That's 3.5 million exams.

As we shall see in chapter 19, the written exam industry as we know it grew out of Oxford and Cambridge universities in the nineteenth century and quite an industry it has grown into. AQA, for example, although a not-for-profit charity, has an annual turnover of £130 million. American company ETS,[2] who were sacked in 2008 for making a bigger farce of the key stage three SATS than they were anyway, waved goodbye to a five-year contract worth £156 million.

But there exists another, more twenty-first century, AQA too – Any Questions Answered.[3]

Text any question you like to 63336 (not 6336 as that, as you may have seen if you spend any time on the UK's motorways, is a catering company, 6336 spelling 'food' if you dial it on a phone with letters and numbers). Within minutes, you will receive an answer. All for £1. Unless they can't answer it, in which case it's free.

The sexy, quirky and useful for more than just pub quizzes (where it is banned) AQA was established in 2002 in the UK and, since then, has answered 20 million questions posed by over two million customers. It boasts that its overriding mission is 'The end of the question mark.'

So, how does it work? (Incidentally this is its number one most frequently asked question, being posed a total of 47,189 times so far. The meaning of life – 31,350 times – and the chicken and egg conundrum – 24,543 times – are second and third, respectively.[4]) It has hundreds of 'employees' in the UK and abroad who log on when they want to and are sent questions to answer. This they do by drawing on the Internet, their own knowledge or from any other source they can come up with, including AQA's own database of answers with 20 million – and counting – responses in it. And they do it with speed, accuracy and a humour that gives the service a very human face.[5]

So, on the one hand you have the AQA of the old world – we'll measure how clever you are by seeing how much information you can cram into your head and regurgitate in an hour or so in an exam hall with millions of other children on exactly the same day and then forget it all the following day – and on the other the twenty-first century AQA – the knowledge will cost you just £1 and then we'll see how clever you are *by what you do with it*. And furthermore, *you* have to come up with what it is you want to know. After all, finding the right answer is easy. Finding the right question can be the hard part.

A few years ago, we were approached by a school in the West Country to see if we knew of any software that students could go and use when their teacher was away for the day and that would help them develop their independent learning and thinking skills. The school had had enough of paying for supply teachers who were satisfactory babysitters at best or, as was more often the case, whose presence disrupted education across the whole school and actually did more damage than good. Such a complaint was a familiar one, echoed the country over by teachers, school leaders, the teaching unions and even the students themselves who could only stomach a certain number of games of 'Make the supply teacher cry' before they started to actually yearn for some real education. When we looked into it we found something we felt was quite mind blowing. It was that England and Wales spend over £800 million a year on supply teachers.[6] Yes, that's right. That much. In fact, the last year we have the figures for, 2005–6, the not so much grand as shockingly awful total stood at £886,783,000![7] No wonder the school was looking for a better way of spending the resources it had, not to mention reducing its budget deficit in the process.

What we came up with, in the end, was a bit of software that was a content-free, teacher-less learning programme we called the *Learning Bug*. When the teacher was going to be away, rather than a school ringing around their lists of local supply teachers and hoping that the one good one wasn't going to the beach that day, the teacher simply tells the *Bug* what the overall topic is going to be. In other words, planning for your cover lesson could be as simple as just typing the word 'Evolution' into the system. Or 'Venice'. Or, if you're feeling ambitious, '21st Century Education'. That's it. And what was at the heart of it? Not rocket science, although the actual software program itself is pretty cool, but simply a process by which we get students to ask each other questions.[8]

With the democratisation of knowledge, where what you need to know is just a few mouse clicks or finger swipes away, the democratisation of learning involves access to the technology. The door to the portals of knowledge, like AQA (the modern one) or Google or Wikipedia or You-Tube or the BBC website or wherever the knowledge needed at that precise moment may reside, needs to be open for all students. But in all but a handful of the many schools I visit each year, computers are locked down; websites are blocked; YouTube is blocked; messaging sites such as Bebo and MSN are blocked; Facebook is sometimes allowed because it has a pseudo-academic feel to it and the teachers are on it anyway; Wikipedia is frowned upon; mobile phones are banned; iPods and other MP3 devices are banned; wifi-enabled PSPs, DS Lites and other 'gaming' devices are banned; interactive whiteboards are jealously guarded by the adult in the room; and students are expected to equip themselves for the digital era with a pen, some paper and a pass to the library.

But there are some schools where every thing you ban is allowed. And the sun still comes up in the morning and goes down at night. And children are learning.

According to Will Wright, the man behind the hugely successful *Sims* series of computer games, gaming is science for children:

> Just watch a kid with a new videogame. The last thing they do is read the manual. Instead, they pick up the controller and start bashing the buttons to see what happens. This isn't a random process; it's the essence of the scientific method … It's a rapid cycle of hypothesis, experiment and analysis. And it's a fundamentally different take on problem-solving than the linear, read-the-manual first approach of their parents.
>
> (*Wired*, 04/2006)

Furthermore, using technology has been shown to improve cognitive ability, with some commentators suggesting that it is children's use of technology that has contributed to the Flynn Effect,[9] the puzzling global rise in IQ scores over the last few decades that I mention in chapter 10.[10] 'Any technology we use will change the brain', according to a fascinating article in *Fortune* magazine where they go on to state that:

> regular computer gamers have improved visual attention and can take in more information. They are better able to pay attention to things that are further apart or more rapidly changing and can switch attention more quickly. Even short-term play produces immediate improvements.
>
> (*Fortune*, 21/04/07)

There is even evidence that the best predictor of a surgeon's skill is not how many years' training they have had or how many procedures they have carried out but how good they are at video games. What, then, are you doing to use the technology your students *already have* to improve their chances of success at school?

I mentioned in the previous chapter how mobile phones, computers and other examples of technology were merging – 'convergence' it is called by those who name these things. Do you know what the next big thing technology will merge with is? You.

The inventor of the Moog synthesizer, among other things, is a genius called Ray Kurzweil. He is the one suggesting that, 'Merging with our technology is the next stage in our evolution'[11] – a process called 'transhumanism'[12] – and that the date of this 'singularity'[13] will be 2045. This he calculates through his understanding of the exponential nature of things. He suggests that information technology power is doubling every year. 'Doubling every year is multiplying by 1000 in ten years,' he points out.

One London prep school told me recently, and only half-jokingly, that the twenty-first century 'was something we are thinking about adopting'. But what about when schools can no longer resist the onset of the twenty-first century without becoming anachronisms themselves? By the time you have overcome an institutional reluctance to dabble with interactive white boards – research from the Institute of Education in 2007 declared that, 'Statistical analysis showed no impact on pupil performance in the first year in which departments were fully equipped', due to what they called the lack of certainty about the best application of the technology to enhance pupil learning in specific subject areas'[14] – and primary schools have decided that an acceptable mobile phone usage policy should be on the next leadership team meeting agenda, by which time the first child with a clip-on brain enhancing device shows up in school for her maths SAT. Science fiction? Not according to Andy Clark from Edinburgh University in another *New Scientist* article entitled 'Will Designers Brains Divide Humanity?' 'It won't be long before clip-on computer aids become available for everybody',[15] he says. Maybe your stance will be to simply un-clip the clip-on device. What will you do, then, with 'IQ chips' embedded in children's brains by well-meaning middle-class parents who see it as a better investment than extra tuition and summer camp? More science fiction? This from James Martin whom we met in Chapter 1:

> In the 21st century, what invention will have the most effect on changing the future? I suspect it may be the creation of wireless links that connect our brains directly to external electronics, including global networks. This may be done with large numbers of nano-transponders in the brain fluid.

He goes on to point out that 'the first direct links between our nervous system and computers have already been made' and elsewhere someone has coined the phrase, 'the outboard brain' to describe how we can tap directly into technology to support what our brain can or cannot do.

As a former teacher of French, I was impressed. I had read about a simultaneous language translation device that, rather than being a fish you put in your ear, was a series of sensors attached around your mouth and throat that worked out the sounds you were making as you talked (we use around 45 in the English language), turned those sounds into your language and then translated that language into the foreign tongue.[16] It was just a prototype that I was reading about and it was 'only' 62 per cent effective at the moment, but still … ! There goes my guaranteed job that I thought I had as a trained languages teacher.

Then I read about the necklace that you wear around your neck and that you synchronize with your thoughts. Whether we speak a word or simply *think* about speaking a word, there is very little difference to our brain. So by loading up the vocabulary into this 'sub-vocal speech recognition'[17] device and synchronizing it with our thoughts, it isn't long before we can get the machine to say the word just by thinking it. One suggested application is that it will allow you to answer your phone and reply without saying a word.

It has been said that the future hot technologies are 'nano – bio – info – cogno'. Advances in any one of these can have huge implications for schools, let alone just one. What about then, something such as *Ritalin*?[18] Apart from being used to help people with Attention-Deficit Hyperactivity Disorder (ADHD), the drug also has short-term memory-enhancing benefits. On top of the four million people in the US who have been prescribed the drug, it is estimated that there are one million illegal users of it, who rely on it to boost their brainpower for things like exams or critical business meetings. In fact, more than 1.6 million people in America had used prescription stimulants[19] for non-medical purposes in the previous 12 months according to US government data in 2007. As the practice of taking 'brain enhancing pharmaceuticals' moves into the mainstream, what will be your school's 'bioethical' standpoint?

And what about sorting out poor behaviour once and for all? According to Arthur Caplan, professor of bioethics at the University of Pennsylvania, 'To the extent that we are born with impulses for aggressiveness, racism and selfishness or limits on our own capacity for wisdom and compassion, we may be morally obliged to modify human nature.'[20] What will your school policy be on accepting children who have been genetically modified to behave better and achieve more highly?

The irony of the distance between my two AQAs is just the start, unless the old world moves to keep up with the new world. In the words of writer Pete McCarthy, 'It's important to have a plan B, especially when there's no plan A'.

By the way, as part of my research for this book, I went onto the website of AQA (the 'old' AQA) and emailed them to ask for their mission statement. I also asked AQA, the modern one, the question, 'Why do I need a teacher when I've got Google?' This, about three minutes later at 11.00 one night, was their reply:

> Teachers express things in a way Google can't. They can make dull subjects seem interesting whereas Google just supplies facts, not all of them correct.

I still haven't heard from the other AQA.

Chapter 6

Your EQ will take you further than your IQ

At the turn of the last century a self-taught Parisian psychologist named Alfred Binet and his colleague Theodore (or Henri, depending on which source you read) Simon were working with children in the Paris school system at the request of the French government. Their purpose was:

> to be able to measure the intellectual capacity of a child who is brought to us in order to know whether he is normal or retarded.
>
> (Binet 1905)

Their major task was to try and work out which of the children who were faring poorly in the French school system could be saved and which ones were, educationally-speaking, beyond hope. This latter group, according to Binet, included the 'unstable', 'moral imbeciles', the 'insane' – including all those with 'decaying sanity' (that is to say less intelligence now than when they started, a group that included 'many epileptics') 'degenerates' and 'idiots'.

Interestingly he is at pains to point out the need for 'great delicacy' when deciding between children who are 'unstable' and those who simply have 'rebellious dispositions'. After all, the symptoms – 'turbulent, vicious, rebellious to all discipline; they lack sequence of ideas, and probably power of attention' – are the same. As he points out in his paper, *New Methods for the Diagnosis of the Intellectual Level of Subnormals*:

> We have insisted upon the necessity of instructors not treating as unstable ... those children whose character is not sympathetic with their own.
>
> (Binet 1905)

The Binet–Simon test they devised involved taking a sample of children whom their teachers had identified as 'average' and then comparing a target child against children of the same age. Any difference of more than two years was deemed to be 'subnormal' and meant the child was in need of remedial help. The process by which the children were assessed consisted of 'medical', 'pedagogical' and 'psychological' methods, the latter of which included 30 different tests of increasing complexity. This third element was not designed to create a measure of intelligence because intelligence 'cannot be measured as linear surfaces are measured' but rather 'a measuring scale of intelligence', comparing children of similar age, a scale 'to determine to what degrees of the scale idiocy, imbecility, and moronity correspond'. I list the 30 tests below not just for historical interest but also to underline the extent to which intelligence testing today, and with it our own view of what clever is, are so influenced by this century-old work:

1 'Le Regard', i.e. 'to follow with his eyes a moving object'
2 Prehension provoked by a tactile stimulus
3 Prehension provoked by a visual perception
4 Recognition of food
5 Quest of food complicated by a slight mechanical difficulty
6 Execution of simple commands and imitation of simple gestures
7 Verbal knowledge of objects
8 Verbal knowledge of pictures
9 Naming of designated objects
10 Immediate comparison of two lines of unequal lengths
11 Repetition of three figures
12 Comparison of two weights
13 Suggestibility
14 Verbal definition of known objects
15 Repetition of sentences of 15 words
16 Comparison of known objects from memory
17 Exercise of memory on pictures
18 Drawing a design from memory
19 Immediate repetition of figure
20 Resemblances of several known objects given from memory
21 Comparison of length
22 Five weights to be placed in order
23 Gap in weights
24 Exercise upon rhymes
25 Verbal gaps to be filled
26 Synthesis of three words in one sentence
27 Reply to an abstract question
28 Reversal of the hands of a clock
29 Paper cutting
30 Definitions of abstract terms.

I particularly like Binet's written instructions for administering number 24. Once it has been pointed out that examples of rhyme are the way in which 'compote' rhymes with 'carotte' and 'baton' rhymes with both 'macaron' and 'citron', children should then be asked:

> Do you now understand what a rhyme is? Very well, you must find all the rhymes you can. The word with which you must find rhymes is 'obéissance'. Come, begin, find some.

(Binet 1905)

Perhaps it was the child who passed the test who asked the examiner why he got all the easy ones.

For our purposes it is well worth listing in full what the Frenchman knew about his work, his methods and the nature of intelligence as a whole according to the Indiana University School of Education's website *Human Intelligence*, citing a 1992 article by R. S. Siegler entitled *The Other Alfred Binet*. What's more, the following is especially ironic given what became of his work when it was adopted and adapted in the US and beyond in the years after his death:

> Binet was upfront about the limitations of his scale. He stressed the remarkable diversity of intelligence and the subsequent need to study it using qualitative as opposed to quantitative measures. Binet also stressed that intellectual development progressed at variable rates, could be impacted by the environment and was therefore not based solely on genetics, was malleable rather than fixed, and could only be used on children with comparable backgrounds.

(Siegler 1992)

In other words, and I am repeating this to make sure I have understood what Binet meant as it makes me furious just typing this, *over 100 years ago* we knew that intelligence testing is limited; there is more than one way to be intelligent; we need to look at the *qualities* of intelligence, not the *quantities*; we develop at different rates even though we have the same birthdays; the environment into which we are born and in which we live will have an effect on how intelligent we end up; intelligence is not determined at – or before – birth; it is not fixed; people can become more intelligent and, if you are going to compare children, at least compare like with like.

Anthropologist Stanley Grant once said, 'If the aborigine drafted an IQ test, all of Western civilisation would presumably flunk it.' If we knew all of the limitations of such intelligence testing in 1905, how did we end up following the shaky concept of IQ down the blind alley that it is?

Eugenics plays a part. In 1910, Binet's test was translated into English by the American eugenicist Henry Goddard who wanted a way of filtering out the 'feeble-minded' from American society. Like the Englishman and cousin to Charles Darwin, Sir Francis Galton, before him, he believed that intelligence, and related defects therein, was hereditary and therefore breeding was at the heart of any attempt to raise a nation's overall intelligence. For Galton this entailed mating the clever people together, namely the well-off and well-educated. For Goddard the key was to stop the stupid people breeding and if, regrettably, forcible sterilization was not palatable to the American people the least they could do was to put them in 'colonies'. Don't worry though as, according to Goddard, 'segregation and colonization is not by any means as hopeless a plan as it may seem to those who look only at the immediate increase in the tax rate.' He claimed that such a capital investment would be more than recompensed by the savings in almshouses, prisons, psychiatric hospitals and 'the reduction in the annual loss in property and life due to these irresponsible people'.

In Great Britain in 1907, The Eugenics Education Society was created to spearhead a campaign to have eugenicist views more widely accepted and, as quoted in *The Making of Intelligence* by Ken Richardson (1999), a book I would make compulsory for all teachers, even the *Encyclopaedia Britannica* waded in, with one contributor asserting as fact that, 'It is cruel to the individual, it serves no social purpose, to drag a man of only moderate intellectual power from the hand-working to the brain-working group.' According to Richardson, the campaign led in no small way to the hugely influential 1938 *Spens Report – The Report of the Consultative Committee on Secondary Education with Special Reference to Grammar Schools and Technical High Schools* – in which it was stated:

> Intellectual development during childhood appears to progress as if it were governed by a single central factor, usually known as 'general intelligence', which may be broadly described as innate all-round intellectual ability. It appears to enter into everything which the child attempts to think, or say, or do, and seems on the whole to be the most important factor in determining his work in the classroom. Our psychological witnesses assured us that it can be measured approximately by means of intelligence tests.
>
> (The Spens Report 1938)

The report goes on to declare, 'We were informed that, with few exceptions, it is possible at a very early age to predict with some degree of accuracy the ultimate level of a child's intellectual powers' before concluding that, given the evidence, 'Different children from the age of 11, if justice is to be done to their varying capacities, require types of education varying in certain important respects'.

The principal 'psychological witness' to which the report refers is the controversial English educational psychologist Cyril Burt, whose later research has been equally controversially discredited. Burt was a member of the British Eugenics Society[1] (as the Eugenics Education Society had become in 1926) and was the author of a 1909 paper which, according to Wikipedia at least, concluded that 'upper-class children in private preparatory schools did better in the tests than those in the ordinary elementary schools, and that the difference was innate'. In his 1963 report 'Is intelligence distributed normally?' on the subject of the normal curve of distribution of intelligence, he stated that:

> Subsequent work in genetics has since furnished strong theoretical grounds for believing that innate mental abilities are not distributed in exact conformity with the normal curve. So far as they are inborn, individual differences in general intelligence are apparently due to a large number of genes of varying influence.

> (Burt 1963)

Compare that with this more scientifically enlightened quote from a twenty-first century professor Robert Winston:

> The kind of child you have depends almost entirely on how you bring it up. Genes and inherited dispositions are pieces of trivia really.

To say that we can measure people at a given time, before their brain has fully matured, and determine how clever or stupid they are, or ever will be, is like determining how good a driver a person is before they have had a lesson. Yes, I understand that not everyone will become a great driver and some will be better than others. What's more, some will learn quickly and others will not pass a test until their fifth attempt. That said, all will be better than when they started. A few years ago I started to learn to sail (partly to fulfil an ambition and partly, after spending so much of my life on the UK's motorways doing this job, to give myself the chance of dying romantically and not on the M62). Learning so many new facts and skills was something I found quite an immense challenge but, on seeing what was going on at sea and in marinas around the country, I consoled myself with the fact that that if stupid people could learn to sail then so could I. As Binet was trying to prove, intelligence is malleable – if we teach children to be cleverer then they will be cleverer. Isn't that the point of education in the first place? What's more, Binet was adamant that his tests were not tests of potential but a way of taking snapshots of an individual's mental faculties *at the time of the tests*. As he declared in *New Methods for the Diagnosis of the Intellectual Level of Subnormals*, his aim was to assess simply whether the child was 'normal or retarded' and that was all:

> We should therefore, study his condition at the time and that only. We have nothing to do either with his past history or with his future. ... We shall limit ourselves to ascertaining the truth in regard to his present mental state.
>
> (Binet 1905)

The eugenics-influenced Spens Report is a very interesting, wide-ranging and thorough overview of the state of education and children's development that had far-reaching implications, the reverberations of which are still sounding throughout the UK today. For example, one of its recommendations was what became the '11+':

> We believe that the examination is capable of selecting in a high proportion of cases those pupils who quite certainly have so much intelligence and intelligence of such a character that without doubt they ought to receive a secondary education of the grammar school type, and also those pupils who quite certainly would not benefit from such an education.
>
> (The Spens Report 1938)

So, as a result of the works and influence of people like Galton and Goddard, we ended up with the 11+ and secondary moderns, a selective two-tier school system and a lot of people with chips on their shoulders who feel they were made to feel like failures at the age of 11. However, it could have been worse. In his 1913 publication, *The Kallikak Family: A Study in the Heredity of Feeble-Mindedness*, in the chapter entitled 'What is to be done' you can discern a certain frustration in Goddard's tone when he writes:

> For the low-grade idiot, the loathsome unfortunate that may be seen in our institutions, some have proposed the lethal chamber. But humanity is steadily tending away from the possibility of that method, and there is no probability that it will ever be practiced.
>
> (Goddard 1913)

Twenty years after the publication of Goddard's work, the *Law for the Prevention of Hereditarily Diseased Offspring* was passed in Nazi Germany;[2]

400,000 people were subsequently sterilized against their will and a further 275,000 killed under Hitler's personal 'T4' programme in which, in Hitler's own words:

> Patients considered incurable according to the best available human judgment of their state of health, can be granted a mercy death.

In 1916, a psychologist (and another eugenicist) from Stanford University named Lewis Terman, adapted Binet's original process and concepts, adding further elements to the test and creating what became known as the Stanford–Binet test, essentially the 'IQ Test' we have today. Building on the success of this test, in 1921, he set about a remarkable longitudinal study entitled *Genetic Studies of Genius*, a project that is still running.[3] In it he identified 1,470 children who had high IQs – and therefore, obviously, great potential – who he then tracked, tested and analysed for the rest of his life, starting a project that will continue until the last one either pulls out or dies. These people became known as his 'Termites'. What did Terman learn? According to Malcolm Gladwell in his enlightening, if a little repetitive book, *Outliers*, Terman wrote in the fourth volume of the study:

> We have seen that intellect and achievement are far from perfectly correlated.
>
> (Gladwell 2008)

Terman's Termites went on to have good lives, but not extraordinary ones. There were a few who ended up as judges or politicians and they earned good salaries on the whole but, as Gladwell points out, 'not *that* good'. But then, the group were predominantly white, middle and upper-class Californians born between 1900 and 1925, whose parents were often Terman's university staff colleagues, none of whom came from 'private, parochial (religious) or Chinese schools' as one later report pointed out (Holahan and Sears 1995). With that sort of background, it would be hard for them not to do quite well.

What is of huge ironic interest to the anti-eugenicists is the fact that none of the children whose 'genius' was predicted by the IQ testing went on to win a Nobel Prize. However, *not one but two* children who Terman's IQ filtering process eliminated did. Louis Alvarez[4] won the Nobel Prize for Physics in 1968, but is best known as the man behind the 'impact theory' of dinosaur extinction. William Shockley,[5] whose work paved the way for Silicon Valley (not to mention whose report to the US War Department paved the way for the use of the atom bombs on

Nagasaki and Hiroshima), was a joint recipient of the Nobel Prize for Physics in 1956. In a double irony, Shockley himself was a particularly controversial eugenicist in later life with views on sterilization, race and the heritability of intelligence that made him very unpopular in many quarters. He was also a high profile donor to the Repository for Germinal Choice – the 'Nobel Prize sperm bank'.[6]

In 1974, a smaller-scale but similar study to Terman's was begun on 70 children in the UK, trying to identify why certain children were labelled as gifted and others not. Although still ongoing, a 2006 report states that:

> a gifted childhood has not always delivered outstanding adult success. Better predictive factors were hard work, emotional support and a positive, open, personal outlook.
>
> (Freeman 2006)

In other words, what we often take for 'genius', as Gladwell joyously points out, supported by the report above, is more often than not cleverness backed up by an awful lot of hard work. Yes, there is a certain amount of heredity involved in how intelligent you are, but nothing that good parenting and a good education (as opposed to a mediocre or damaging schooling) can't influence significantly.

Just how much hard work is needed has also been the subject of much research, and the findings come down to a remarkably precise and consistent number, one that seems to be true no matter what the field in which you aspire to excel – 10,000 hours. Research by Anders Ericsson[7] at Florida State University, quoted by Gladwell but pre-empted two years earlier by Daniel Levitin in his book *This Is Your Brain On Music* shows that:

> In study after study, of composers, basketball players, fiction writers, ice skaters, concert pianists, chess players, master criminals ... this number comes up time and time again.
>
> (Levitin 2006)

You want to have a chance of turning an innate talent into genius – practice for three hours a day, twenty hours a week for ten years. So that's nature, nurture and now a number.

There is, according to Ericsson, one other factor at play here. 'Practice doesn't make perfect', as they say. 'Perfect practice makes perfect'. And what separates one from the other? You do. According to Ericsson, the formula for genius is '1 per cent inspiration, 70 per cent perspiration and 29 per cent good instruction'.

But very few people are in the position where simply being very good at something puts bread on the table. Unless they are a baker. We are sociable creatures who, like ants, bees and celebrities, need others in order to live. Your IQ may contribute to who you are; your EQ (Emotional Quotient) will determine how far you go.

If there are any teachers out there who haven't yet read Daniel Goleman's (1995) paradigm-shifting, first book *Emotional Intelligence* then put this one down and go and get it. (Or, in the spirit of this book, don't put this one down, just log onto Amazon and order it. Or go onto iTunes and download it. It can be playing to you in just a few minutes. Or plug your Kindle in and download it. Or go onto YouTube. Or go to www.ted.com/talks/daniel_goleman_on_compassion.html and watch him talking at a TED conference. Anyway, you get the idea ... .)

The basic premise is, in a nutshell, your 'softer skills' such as dealing with yourself and others at an emotional level, are far more valid in today's world than IQ alone. There has been a phrase doing the rounds in the world of business for a while which is the 'death of competition'. Although the economic crisis nearly pushed companies – and countries – backwards again towards pulling up the figurative drawbridges on collaboration, most seem to have hung onto the fact that we will achieve more by working together. Certainly, in my own company we don't 'do' competition. All the people who work under the Independent Thinking umbrella are, or could be, direct competitors of mine personally, but it makes far more sense to work together. (With some healthy internal market forces at play to keep everyone moving forward and improving their game. It's not a communist collective!) Better this way, than all of us ploughing our own lonely furrows. We share ideas, we give ideas away, we meet as a whole group once a year up in the hills somewhere, we share platforms, we do 'tag' presentations, we are a collection of unconnected individuals who actually work together very well, as if shifting molecular state from gas to water to solid depending on what's needed. In their powerful book *Funky Business* (1999), the world's best-known bald Scandinavian business professors, Jonas Ridderstråle and Kjell Nordström describe the nature of teams in the new world of business. Rather than locking people into working together for long periods of time until an employee is fired, made redundant, leaves or dies, they suggest organizations will work more like Hollywood production companies where the very best team will come together for however long it takes to make a particular film and then disband with a different, but equally good, unit coalescing around a new project a few weeks or months later.

These ways of working demand a level of sociability, personal motivation and self-confidence that working with the same team year in year out does not. In other words, regardless of how good a technician you may be in your chosen field, there are certain demands on you where success is down to your EQ. You would have to be very, *very* good to succeed and be a complete plonker when it comes to working together quickly and effectively as a team.

In a 2006 *Fortune* article entitled 'Teamwork is an Individual Skill' the magazine suggests that, 'Becoming skilled at doing more with others may be the single most important thing you can do.'[8] Are you teaching, then, this most important of skills – the ability to work well in a team? And it *is* a skill and as such *can* be taught. The article quotes Stanford sociologist Elizabeth Cohen who explains that if children are simply told to get themselves into teams then one child will often dominate. However, if the teacher sets out roles, goals and responsibilities, 'not only will [the children] behave according to the new norms, but they will enforce rules on other group members'.

Schools are, at one level at least, tremendously sociable places. Children are practically never alone and usually working with dozens of other children on the same piece of work or task at the same time. You have to exhibit a certain amount of team-working prowess when there are 1,500 of you all in the same building and all wearing the same uniform. And right from when we start school we exhort children to share – share the paints, share the toys, share the book, share the Bunsen burner, share the basketball, share the computer … . Yet there is a cruel irony in the fact that we force children to interact, but then measure them as individuals. They spend all their school careers made to share but when it comes to their exams, all that grinds to a halt and we say, 'Right, you're on your own now. And in silence!'

While schools are sociable, schooling is a very solitary process, where you can have the highest levels of emotional intelligence and team-working skills and still fail or, conversely, succeed yet have all the social skills of the academic hall of fame board your name is etched on. In fact, this says something about the nature of schooling itself. Independent Thinking's 'tame' paediatric neurologist (and I use the term 'tame' loosely), Dr Andrew Curran, quotes research he has come across that showed how 75 per cent of teachers, 85 per cent of GPs and 95 per cent of managing directors scored highly along the autistic spectrum. They have the IQ skills needed to perform well in school – high boredom threshold, ability to fixate on a single task for extended periods, good organizational skills and no real social life to speak of – which means they can revise for and sit exams. But when it comes to human interactions, some, not all, can be particularly lacking. The teacher who can't look young people in the eye and teaches subjects, not children; the doctor who looks at his screen rather than look his patient in the eye and treats symptoms, not people; the managing director who looks someone straight in the eye and says with relish, 'You're fired!'

In one of Malcolm Gladwell's previous books, *Blink*, he describes research on GPs in the US who were, or were not, sued for malpractice (Gladwell 2005). What the research showed was that the decision on whether or not to sue the doctor depended on the extent to which the patient liked them. 'People just don't sue doctors they like', according to a lawyer quoted by the author. In other words, their EQ saved them from where the GP-related IQ had let them down. This, and other such research, prompted Dr Curran and Independent Thinking to put a programme together for medical undergraduates which is in its third year, taking the trainee GPs through an EQ-training programme that runs parallel to their traditional medical training. We called it HiOP to see if anyone would ask what it stood for. Only one or two have. (Hell is Other People. After Sartre. But before Big Brother.)

We all know doctors whose 'bedside manner' is exemplary, teachers whose ability to get on well with people changes lives for the better and bosses you just love to work for. So, we know combining EQ with IQ can be done. And it can also be taught. What, then, are you doing at your school to develop EQ in your children and your colleagues? What are you doing to be the embodiment of an emotionally intelligent adult? Some of your children may never have seen an emotionally intelligent adult. They've seen grown-ups but that's not necessarily the same thing at all.

Remember the UK research I mentioned above on gifted and talented students? This is how it closes:

> After innumerable hours of interaction and investigation with the individuals in this sample as they grew to adulthood, I had to conclude that many influences on happiness and success are like love – it is possible to say how it feels and what happens because of it, but there is no sure recipe to apply to others. For the rest we do have very clear information about what the gifted and talented need by way of support towards self-fulfilment – an education to suit their potential, opportunities to flourish and people who believe in them.

Amen to that.

Chapter 7

Nothing is more dangerous than an idea when it's the only idea you've got

Teacher: What did the Vikings come in, children?

Class: Longboats, Miss!

Teacher: No, no, now come on, we did this last time, remember ...

Class: Er, ships, narrowboats, er, don't know, Miss!

Teacher: Oh come on, we did this! They came in 'hoards', class. What did they come in?

Class: 'Hoards', Miss ...

This, as told by comedian Mark Steel in one of his 'lectures' for the Open University and the BBC,[1] is a great example of the 'guess what's in the teacher's head' game we so often play with children, encouraged to do so by the nature of the schooling system. As we prepare them for the right or wrong 'zero sum game' of the exam system, we drill them in our class-rooms, almost without being aware of it, in getting the 'one right answer', that is to say the one answer we are thinking of to the question we have asked. I know there are many teachers out there who don't work that way, but I've been in too many classrooms in all sorts of schools to ignore the fact that it happens and has a pernicious effect on children's creativity and, linked to that, their self-esteem.

The game is a quick and easy way of playing the bigger game of school, quickly sorting out those who 'know' from those who 'don't know' and efficiently ending up with winners and losers and a set of scores in a mark book. It is a game that is replicated in most game shows, quiz shows and crossword puzzles across the world. But can we really say that the *Brain of Britain* is just that? Or should it be called *Memory of Britain*? Along with

Mastermemory? Who Has the Memory to be a Millionaire? At least *Deal or No Deal* makes no obfuscatory claims about the nature of its vacuousness.

But, as the title of this chapter points out, nothing is more dangerous than an idea when it's the only idea we've got. If all we are skilled in and duly rewarded for is the one right answer then we seriously narrow down our creativity and significantly reduce the opportunity we have to use the tremendous power of the human brain to take amazing cognitive leaps sideways in many different directions at the same time.

American psychologist J.P. Guilford[2] worked in the US military during the Second World War, looking at ways of assessing intelligence in the air force, in particular why so many trainees were not graduating. He identified eight specific cognitive abilities that were needed to successfully fly a plane and later went on to identify 180 different factors at play in determining how 'clever' someone is. These ranged across three 'dimensions' he called 'operations', 'content' and 'product'. 'Operations' related to aspects such as memory and evaluation. 'Content' related to aspects such as visual or auditory inputs or semantic understanding. 'Product' related to units such as single items of knowledge or relations. So, your ability to recall visual memory about things as a police officer might do is a different sort of intelligence from your ability to, say, evaluate the implications of group behaviour as a psychologist might have to. It was Guilford's work that really brought out the idea of 'convergent' and 'divergent' thinking, linking the latter with greater creative ability.

Consider, then, the following list (that I have just made up as I typed it):

Hamster
Radio
Caravan

Convergent thinking would ask the question, obviously, 'Which is the odd one out?' Equally obviously, the answer would be 'Caravan' because no one wants the owners of radios or hamsters shot.

Divergent thinking would ask the question 'Why each one is the odd one out?', with a bonus ball for anyone who can both explain why none of them is and why all of them are? And, if you really want to stretch their brains even further you could ask them what the fourth item in the sequence would be and why?

They are using the same three items you could also ask children why your, let's say, geography lesson is like a hamster or a radio or a caravan; what profession would use all three; what you would get if you combined all three; why all three should be legal tender in Norfolk; and how would the world change either for the better or for worse if all three were banned (and not just the obvious one)?

I could go on, but then I am a divergent thinker. And thought is 'Infinite in all directions', to use a phrase from the theoretical physicist Freeman Dyson.

Guilford wasn't saying one is better than the other. He gave each equal footing depending on the task the one doing the thinking was supposed to pull off, which is what you would hope for a pilot. My challenge to you, the teacher of the twenty-first century, is, are you giving equal footing to them too? Do you favour the reassurance of the right or wrong answer to the giddy flurry of a class of 12-year-olds in full divergent swing?

I have already mentioned 'The Great Educational Lie', one of two big aspects of my own schooling I didn't pick up on until after I left full-time education. The other relates to what I later identified as the secret of my success at school which was, in a well-behaved nutshell, 'Wait to be told what to do and do it well'. Don't think for yourself. No independent thinking. Just sit there and be a good boy and you'll go far. And, in the world of education, I did. Top grades and a top university, the stupid man's Oxford. But it suddenly dawned on me, and I have been struggling with this all my working life, that the secret of my success at school, as a strategy, will get in the way of my achieving what I'm capable of achieving beyond school. Because while I'm sitting there waiting to be told what to do, others are out there doing it. A lot of them a lot less qualified than I am. The German philosopher Emmanuel Kant[3] wrote about what he called 'nonage', something he defined as our 'inability to use one's own understanding without another's guidance', before adding the challenge:

> Dare to know! (Sapere aude.) 'Have the courage to use your own understanding,' is therefore the motto of the enlightenment.

This is something I feel very strongly about, how my success in education came not as a result of having the strengths of my convictions but knowing how to express the strength of the convictions of others and do it well. Like Marco Pierre White, the great chef, when he said, 'It started to dawn on me that I had spent my whole career being judged by people who had less knowledge than me' (White 2006). But it is the single-minded people who often achieve so much more than the broad-minded ones.

What's more, learning how and when to break the rules might just save your life. Research by engineers in the aftermath of the 9/11 bombings showed that nearly 2,500 people saved themselves by ignoring fire marshal instructions, using the lifts in the early stages of the alert and not staying put when they were told to.[4] Interestingly, this wasn't out of belligerence or panic, it was because, in our new connected world, their use of technology meant they knew more than the authorities did.

The 'guess my thought and I'll throw you a fish' approach to teaching and learning has got to change if we want confident creative thinkers capable of both convergent *and* divergent thinking according to what each individual situation merits. And part of that thinking skill set needs to be the ability to confidently and without malice throw out an old idea and come up with a new one. 'Every act of creation starts with an act of destruction,' said Picasso. 'What might you have to go away and break', I say to teachers in the sessions that I run, 'in order to move things forward in the 21st century for the children in your school?' After all, in the words of advertising guru, David Ogilvy, 'The cracked ones let in the light.'

But I bet you, like me, got where you are by the same secret of success that I used – be a good boy or girl and do what you're told. So, going away and breaking things goes against every bone in our bodies. I was in a Northern town with a chip problem a while back and was talking to an LA advisor about the nature of the presentation I was about to give to a group of teachers. She liked some of the ideas but could see they could be quite challenging to some of the staff in what was a conservative Catholic (as opposed to Conservative catholic) secondary school. 'Oh yes, the revolution starts here!' I joked with her. 'I'd get into trouble for starting a revolution,' she replied in all seriousness.

Often we feel in Independent Thinking that our job isn't so much teaching teachers anything new as it is simply giving them permission to do the thing they would like to do but were scared to in case they got into trouble. But how can we have children who are happy with diverging away from the concrete world of right answers if we're not modelling to them how to take risks, try new solutions and innovate?[5]

If we are going to learn anything from Einstein and his assertion that 'We can't solve the problems by using the same thinking we used when we created them', then the more you are comfortable with rollercoaster divergent thinking and, better still, the more you can actively develop it in your classroom, the better our chances of survival. Yes, you have to teach them the hoop-jumping skills to get them through exams (less so maybe in areas like Humanities and English where there does seem to be more scope for divergent thinking) but don't let the hoop take over. In doing so, ensure you are genuinely preparing them for the task ahead of them where the only way of doing something (oil, cars, baths, beef, coal, holidays abroad, cotton, newspapers, mobile phones, air conditioning, chips, stocks and shares, having two or more children, living in villages, central heating, wooden furniture …) may be the thing that finishes us all off.

Chapter 8

It's the brain, stupid

President Clinton, the last time he was elected, famously put a sign on his fridge door (or on his election headquarters depending on what you read[1]). It was designed to remind him what he had to focus on in order to win. Along with 'Change v more of the same' and 'Don't forget health-care' it said, 'The economy stupid'.[2] The slogan became something of a catchphrase appearing on bumper stickers and fridge magnets and in newspaper columns ever since. For the fridge door in your staffroom I would like to suggest something similar, however this one says:

It's the brain, stupid!

Everything that takes place in your classroom from the achievements of your favourite student to the misbehaviour of your bottom set nemesis to the apathy or otherwise of the ones in the middle, is down to some form of electro-chemical combustion taking place between ears – yours and theirs. The more you know about that process, the more you can make sure you are doing the right thing to influence it for the better.

If you were a doctor or a nurse, the general public would expect you to keep up to date with medical research, breakthroughs and innovations in your area. Surely, it should be the same for teachers. You have the same moral, professional and ethical obligations to keep up to date with learning science – so much of which relates to brain science – as the medical profession has. And yes, I know teaching isn't about life and death. It's more important than that.

Two years before Bill Clinton was sticking slogans on his fridge door, his rival in that 1992 election was making the following declaration:

To enhance public awareness of the benefits to be derived from brain research, the Congress, by House Joint Resolution 174, has designated the decade beginning January 1, 1990, as the 'Decade of the Brain' and has authorized and requested the President to issue a proclamation in observance of this occasion.

Now, therefore, I, George Bush, President of the United States of America, do hereby proclaim the decade beginning January 1, 1990, as the Decade of the Brain. I call upon all public officials and the people of the United States to observe that decade with appropriate programs, ceremonies, and activities.

(Presidential Proclamation 6158)

As I pointed out in my foreword to Dr Andrew Curran's book for the Independent Thinking Series, *The Little Book of Big Stuff About the Brain*, this was how George Bush Snr opened the Decade of the Brain and this was how George Bush Jnr opened the 2007 APEC Summit: 'Mr. Prime Minister. Thank you for being such a fine host for the OPEC summit'.

The 1990s saw a tremendous surge in our understanding of the human brain with various claims such as '90% of what we know about the brain we've learned in the last ten years or so' and, even though we've come a long way from sticking ice picks through our eye sockets as a cure for schizophrenia (effective in some but not all cases (El-Hai 2005)), we still know so little in the big scale of things. And even what we do know can change as new discoveries outdate older assertions. (For more on this have a look at the next chapter where the OECD and I debunk a few neuromyths.)

But can we apply what we now know in a classroom setting? That is one of the most relevant questions of twenty-first century education and one that was vexing the minds of various experts from around the world at the Decade of the Mind[3] Symposium[4] held in Berlin in September 2009. There is even a Transfer Centre for Neuroscience and Learning[5] whose mission is to take the proper academic research about the brain – not the pop science stuff – and apply it in a proper academic way in classrooms – not in a pop-sciencey way. Again, to use the medical analogy, medicine moves forward by active research conducted by all medical professionals, from the nurses to the professors, in a work setting where constant improvements are sought, collected and distributed. It should be like this in education too.

As told to the *New Scientist* by Manfred Spitzer from the University of Ulm in Germany:

In medicine, we have an excellent system in place to go from basic research to clinical practice, while in neuroscience we have the basic understanding of how the brain learns but still need to figure out how to translate this into the classroom.

(Same Sex, Different Rules, *New Scientist*, 29/04/06)

According to the article, one of the big things to come from the symposium is that you can improve how well children learn by improving the child's 'executive function'. This, although the exact definition varies between the experts, is the way they approach the things they are approaching at a neurological level. According to Sheldon H. Horowitz, Ed.D, director of professional services at the National Center for Learning Disabilities (NCLD),

> Executive functioning involves activating, orchestrating, monitoring, evaluating, and adapting different strategies to accomplish different tasks. ... It requires the ability to analyze situations, plan and take action, focus and maintain attention, and adjust actions as needed to get the job done.
> (www.greatschools.net/LD/identifying/executive-function-lens-to-view-your-child.gs?content=1017)

To what extent, then, are you helping your struggling learners to do better by improving their executive functioning? Are you helping them with organizational and planning skills? Are you helping them learn how to focus, pace themselves, manage their time and resist distraction? Do you teach them how to respond when they feel themselves becoming frustrated?

And to what extent are you tapping into other insights about the human brain to help your students be the best they can be? For example, do you 'differentiate by gender'? And by that I don't mean have single sex lessons; after all, recent research found that one in ten women have male-type brains and one in five men have female-type brains.[6] According to the previously mentioned article entitled, 'Same Sex, Different Rules' in the *New Scientist*:

> Men and woman differ from each other, statistically at least, in cognitive traits such as visuospatial skills, navigational strategies, verbal fluency, memory skill and mathematical reasoning and in aspects of personality such as aggressiveness, competitiveness, self-esteem, risk-taking, neuroticism, emotional sensitivity, agreeableness, interest in casual sex and pornography and jealousy.
> (Same Sex, Different Rules, *New Scientist*, 29/04/06)

Or, are you aware of the specific differences noticeable in MRI scans between the brains of children and adults with ADHD and those without?[7] And have you read the US National Institute of Health report that, according to the Financial Times, 'seems to suggest that ADHD is a neurological reality, but does not establish that it is, in the long term, either abnormal or permanent'?[8]

With all the fuss about water in the classroom, are you aware there is no proper academic research to substantiate any claims about its efficacy in helping young people concentrate? Or that, with all the pressure on children to have a good breakfast to help with learning, different foods have different effects on their brains anyway, depending on their genetic make-up and that there is a naturally occurring hormone, grehlin, that we produce when we are hungry that actually increases concentration and learning?[9]

And are you tapping into the growing field of evolutionary psychology and understanding that, due to what is called the 'environment of evolutionary adaptedness', some of the problems you are facing in the classroom, with 'naughty boys' for example, have been millions of years in the making? We are like we are because of how we've been. Your job isn't to squash such behaviours so much as to channel them in new ways.

And what about the fact that you can't be older than your brain? That if you are working with a 14-year-old who has the emotional maturity of a 12-year-old then, to all intents and purposes, they are a 12-year-old, so you should work with them as such to develop their delayed potential, not treat them as a defective 14-year-old.

I could go on, but you get the idea. I once heard Andrew Curran say that 'The core to understanding all learning is to understand how to get the right neurochemistry in the brain' and who am I to argue? It is so important that you keep learning about how best to do that and keep stretching your brain to help them get the best out of theirs.

Chapter 9

Neuromyths debunked![1]

In my work with teachers one of the things I do is try and bring them up to date with some of the most relevant brain discoveries of recent times and, like any good teacher, I always start with 'assessing prior knowledge'. Occasionally I meet teachers who know a great deal about the nature of the brain. Occasionally. For the most part, though, I would suggest that teachers as a profession know very little about it. This is especially true of the NQTs or 'Not Quite Teachers'. I always ask the question of them, whether they are primary or secondary, PGCE or BEd or whatever route it is by which they came into teaching, 'What did you do about the brain in your training?' The answer, nine times out of ten, is 'Nothing'. Or 'A little bit'. Or, 'We did brain gym!', which, as I point out to them, is not about the brain, it's just a phrase with 'brain' in it. You wouldn't train to be a car mechanic without lifting up the bonnet so why should you be allowed to train to be a moulder of the physical and lasting structure of young brains without having to have some understanding of the neurological effects of your actions?

When there is some claim to prior neurological knowledge it often boils down to a hazy understanding of left brain, right brain theory, combined usually with an inability to remember which side is 'responsible for' which attributes. So, let's put that one to bed straightaway. The whole left brain does this, right brain does that story is not true. Not in the way you think it is anyway.

This particular myth came about due to the Nobel-winning work of a neurobiologist called Roger Sperry,[2] who identified what he called 'two spheres of consciousness' when working with people with epilepsy in the 1960s. The severing of the corpus callosum, the 'bridge' that links the two hemispheres and allows messages to pass between them, seemed to have a beneficial effect on people suffering from epilepsy and, in studying why this was, Sperry and his team identified that, among other things, the left side of the brain was the 'language center' whilst the right side had no language but was where we processed music and space perception. And from some hard science, a whole industry of pop-psychology was born.

But it's not so much not true or false as, like everything with the brain, far more complicated than that and even now the cause of a great deal of heated debate in neuroscientific circles. In a *New Scientist* article in 1999, the freelance neuroscience writer John McCrone described how advances in brain imaging techniques were revealing how we are not a person made of two split brains but a person made up of one very complicated, very linked, single brain:

> language turned out to be represented on both sides of the brain, in matching areas of the cortex. Areas on the left dealt with the core aspects of speech such as grammar and word production, while aspects such as intonation and emphasis lit up the right side. In the same way, the right brain proved to be good at working with a general sense of space, while equivalent areas in the left brain fired when someone thought about objects at particular locations.
>
> (www.newscientist.com/article/mg16321934.600-
> left-brain-right-brain.html published in full at: http://painting.
> about.com/gi/o.htm?zi=1/XJ/Ya&zTi=1&sdn=painting
> &cdn=hobbies&tm=20&f=00&tt=14&bt=0&bts=0&zu=
> http%3A//www.rense.com/general2/rb.htm)

It's not that one side does one thing and one does another, it's that they both have different but complementary subtle processing functions that allow us to grasp reality and process it as effectively as possible. He concludes with the affirmation, 'It is how the two sides of the brain complement and combine that counts.'

Another example is the processing of music. Whereas we tend to associate listening to music with the right brain, studies have shown that trained musicians use their left brain to appreciate music when listening to it. A study in the *Journal of the Royal Society of Medicine* refers to such research as a 'hotly debated topic' and, in describing some of this research, concludes by saying: 'A point to note is that, for musicians, mere passive listening is more difficult because of their spontaneous analytical processing, and this possibly contributes to the left lateralization.'[3,4]

Where does that leave the teacher about to go into a history classroom and engage the 'whole brains' of 30 14-year-olds? Well, if you look at the traditional (but not accurate) demarcation of what both hemispheres were up to – left brain was words and sequences and analysis and right brain was the big picture and colour and shapes and rhythm and move-ment – just make sure you are doing *all* of it. So, where you have words make sure you have pictures too, where you have black and white make sure you have colour, where you have discussion make sure you have music, where you have stillness make sure you have movement too, you get the picture … .

While we're on the subject of false 'facts' we know about the brain, here are a few more that I have come across on my travels in schools, as debunked by, of all people, the OECD and their Centre for Educational Research and Innovation.

We only use ten per cent of our brains[5]

No we don't, we use a lot of our brains a lot of the time, even when we're asleep. This idea, unattributably attributed to Einstein amongst others, may well have come out of a self-help book from the US on how to improve your memory from the nineteenth century. It just simply isn't true. As the good people of OECD state categorically:

All existing data shows that we use a 100% of our brains.
(www.oecd.org/document/23/0,3343,
en_2649_35845581_33831575_1_1_1_1,00.html)

When you start talking about the brain's *potential* though, now you're onto something. Brain 'plasticity' relates to the extent to which we can grow our brain, not in size, but in the way it is wired up. As we learn we make new connections, the more connections we make, the more we can go on to make. In other words the more we use it, the more we can use it. Stands to reason in an exponential way. But simply having plenty of connections doesn't necessarily make us cleverer. As John T. Bruer, president of the James S. McDonnell Foundation,[6,7] says in his article *Neural Connections: Some You Use, Some You Lose*, 'despite what we read in the papers, the neuroscientific evidence does not support the claim that the more connections you have, the smarter you are.' What we are talking about is the brain's capacity for growth. Don't tell me you can't sing, draw, rock climb, write a poem, bake a soufflé, do Soduku. Just tell me you can't do those things *yet*. And, what then, is the potential of our brains? My favourite estimate is that there are more potential connections in a single human brain than there are atoms in the visible universe (for which the number has been calculated as ten to the 80th power[8]). But this is not infinite as some self-help gurus would have us believe. According to Dr Curran, there is a genetic limit to our potential, the thing is we don't know where it is. So, how high is high? We can't all sing like Pavarotti sang, but we can all sing better than we have done up to now. To achieve this we need to go through a three-step process. We need to have the desire to sing better. We need to believe we can sing better (and put to bed the 'I can't sing' myth). Then we need to do something different from what we did before when we failed, which usually means not going back to that music teacher who made you mime in the school choir because you were putting the pianist off. When I was teaching French we had 'C/D borderline' students back after school in their own time and we, basically, gave them more of the same. What did this change? It made them *better* C/D borderline students. As the saying goes, you'll get what you got if you do what you did. We, like many schools and governments seem to do, overlooked the first two steps.

There is a 'critical' window of opportunity to stimulate and enrich the brain, up to the age of three that will have an effect on an individual's success in later life

I meet teachers sometimes who are in despair about the damage that parents do to their children, especially when they feel that so much of this damage in the early years of the child's life is irreparable and permanent. I do my best to reassure them that they must believe, as teachers, that they can make a difference because if not, we could all throw our hands up in despair. The debunking of this neuromyth should bring hope to all those teachers who wonder if they really can change children's brains for the better. According to the OECD, the idea of a 'critical period' of development has been replaced with what they call a 'sensitive period', where we make connections more easily but if we miss out there is still hope. As they go on to point out:

> While there might be sensitive periods for some stimuli, the capacity to form synapses, i.e. plasticity, is not limited to the first three years of life. Thus it can not be generalized that there is a sole sensitive period (up to 3 years) for every possible stimuli. Any kind of specific environmental stimulation causes the brain to form new connections. This ability is conserved throughout life.
> (www.oecd.org/document/4/0,3343, en_2649_35845581_33829892_1_1_1_1,00.html)

What it does boil down to is the adage 'use it or lose it'. The brain will last a long lifetime and new connections can be made right through to old age, but you do have to keep on using it. Read a brain book inches thick and it still seems to boil down to those five words. This is particularly relevant when, with the increase in age-related brain diseases such as dementia and Alzheimer's disease, we look at the controversial topic of 'neural reserve'. This suggests that using our brains well during our lives doesn't protect us from these diseases but means that we have built enough richness in terms of brain connectivity that, as we start to lose these connections, we can last for much longer before the symptoms start to appear. In the words of Dr. David A. Bennett, director of the Rush Alzheimer's Disease Center in Chicago:

> We think that education and factors related to education may affect the way the brain responds to the abnormal proteins that accumulate in the brains of people with Alzheimer's disease. In other words, in people with similar amounts of these abnormal Alzheimer's disease protein deposits, those with more educational experiences will be less likely to have memory loss than those with less education.
>
> (www.scienceblog.com/community/older/
> 2002/D/20024932.html)

I heard the story on the radio of a man who was a very good chess player who went to his doctor to complain that the number of moves ahead he could work out had reduced slightly and it was impairing his game. After an intensive course of neural investigation, doctors concluded there was nothing wrong with his brain. He died shortly afterwards 'riddled' with Alzheimer's, something that can only be positively identified by looking at brain tissue after death. It would appear that his university-level education and his intellectually active lifestyle had delayed the onset not of the disease but of the outward appearance of its symptoms. Again, to quote Dr David A. Bennett:

> it is possible that education and related factors could increase neural reserve and allow the brain to tolerate pathology without manifesting memory loss and other clinical signs.

Or, in the words of *New Scientist*:

> Study after study has shown that intelligence, good education, literacy and high status jobs all seem to protect people from the mental ravages of old age and provide some resistance to the symptoms, if not the brain shrinkage, of dementia.
>
> (*New Scientist*, 03/06/06)

As we live longer in the West, we are increasing our likelihood of having a range of awful neurodiseases. In fact, studies show that once you reach 65, your life expectancy increases by five hours a day, which also means that your risk of Alzheimer's increases exponentially.[9] We need to educate our children not only to take their place in the twenty-first century, but also to keep healthy into the longer old age they will experience. This is where you come in.

We need to immerse babies and children in multisensory enriched environments to enhance their ability to learn

Not true according to the OECD[10] citing the article mentioned above by John T. Bruer, especially when matched with the idea that if the baby's nursery doesn't have enough stimulation before the child reaches the age of three you may as well cancel that place you've reserved at Roedean.

As Bruer points out, there is a 'misconception that early environmental stimulation or experience causes synapses to form. This ... runs counter to the existing neuroscientific evidence. Rather, the research suggests that genetic and developmental programs, not environmental input, control early synapse formation.'

So, nature, as opposed to nurture, has the upper hand in the early years. It's not the wallpaper your parents buy, but the genetic material they give you that will count in those early years. So, where do you come in as a teacher? Look at Bruer's quote again: 'genetic *and* developmental programs'. In other words, what you are born with and, not Classic FM on in the nursery, but the way good parenting and professionals like you work to develop young brains effectively and consistently over time. In the words of another neuroscientist Patricia Goldman-Rakic:

> While children's brains acquire a tremendous amount of information during the early years, most learning takes place after synaptic formation stabilizes. From the time a child enters first grade, through high school, college, and beyond, there is little change in the number of synapses. It is during the time when no, or little, synapse formation occurs that most learning takes place.

In other words, as I keep saying, you are powerful, powerful professionals, directly influencing young people right down to the actual physical architecture of their brains. Some scientists are even suggesting that children are 'hardwired' to believe and trust adults from an evolutionary point of view. Beware, too, that because so much of what is going into their heads from what you say and do is working at a subconscious level, then, in the words of Dr Curran, 'The child may never have an insight into what you have hardwired into their brain.' Like a hypnotist, you *suggest* messages into impressionable young minds through your every word and deed, messages that are the building blocks of that child's sense of self-worth and their self-image. And because this is a subconscious process, the child's self-esteem never really knew what hit it. That's why you need to know about brains, neural development and your role in it. And why you need to watch out for the things that just aren't true.

Chapter 10

Your hands in their brains

Just when you thought the whole 'nature v nurture' debate had quietened down along comes the concept of epigenetic theory and it kicks off again. Epigenetics is all to do with the way genes can be reprogrammed by cultural, maternal and environmental influences and, although you, as a teacher, may have no input with regard to the 'nature' element of the equation, you need to be aware of the effects of 'nurture'. Not least because your actions actually change the very nature of the DNA of the children in your care.

The truce between those expressing the view that our genes determine who we are more than our environment and those declaring, on the contrary, that it is our environment that moulds us into who we become, overriding our genes, the naturists versus the nurturists, was best summed up by science writer Matt Ridley when he wrote:

> No longer is it nature-versus-nurture, but nature-via-nurture.
>
> (Ridley 2003)

To look at this properly we need to go back to the whole question of the very nature of intelligence, not IQ this time but the related concept of 'g'. In a nutshell, 'g',[1] which stands for 'general intelligence' and was coined by statistician Charles Spearman who was a follower of the Francis Galton, we met in chapter six and a 'fervent champion of heredity' in Ridley's words, is a way of summing up that special ingredient that is common to all the various intelligence tests. In other words, that special ingredient possessed by the child who seems to do well no matter what you throw at them.

What's more, there is something called the Flynn Effect[2] these days that shows that IQ scores have actually been rising significantly across the world. And no-one really knows why. Is it diet? Is it the increasingly enriched environments children are living in with access to various forms of media? Is it more experience in dealing with the sorts of questions and the sort of questioning techniques the tests use? And before you declare that it must be schooling, the sorts of 3-Rs type learning to be found in schools have not shown any significant increase and have even shown declines. What's more, the biggest gains have taken place at the lower end of the intelligence scale with the higher end remaining pretty much the same. In other words, all over the world stupid people are becoming cleverer. (Although, in the UK, this growth in intelligence of young people peaked in the 1980s and has held steady since then. I don't know about you but I get a warm glow from being part of such a peak.) What's more, if you extrapolate backwards, according to controversial professor Arthur Jensen,[3] Aristotle would have an IQ of -1000.

So, here, as we have seen elsewhere, the whole idea of measuring intelligence in a meaningful way is a very tangled web. That said, it still seems to be the most consistent way of roughly saying – this child is 'intelligent'. Which brings us back to genes. No-one has yet discovered an 'intelligence gene' (although Ridley does point out that one gene that does seem to play a part in IQ contains a repeating code that always begins with the amino acids isoleucine and glutamine or, to give them their standard abbreviation, IQ). But there do appear to be genetic factors at play. For example, there is a correlation between brain volume and IQ of around 40 per cent. Having a big brain doesn't guarantee you are a genius but it starts to tip things in your favour. Yet environment still plays a part with studies of twins showing it to be around the nice and non-confrontational 50–50 mark. But there are other factors at play too, as research shows that how well you inherit your parents' IQ depends on your socio-economic status too. If you're middle class or well off, your environment doesn't make much difference to the brainpower you were born with. If you're poor, that poverty outweighs practically any of the IQ-related potential you were born with.

Think about the implications of that at a national level – where should governments be targeting their resources if they want a 'cleverer' population? But also think about it with regard to schools. What can you do to work with the poorest families in your catchment area to help to try and make a difference and, if you are in a secondary school, why are you waiting until they come to you at the age of 11?

On the subject of age, throw into the IQ pot too the research thrown up by *New Scientist* in July 2009 showing that, as we progress from childhood through adolescence to young adulthood the part genes play in the variation in our intelligence changes too.[4] As children it can account for 40 per cent of this variation, as adolescents it is 55 per cent and as young adults it rises to 66 per cent. But, as we have seen, being born that way doesn't mean you need to stay that way. Research shows that you can tap into the brain's wonderful ability to be moulded, its plasticity, and make a difference, with researchers finding that the biggest gains in IQ tests were in individuals who had the lower scores in the beginning. Again, what does that mean for where governments at national level and schools at community level target their resources?

The brain's yearning to be great, stifled by both genetic and environmental factors in our most needy young people, can be addressed if we can be bothered to do so. How? Well, apart from specific training in how to use our brains, a curriculum that actually responds to the needs of the individual will help. Research from Robert Planin from King's College in London quoted in *New Scientist* found that these genetic differences are even greater when everyone endures the same curriculum rather than one that is better matched to the child's natural strengths and abilities. Our challenge, then, is to strive to match the curriculum to children's natural abilities with a special focus on those currently struggling the most.

Which brings us back to multiple intelligences, which, as a theory, may have its detractors from a scientific point of view but has a powerful role to play in what I call the 'dumbing up' of learning – giving more people access to the knowledge that is there rather than dumbing it down so only those with good IQ scores – those who have high logical/mathematical and verbal/linguistic skills – can access the pure knowledge. As an example of what I mean take the example of a young man I met who was working as an IT technician at a further education college in the Midlands. He had hated school and had pretty much failed at everything he had attempted. On arriving at the college where he now worked, he had been identified as having dyslexia and given the appropriate support. This included learning how to use non-verbal techniques such as Tony Buzan's *Mind Maps*, moving away from what I call the 'tyranny of syntax'. With the tools to overcome his particular neurological handicap, he was able to access the learning and excel in a way that he never managed at school. Failing his exams makes him look dumb but there are many ways to fail an exam. For this boy being dumb wasn't one of them. Being expected to learn in what was, for him, a dumb way was what did it, that and a system dumb enough to do the same failing strategy over and over again and expect a different result. Yet he was the one who came out looking dumb.

You are a teacher. You are one of the most powerful people in the world. You mould young minds. More than that, though, you mould young brains – literally. Your actions (or lack of them, remember we are often marked out by what we don't do as much as by what we do) directly impact on the actual physical architecture of the brains of the young people in your care on an hourly basis. You are directly influencing the neurological structures of the future of the world.

One of the aspects of neuroscience that most people seem to under-stand these days in my experience is that learning, at a very simple level, is the process of making and then strengthening connections between brain cells. As we experience new things, we make new connections. As we re-experience them and make sense of them, those connections become more stable, creating templates or Hebbian assemblies named after the Canadian neuroscientist Donald Hebbe who first identified this process. In this way we create a unique structure between our ears that determines how we respond to novel situations, how well we speak French, what happens when someone asks us a maths question, how well we perform on *Who Wants to be a Millionaire* and what we think of cheese. The brain is cap-able of making – and breaking – a million new connections per second and retains the ability to make new connections into old age despite the best intentions of daytime television. This process of constructing our neural architecture is matched, though, by a process of deconstruction known as neural pruning. This is the brain getting rid of the connections it no longer feels are necessary, a deliberate, inevitable pruning away of untapped potential.

According to Ian Robertson in the wonderful little book *Mind Sculpture*, the seven-year-old's brain looks and weighs pretty much the same as an adult brain yet there are around 40 per cent more synapses, the connec-tions between brain cells, per brain cell in the child's brain than in the adult one. This explains why, when you ask a young child to tell you what they did last summer, you are regaled with a 30-minute monologue full of the most excruciating detail about every last little aspect of their trip to the Dordogne. Everything is still linked to everything else at a synaptic level and when you trip the switch with your ill-advised but well-meaning question the whole lot is downloaded in one breathless, unstoppable mess.

As we mature, both physically and neurologically, the brain has pruned away many of these spurious connections, which means we can get straight to the point far more readily (although I'm sure you could point to – or, if you are sitting in the staffroom reading this, point at – people for whom this is still not the case).

What is the deciding factor as to whether a connection remains or is pruned away? You are.

As Robertson points out:

> One of the main things which determines which synapses stay and which go is learning. Those synapses which don't become connected to other neurons, through learning and experience, simply wither away in the great competitive free-for-all which is brain activity.
>
> (Robertson 1999)

So, we have nature and nurture interacting with and influencing each other in various ways and to various extents depending on where we are born and who we are born to and this whole process contributing to the actual architecture of the brains we carry in our heads for the rest of our lives. What's more we have education – you – right at the heart of this wonderfully complex web, capable of significantly influencing the whole process for the better when done well. But let's take another look at the darker side of epigenetic theory. In May 2009, the *New York Times* quoted an article from the journal *Nature Neuroscience*, where researchers in Montreal found, whilst researching into people who had committed suicide, that:

> people who were abused or neglected as children showed genetic alterations that made them more sensitive to stress.

If I hit you, you bruise. If I hit you repeatedly your brain structure changes to create a template that says, don't go near him – or people like him – because it hurts. If I persist in my abuse of you, you change physically, not only internally and externally, but also at a chemical level right down to your very DNA, the very building blocks of who you are. Research from Germany and quoted on the BBC news website in November 2009,[5] showed how raising levels of stress in young mice by separating them from their mothers at an early age for just three hours a day for ten days, created specific and tangible changes in their DNA leading to an inability to deal with stressful situations in adulthood and, what's more, poorer memories. The researcher, Dr Christopher Murgatroyd from the Max Planck Institute of Psychiatry in Munich, describes how the high levels of stress hormones produced by the baby mice 'tweaked' the DNA of a gene that codes for a vasopressin, a stress hormone.

'This leaves a permanent mark at the vasopressin gene,' said Dr Murgatroyd. 'It is then programmed to produce high levels [of the hormone] later on in life.'

The BBC article also quotes Professor Hans Reul, a neuroscientist at Bristol University, as saying that 'There is strong evidence that adversities such as abuse and neglect during infancy contribute to the development of psychiatric diseases such as depression.' This is something backed up by *New Scientist* in April 2009:

> Maternal rejection or trauma early in life, for example, may affect a person's emotional reactions to stressful events later on, potentially predisposing them to depression and anxiety disorders.
> (www.newscientist.com/article/mg20227022.800-the-five-ages-of-the-brain-childhood.html)

So, the more stressed your life as a child – and remember with these mice it wasn't overly harsh abuse or neglect, it can simply be the stress caused by having a non-demonstrative mother in early childhood – the more susceptible to stress you are in adulthood *at a genetic level*. And, according to the World Health Organization, depression is currently the leading cause of disability in the world, is fourth in the world in terms of productive days lost and lives shortened by it and is heading to the number two slot by 2020.[6] For people aged 15 to 44 it is already there.

Who we are is a complex series of interactions between what we were born with and what we were born into, none of which is written in stone. If to be poor and stupid is your fate then what is the point of school? I am often asked by teachers if there really is anything they can do to help children who have already suffered at the hands of the people and life they were born into and, even before I came across this research, I felt I had to say yes, absolutely, or else what's the point! What the latest research findings are showing teachers everywhere is that yes there is a point, you don't just make a difference; you make everything different. Because, as Ian Robertson points out:

> Schooling and education, without doubt, physically change the brains of children.
>
> (Robertson 1999)

Chapter 11

Talk to the hand coz the nucleus accumbens ain't listening

How often have you said the words 'Grow up!' to a child? Or, 'You're acting childish!', or 'Act your age!'? Yet what the neuroscience is showing us is that to say 'grow up' to a child is like saying 'be thin' to a fat person or 'speak English' to a badger.

In the words of the great Swiss researcher into children's development, Jean Piaget:

> Education, for most people, means trying to lead the child to resemble the typical adult of his society ... but for me and no one else, education means making creators. ... You have to make inventors, innovators— not conformists.
>
> (Bringuier 1980)

Remember these words – adolescents are not people.

I mentioned in chapter 10 that one of the few accurate aspects of neuroscience that seems to have percolated out of the ivory neurological towers is the idea that we 'grow' our brains, that brains learn through making and strengthening connections between brain cells. The making of connections contributes to what is called 'grey matter' in the brain. The strengthening is a process called myelination, myelin being a fatty substance that acts as an insulating sheath around the connections and helps make the passage of electrical impulses down these connections more effective. As this builds up in the growing brain, it is known as 'white matter' and it is something whose importance is only just beginning to be discovered by scientists.

In between growing and consolidating though, there is the equally important process of neural pruning, the brain getting rid of connections it doesn't use. More of that in a minute.

How many years does this process of growing, wiring, pruning and consolidating take until we can say this is an adult, mature, human brain?

Between 20 and 30. Remember that next time you are berating a 13-year-old for 'acting like a child'. A 13-year-old acts like a child because they *are* a child and a child is not a 'mini-me'. They are not small versions of us walking around doing bad things. They are a work in progress. And if they can't get it wrong – and then learn to get it right under your professional care – where will they learn to get it right? In the words of *Scientific American Mind*:

> Society should not be fooled into thinking that a teen has the mental prowess of an adult just because he or she looks, and most of the time, acts like one.
>
> (*Scientific American Mind* 09/2006)

This maturation process, which has different rates according to gender but with both sexes reaching the finishing line about the same time, does not happen in a haphazard way. Rather it follows a pattern that appears to be hardwired into our genes with only serious malnutrition having any disruptive impact on it. It is a process that, like the filling up of a school hall on a training day, starts at the back and ends up at the front. And, as it can feel like on some mornings in a cold school hall, it is a process that takes years, something that has serious implications for the way in which we treat young people in schools.

The first part of the brain that goes through this process of wiring up in the baby is at the back of the brain and relates to areas of the cortex to do with the senses, notably touch and sight.[1] This makes perfect sense if you think about babies 'in the wild'. The sooner you can see and feel safety (your mother) or see and feel danger (not your mother), the more chance you have of surviving.

The process of building, in over-abundance, grey matter in the part of the brain that deals with senses, known as the parietal lobes, is not finished until around the age of 12. Then the pruning starts. The growing of grey matter in the temporal lobes, an area of the brain associated with emotional behaviours and language, does not finish until around the age of 16 and, even then, there is still the growing of white matter and the pruning process to take place.

So, from these early stages of myelination, what else does the young brain go through, especially in those critical adolescent years? Well, for a start, those mood swings and that newfound interest in loud music, extreme sports and people of the opposite, or indeed any, sex is not down to hormones. They are all down to the fact that the brain is a work very much in progress and, in the same way that you have to make a mess to build a house and for most of that time it is completely uninhabitable, the brains, thoughts and minds of the average teen are equally a vast and dangerous building site where no-one would want to live.

One of the biggest factors contributing to this is a process called hairy dendritic sprouting. During adolescence, there is a massive spurt in the number of connections in the brain, as if it is readying itself for one last gasp effort in preparing the soon-to-be adult carrying it around for whatever life may throw it at it. This is then followed by a significant period of neural pruning as the brain starts to mould itself to what is effectively going to be the life it's going to lead (and remember that in the millions of years it has taken for this process to evolve, delaying the onset of adulthood by 'having a year out' is a recent addition).

As the brain starts to 'equip' itself for the years ahead, the teen years become a wonderful opportunity to ensure none of this 'equipment' is lost. How? By exposing young people to as many opportunities and novel encounters as possible to send the message to the brain that says, this potential is going to be needed, so don't prune it away. It really is – and this phrase is basically what all the books about the brain that have been written in the last 50 years are saying – 'use it or lose it'.

Which leads us to the fascinating phenomenon that is 'pseudostupidity'.

Ask an adolescent a really straightforward question like, 'Swimming with sharks – good idea or bad idea?' and see what happens. This is exactly what researchers did; measuring the time it took for the adolescent to come up with an answer. An adult brain knows immediately the answer is bad idea, without a great deal of thinking. The child's brain would probably want to know what the shark's name was and if they could bring a friend. The teenage brain, on the other hand hesitates because, well, there are lots of answers to that question and, hey, I want to make sure I'm not missing anything here. The spurt in neural connectivity they are experiencing, especially in their immature pre-frontal cortex (PFC), means that their brains have many, many possible ways to get from A – Is swimming with sharks dangerous? – to B – Well, duh! A mature brain has fewer connections but the ones we do have, have been honed by experience, by learning, making our thought processes far more efficient. We rely less on our PFCs and more on our memories. We don't have as much potential for creativity maybe, but equally we don't have as much potential for coming up with dumb answers.

Another way of thinking about it – and one that resonates with me as I have just recently started living in Dubai and anyone who has been there will know what I mean – is to imagine you have just moved to a new city whose roads are a tangled web of motorways, intersections, roundabouts, traffic lights, road works, speed cameras and traffic jams. You want to go from A to B for the very first time. You have a map, a sense of direction, a full tank of gas, half a pack of cigarettes, it's dark and you're wearing sunglasses. The very first time you set off from A to get to B you are overwhelmed by everything the trip is throwing at you and you have so many choices about how to get there it is hard to know which one to make. It would be so much easier if the place had just two roads, one leading in, one leading out. Like Cromer. If you get to where you want to go quickly it is more by luck than judgement and you usually get home tired, confused and stressed. The second time you make the journey, however, it suddenly becomes a whole lot easier. You still may make the odd wrong turn but that may be more through lapse of concentration than anything else. It doesn't take very long before, despite all the factors being the same as they were the first time you travelled, you can make that same journey on autopilot, without even having to think about it.

This process of learning how to get quickly from A to B, as if all the other roads and possible routes were no longer there, is what is going on in the adolescent brain and explains so much about the bad choices, the wrong turns, the dumb decisions, the obviously stupid things they do. Contrary to existential values, they are not stupid, they are just acting that way.

There are other ways in which their brains differ from ours too. The nucleus accumbens are part of our slow-maturing PFC and have a role to play directing our motivation to seek out rewards. Yet in the adolescent brain, research shows there is less activity here, explaining the need for using short-term goals when working with young people as well as encouraging them to develop a longer-term perspective. The nucleus accumbens[2] also have a role in the processing of rewards such as food and sex. Hence the title of this chapter. Another difference is seen, not so much in going to bed but getting up. Waking in the mornings for adults involves a process where daylight seeps through our eyes into our brains to activate the pineal gland to produce melatonin which suppresses our feelings of sleepiness. The teenage brain's decision about when to be awake and when to be asleep does not work in the same way, with melatonin[3] being produced later and being less affected by daylight. Yet the teenage brain also needs the right amount of sleep, with research quoted by Sheryl Feinstein in *Secrets of the Teenage Brain* indicating that 'the majority of high school students were sleep deprived resulting in 20 per cent of high school students falling asleep in school'. She goes on to add that 'Research studies show that high school students not receiving enough sleep suffer in grades and overall school success' (Feinstein 2004). A more disturbing side to the teenager's irregular sleep patterns was highlighted by research that found that going to bed after ten o'clock at night led to a 24 per cent increase in depression in people aged between

12 and 18.[4] They were also 20 per cent more likely to experience 'suicidal thoughts'. Furthermore, young people who had fewer than five hours' sleep were 71 per cent more likely to become depressed.

What can schools do about this? In an article in *The Independent*, Professor Dirk-Jan Dijk, director of the Surrey Sleep Research Centre said, 'There is something to be said for the idea that making school schedules fit in with adolescents' natural rhythms would make youngsters more productive.'[5] Such insights have encouraged some schools in the UK to use their new-found flexibility with the timetable to start lessons later in the day and finish later in the evening to fit around the adolescent brain a whole lot better. Where this has been adopted in the US, it has been shown to raise achievement. Most schools, however, still operate the traditional system of making young people arrive at 8.30 even though they don't wake up until 11.

As with all educational innovations, though, such an idea comes up against the *Daily Mail* who reported the story under the headline 'School trials 10am starts "to give tired pupils a lie-in"'.[6] Here they quote Ruth Lea, an economic advisor to an unnamed banking group and former head of policy at the Institute of Directors, who 'branded' the idea as 'fatuous', saying, 'If teenagers need nine-and-a-half hours sleep, they should go to bed earlier.' Yet, as Feinstein points out, citing research on tired and underachieving adolescents, 'forcing them to bed earlier did not solve the problem'.

Perhaps one day we'll stop bankers and journalists from setting educational policy. Although it could be worse. We could just leave it to politicians.

Talking of politicians, let us continue our exploration of the teenage brain by considering a species of spineless bottom feeder known as a sea squirt.

Known colloquially to East Coast fishermen as a 'pisser' – for obvious reasons if you have ever squeezed one (a sea squirt that is, not an East Coast fisherman) – the sea squirt is a member of the tunicate family[7] and has a life cycle that goes something along the lines of (1) drift around for a while as a larva, (2) find a rock and attach itself to grow into an adult and (3) never, ever move again. Because of that it is has been shown to digest its own cerebral ganglion, effectively the primitive brain that deals with movement. In other words, because it no longer moves at all, it eats its own brain. Some of the boys do that during year nine.

Movement and learning go together and strapping young people down for hours on end to uncomfortable chairs is all about teaching and control and nothing about learning. Not only that, by helping them develop their motor skills you are actually enhancing the part of the brain that deals with coordinating thinking too. Why? Because both skills employ the same part of the brain, the cerebellum.[8]

Touch your nape and you are only centimetres away from this cauliflower-looking primitive part of the brain, that is packed with more neurons than, according to some sources, the rest of the brain put together. In the same way that it helps with balance and posture, it also aids thinking and reasoning by keeping us on task, organized and, effectively, balanced. And, according to Feinstein again, 'the more complicated a task facing us, the larger the role the cerebellum plays in resolving it'. It is also linked to reading, although the understanding of the words part is performed elsewhere, and even song lyrics and lines from films are stored there. I once met a teacher who used to let her 'remedial' children walk up and down in the primary school hall whilst reading as it 'seemed to help them'. Another example was the primary head who saw a significant increase in the achievement of her 'naughty boys' in reading after they had had drumming lessons.

In a similar vein, Darwin used to have what he called his 'thinking walks' in a part of his garden he designed for that purpose, part of a process he called 'long pondering'. Not only does movement stimulate the thinking brain it also changes the neurological 'state' you are in. We tend to have children in the same state – i.e. sitting at a desk – whether they are taking new information in or trying to process that information. But, as Darwin found, maybe the second process would benefit from a different state to the first.

One final insight about the cerebellum from the wonderful Feinstein book is that it is in this part of the brain that we find the most differences between the male- and female-type brains, with the cerebellum of adolescent boys 'being about 14 per cent larger than cerebellums in adolescent girls', adding that 'the difference remains throughout adulthood'.

So, to sum up, brains need to move, thinking is neurologically linked to movement and boys need more of it than girls. This brain science is hardly rocket science is it! Let's move now, though, from sea squirts to eels. Or rather EELS. An article in *Time* magazine in 2004[9] gave a detailed account of what is known about the teenage brain that could best be summed up with that one acronym, that is to say:

> *Experiences* – to grow the brain. They need things that are novel, that are new, that are unpredictable, that stand out from ordinary day-to-day experience. This is what grabs them. They are bored and turned off by predictability and commonplace.
>
> *Engagement* – to focus it properly. They need to be involved in things that they find interesting, challenging and relevant or, preferably, all three. They need to be given the time to get involved in things and receive feedback as to whether what they are doing is working or not and what they can do to become better.

Love – to help it grow well. They need to know that, *whatever they do*, they will have unconditional love of the significant adults in their life, be it parents or teachers. You might hate their actions but it will never stop you loving them for who they are. They might annoy you, frustrate you, exasperate you, they might have crashed your car, left the shower running for three days or killed the neighbour's cat by accident, but your love for them is non-negotiable and something they can always rely on, until the day one of you dies. In fact, Dr Curran's whole analysis of millions of years and billions of dollars-worth of understanding about the brain boils down to that one four-letter word. And, in the classroom, if they know you love them then 'neurochemically they will have no option but to learn from you'.

Structure – to help it grow safely. They need clearly defined boundaries that they will push against because that is what adolescents do, it's their job. But that doesn't mean to say they don't want them or need them. They do, very much. Remember, too, that love and structure does not equal stifling them. They need the chance to go it alone too within the parameters you have set. Think of it as 'tender loving neglect'.

Let me finish this chapter on the teenage brain by sharing with you 'A Teen-Age Bill of Rights'[10] published in the *New York Times Magazine* in 1945, the year after the birth of the 'teenager' and quoted in a book by Jon Savage, *Teenage – The Creation of Youth 1875 – 1945*. Although described as 'distinctly wussy'[11] by the *New Statesman* when reviewing Savage's book, the charter seems to be an eloquent call for what the neuroscience tells us – give me excitement, engagement, structure and love.

1 The right to let childhood be forgotten
2 The right to a 'say' about his own life
3 The right to make mistakes, to find out for oneself
4 The right to have rules explained, not imposed
5 The right to have fun and companions
6 The right to question ideas
7 The right to be at the romantic age
8 The right to a fair chance and opportunity
9 The right to struggle toward his own philosophy of life
10 The right to professional help whenever necessary.

(Savage 2007)

Measuring how many of these rights the teenagers in your school have may be a good starting point.

Chapter 12

Is that an iron bar through your frontal lobes or are you just pleased to see me?

What do all these activities have in common?

- Working out if I should get a job in McDonald's to pay for my trip to Ibiza next year
- Explaining why I think use of nuclear power is a good or bad thing
- Persuading my dad to let me off the hook for being out till three am last night
- Being out till three am last night and feeling a bit guilty about it
- Coming to the conclusion that my homework is/is not important
- Wondering what it's all about
- Wondering whether it's all worth it anyway, even if you did know
- Choosing to smoke that strange-looking cigarette because bad things only ever happen to other people and I'm not dead yet and see no reasons why things should change.

Apart from that strange feeling you have that I've just read some of your teenage diaries, what they all share is that they have involved a part of the brain called the pre-frontal cortex, the very last part of our brain to mature.

The pre-frontal cortex, or PFC, is the part of the brain we use when we are comparing short-term gains over long-term goals, balancing risk and reward, using intellectual language, making choices based on morals and exploring right versus wrong. It is what is at play when we move from what is called 'exogenous' behaviour control, that is to say we are simply responding to stimuli like a stick or a carrot, to 'endogenous' control, where we behave according to a personal and voluntary plan. In fact, the PFC is right at the heart of the sort of thinking that separates grown-ups from children. And it's the bit alcohol shuts up.[1] No wonder it is also known as 'the area of sober second thought'.

Once you understand this it helps you put all those stressful and infuriating situations you have with your class – or your own children – very much into perspective. Now you, too, will be able to go up to that colleague who is tearing her hair out because of the behaviour and attitude of that group of 15-year-olds, tap your temple and say knowingly, 'It's just their immature pre-frontal cortex so don't worry about it.'

The PFC has been the subject of a great deal of debate and research ever since an unfortunate man named Phineas Gage ended up with a metal rod in his after an accident whilst building a railroad in America in 1848. As recounted by Rita Carter in *Mapping the Mind*, the doctor who treated Gage described how he had changed from being a hardworking conscientious employee to become a drunken vagrant who was 'at times pertinaciously obstinate, yet capricious and vacillating, devising many plans of future operations which are soon abandoned ... a child in his intellectual capacity and manifestations yet with the animal passions of a young man' (Carter 1988).

Sound like any adolescent boys you know?

One hundred years later, the influence that the PFC has over our behaviours fell under the spotlight of one Walter Freeman, a neurologist who pioneered the 'transorbital lobotomy', that is to say the practice of sticking a kitchen ice pick up through the eye sockets of patients with mental illness and having a bit of a scrape around their frontal lobes. The arrival of antipsychotic drugs in the 1950s helped eliminate this barbaric practice and his work became quickly discredited, but not before Freeman, travelling across America in his 'lobotomobile', had performed 3,500 of these procedures (El-Hai 2005).

There is even new evidence about the influence of the PFC on lying, something that has been shown to employ a great deal of PFC action, with structural differences in both the grey and white matter components in this part of the brain between liars and non-liars.[2] A fascinating online article entitled *Liar, Liar, Your Prefrontal Cortex Is On Fire* quotes the *British Journal of Psychiatry* when it describes how liars have 22 per cent more white matter and 14 per cent less grey matter than non-liars. The researchers' conclusion was that this difference meant that liars had the wiring (white matter) necessary to tell 'big whoppers' but not the necessary brain cells (grey matter) to keep an adequate moral check on things. Interestingly, they also found that the complete opposite was true in children with autism, a group that research has shown find it difficult to lie. These children had an equivalent but opposite ratio of grey matter to white.

In his seminal book on the pre-frontal cortex, imaginatively named *The Prefrontal Cortex*, Joaquin M. Fuster describes how planning and decision-making are two of the three main functions of the pre-frontal cortex.

If there is a unique and characteristic feature of that part of the brain, it is its ability to structure the present in order to serve the future.

(Fuster 2008)

In other words, tapping into our innate teleological or goal-oriented cognitive faculties is when we really start to tap into what the PFC can do for us. Once again, with brain research catching up with the best advice from the wise man in the Ferrari, goal setting is a vital tool for helping us to move closer to our potential.

The third of the PFC's main functions is, according to Fuster, the executive functioning[3] we met in chapter 8. We employ the PFC to prepare ourselves properly for the task in hand, to have enough 'working memory' to be able to process what we are doing and to be able to stop ourselves from drifting off to go and find something more interesting to do part-way through.

Sheldon H. Horowitz, Ed.D, director of professional services at the National Center for Learning Disabilities,[4] goes further, explaining that:

> Executive functioning involves activating, orchestrating, monitoring, evaluating, and adapting different strategies to accomplish different tasks. … It requires the ability to analyze situations, plan and take action, focus and maintain attention, and adjust actions as needed to get the job done.

For children with Attention-Deficit Hyperactivity Disorder (ADHD) and other learning difficulties, it is often issues to do with this part of the brain that are leading to their problems in the classroom. A report entitled '"Executive Functioning"——New Research About Familiar Behavior' from the 2003 Independent Educational Consultant Association conference in Washington, DC, reported on the website www.strugglingteens.com, describes how problems with executive functioning can lead to learning difficulties in 'reading, writing, math skills and content area learning', outlining the problems as follows:

> For example, dysfunctions in working memory, an important aspect of executive functioning, can cause difficulties in reading comprehension. Also, poor readers have trouble suppressing the activation of irrelevant information. Writing is adversely affected by problems with sequencing, organizational and self-monitoring skills, and holding ideas in working memory. There is also a strong overlap between dysgraphia and ADHD. Students with poor math skills have trouble with multiple-step procedures that require working memory. Executive dysfunction can also cause difficulties using mental strategies involved in memorization and retrieval.
>
> (www.strugglingteens.com/news/executivefunctioning.html)

Take another look at that list and have a think about how much of what goes on in your classroom involves being able to master these skills. Then imagine how hard it must be to be asked to do these things – to want to do these things – but, for whatever reason, simply not to have the tools to do them.

Consider, too, research on executive functioning in children and adults with dyslexia from the University of Greenwich. Researchers here found that:

> dyslexic individuals show deficiencies in executive functions relating to inhibition of distractors and to sequencing of events, a set of tasks associated with left prefrontal cortex functioning.
>
> (Brosnan *et al.* 2001)

In other words, and I have seen this so often with my dyslexic daughter, it is not their brainpower that means they get the answer wrong and feel stupid but their brain process. They don't need extra maths lessons, they need extra 'how to focus and organize things properly' lessons.[5]

As we have seen, the twenty-first century teacher does not teach subjects; they teach children. You may be helping them to learn a particular body of subject-specific knowledge (a process that may include, but not exclusively, teaching) but remember the premise of this book – they can get that body of facts from Google without getting out of bed. What you can do, though, is to help them develop the skills they need to be able to find, identify, co-opt, employ, store and recall as necessary the new knowledge they are acquiring under your guidance. In other words, your number one priority is not so much teaching them as helping them reduce the obstacles to learning, so many of which relate to the functioning of the PFC. As the Struggling Teens website goes on to point out, citing the research as it goes:

> There is evidence that aspects of executive function can be improved, especially in terms of working memory (Schweitzer, et al), rapid shifting (Cedpeda, et al) and effortful processing (Tannock, et al). One of the more unusual findings is that kids with ADHD who looked in the mirror while working had better executive functioning, suggesting that it enhances emotional regulation. Cognitive rehabilitation studies by Mateer, Kearns, Selmud-Clikeman and others show that attention training is beneficial for children with attentional difficulties. Also, deep rest has been shown to heal the nervous system of stress, in part by lowering cortisol levels. Certain meditation techniques have been documented to improve emotional regulation and sleep, and reduce blood pressure as effectively as medication. Meditation

techniques have also been shown to increase one's ability to focus attention.

(www.strugglingteens.com/news/executivefunctioning.html)

We have had the capacity to teach thinking skills – to educate the prefrontal cortex and develop executive functioning in our children – for a long time now. Are you teaching your children *how* to think as well as *what* to think?

Chapter 13

Don't make 'em mad, make 'em think?

Pick up most brain books and you will find the authors waxing lyrical over the way our brain works, some even arguing that its wonderful design must be the hand of some Divine Creator at work (although the more I have learned about how weird the universe really is, for example how it may have gone from microscopic to astronomical in the blink of an eye according to Inflation Theory, the more I think Intelligent Design makes sense as the least weird option). *Accidental Mind: How Brain Evolution Has Given Us Love, Memory, Dreams, and God* by David J. Linden, professor of neuroscience at the Johns Hopkins University in the US, suggests otherwise. He picks up the triune brain theory research of Paul Maclean, which shows that we don't just have one brain, we have three brains; the oldest is the reptilian brain,[1] the next one to evolve being the limbic system or the mammalian brain and then the 'newest' part of our brain, the bit that makes us human, the neo-cortex. According to Linden the first two parts are essentially a lizard brain 'with some extra stuff thrown on top' to make a mouse brain, with the grand three-part total being no more than 'a mouse brain with extra toppings' (Linden 2008).[2]

So much for the 'most powerful computer in the universe'! In fact, in Linden's words, the brain is quite categorically *not* 'an optimized, generic problem-solving machine, but rather a weird agglomeration of ad hoc solutions that have accumulated throughout millions of years of evolutionary history' (which we will see in chapter 19 is also the process by which we have the education system we do today).

Yet, this 'cobbled together mess' somehow gives us poetry, the fiscal system and the Eurovision Song Contest.

What is interesting to note is the way in which our oh-so-clever neo-cortex is still at the mercy of our basic and millions-of-years-old reptilian brain, whether we like it or not. It's the reason we all watch *Dr Who* from behind the sofa. Understanding this can help us in the classroom when dealing with inappropriate behaviour, can inform our responses to these behaviours and shows that, quite often, our responses make the situation so much worse anyway.

But let's start in Mexico and the watching of lizards. Neuroscientist Paul D. Maclean is the man behind this widespread 'triune brain theory' (which like much in brain research has since been superseded by a more complex model of our evolution, one that now allows us to explain intelligent octopuses and the ability of an African Grey parrot named Alex to name 50 different objects). Maclean drew on the research of a visionary 1930s naturalist, Llewellyn T. Evans, who had spent a great deal of time watching and recording the behaviours of 22 lizards on the wall of a cemetery near the village of Acapancingo in Mexico.

In his seminal book *The Triune Brain in Evolution: Role in Paleocerebral Functions*, Maclean notes that:

> One of the surprising results of studying a variety of terrestrial animals is to discover how relatively few kinds of behavior one can identify in each and how most of these are common to all.
>
> (Maclean 1990)

He identifies a neat list of just 25 lizard behaviours including acts such as 'establishment of territory', 'hunting', 'hoarding', 'mating', 'flocking', 'greeting', 'grooming' and, of course, 'the use of defecation posts'.

The interesting thing is that we humans still carry with us these same behaviours and can resort back to them at any point, without being able to stop ourselves. Consider the daily routine of the average lizard:

1 A slow, cautious emerging in the morning;
2 A preliminary period of basking followed by:
3 Defecation;
4 Local foraging;
5 An inactive period followed by:
6 Foraging further afield;
7 Returning to the shelter area; and
8 Retirement to shelter or roost.

Swap foraging for shopping and add something about football and you have a typical Saturday for many men.

For Maclean, at the heart of this reptilian brain were two small constructions known as the amygdalae after the Greek word for 'almond', which best describes their shape. Known more commonly as the single 'amygdala', it is this basic but powerful part of our brain that determines how we deal with challenge, how we respond to threat and, because of the direct link between emotions and long-term memory, how long we remember what we have learned. As Daniel Goleman points out in *Emotional Intelligence*, the amygdala is what is responsible for 'neural hijacking' when it perceives a dangerous situation and sends a whole torrent of messages and chemicals across the entire brain to help us, effectively, fly, fight, freeze or flock (Goleman 1995). This is something commonly seen in examples of road, air and IKEA rage.

It is worth noting too that the teenage brain relies heavily on its amygdala, far more so than on its work-in-progress pre-frontal cortex. This means that where we may have been expecting a balanced and well-reasoned counter-argument to why they should be allowed to sit with their friend at the back of the classroom, we are met instead with a bag thrown across the room and a hefty kick to the chair that's in their way. What's more, research shows that the teenager's reliance on the amygdala can impair their ability to interpret body language and facial expressions.[3] Research at San Diego State University in the US quoted by Feinstein showed that the ability to read other people's emotions decreased in puberty by up to 20 per cent without reaching normal levels again until the age of about 18 (Feinstein 2004). Further study by Yurgelun-Todd, and cited in an online article entitled *The Teen Brain: Implications for Paediatric Nurses: The Brain Matures: Emotions and Development*, has found that:

> teens were noted to be less skilled in emotional reasoning, showed fewer signs of emotional insight, exhibited more impulsive behavior, and were noted to misread the emotional cues of others more than adults.
>
> (www.medscape.com/viewarticle/504350_4)

One interesting thing about this amygdala-driven reaction process is the fact that all of this happens in a way that entirely bypasses our rational, thinking brains. We respond to threats at a neural and emotional level *before we intellectually realize they are there*. Just by walking into the school grounds your students may be in a neurally hijacked state without even being aware of it. One of the reasons why helping them to get into the right state for learning is so important at the beginning of the day. (Something that a smile can achieve, by the way.)

One of the most important elements of developing emotional intelligence – our EQ – is the ability to identify these neural hijackings and seek to manage them. Not to suppress our feelings or ignore them but not to be at their mercy either. To achieve this state of psychological nirvana – the difference between 'I'm feeling anger' and 'I'm angry' or 'When you do that thing I experience feelings of annoyance and irritation' and 'You make me sick' – we need to re-establish chemical control of our brains and quieten down the amygdala. To do this we need to fight fire with fire or, in this case, chemicals with chemicals. Where do these amygdala-dampening chemicals come from? We're back to our friend from the previous chapter – the pre-frontal cortex.

According to the research, 'The prefrontal cortex and the amygdala have synergistic roles in regulating purposive behavior, effected through bidirectional pathways.' In other words, there are direct lines of communication between our survival-driven ancient lizard brain and our rational, thinking and intellectualizing human fore-brain. What's more, they travel in both directions. Although there are more links going up from the amygdala than coming down to it, it still means that not only do our emotions have a direct input on our thoughts, but also our thoughts can have direct input into our emotions.

What does all this mean for you in your classroom when little Darren is standing with a face like thunder and a pot of red paint in his hand and you know he is just about to lose it completely? It means that you have to do what you can do to give Darren the space, time and especially the strategies to allow him to use his developing pre-frontal cortex to take back over the neurological reins from his currently highly activated amygdalae, something you can help them learn to do by way of a simple acronym – STAR:

Stop
Think
Act
Reflect

This four-step process starts to teach the brain to buy itself time before acting (although in the situation above, it could well be a little late for Darren as his finger is already on the proverbial trigger). The key here, and this is another critical element in the development of emotional intelligence, is to learn to spot when the amygdala is starting to kick in and do something then before it's too late. In my experience, children can do this, even quite young children. The important thing is to teach them the strategies about what to do next. Again, in my experience in classrooms, children usually have two options at this stage – either (1) lose it completely, throw stuff about, hit someone or swear at the teacher and get thrown out of the lesson and onto the slippery slope or (2) suppress these feelings, thus sending a message to their growing sense of self-worth and self-esteem that says, my feelings don't count. STAR offers a third way. One primary school we worked with has a 'STAR corner' where children who know they are about to lose it can go in order to move away from whatever or whoever it was giving them so much trouble, regain control over their neurochemistry and then, when they feel they are ready, rejoin the lesson as if nothing had happened.

What do they do in that critical period between stopping and acting? There are a number of things, but simple visualization and breathing techniques can help. Teaching children simple meditative strategies has been shown to have beneficial effects on stress levels. As the Independent Educational Consultant Association conference that we met in the previous chapter was told:

> Certain meditation techniques have been documented to improve emotional regulation and sleep, and reduce blood pressure as effectively as medication.
>
> (www.strugglingteens.com/news/executivefunctioning.html)

I mentioned this STAR process to a group of teachers from a secondary school recently and one of the deputies spoke to me during the break to thank me for explaining why something he did instinctively worked so well. He was known as 'The Jailer' as he used to be a prison warden and in his inner-city school he was the one who was called on when things were getting out of hand in a particular classroom. One of the things he did was to take the stroppy or threatening student and rather than whisk them away to some exclusion base for a period of solitary confinement in a scholastic version of extraordinary rendition, he would take them for a walk around the school quad. And he would talk to them. And walk. And talk. And let them talk. He said it was not very long before they were able to talk rationally and maturely about what they had done and why it may not have been appropriate and what they maybe could have done differently.

This is STAR in action.

The state they were in which prompted the class teacher to hit the panic button was one of obvious high amygdala arousal. How they got there we can think about in a minute. If 'The Jailer' had entered the classroom all guns blazing as I have seen other members of senior management teams do on occasions (often because they think this is what the teacher who called them expects them to do) then it would be seen by the student as simply another form of attack to go with the one he or she is already experiencing. The amygdala and all associated 'fight or flight' mechanisms will be even more active than before. Even if the deputy had come in and tried to reason with the student at this stage it would still not be particularly effective, as you will know if you have ever tried to persuade a lizard anything. You are trying to reason with a part of the brain that doesn't do reason. And you're trying to use language on a part of the brain that doesn't do language. By taking the student away from the perceived – or real – threat and by engaging him or her in a distracting activity you are giving the brain the time and space it needs to re-balance itself at a neuro-chemical level. And the fact that he engaged the students in a physical activity meant that, as we have seen, he was also tapping into the cere-bellum's dual ability to help us both move and think in a balanced and, quite literally, level-headed way.

If we punish a child when their amygdala is aroused it is seen as another attack. If we punish them when our amygdala is aroused, it is an act of vengeance. Punishment should never be emotionally driven. It should be a simple process of 'cause and effect', clearly demarked. If you do this, this is what will happen.

Sometimes in the classroom our interventions make a bad situation worse. We match their state with a similar one of our own and the whole thing can degenerate into an ever-escalating 'Well, you said that!', 'Well you did that!' war of attrition that is, at the end of the day, two lizards shouting at each other. We need to model the emotionally intelligent STAR approach ourselves. Nipping such a situation in the bud by saying, 'Look, this is getting us nowhere. I'm going to walk over here and breathe and have a think about things and I suggest you do the same and then we'll talk to each other again at the end of the lesson and work out what we are going to do.' While I know this can be hard at times, especially when we are at the mercy of our own amygdalae, the ability to model emotionally intelligent behaviour is one of the most important things you can do for young people. Remember, they may never have seen an emotionally intelligent adult before.

On those occasions when you do lose it completely, afterwards you say 'Sorry'. And remember, 'sorry' is a word that should always be followed by a full stop. Not 'Sorry, but ... if you hadn't done this or that!' Just 'I'm sorry. Will you forgive me so we can move on?'

After all, if we want children to grow up then we must be grown up too.

Chapter 14

Teacher's little helper

There has been a great deal written about the neurotransmitter[1] dopamine[2] in recent years, much of it because of the part it plays – or the lack of it plays – in diseases such as depression and Parkinson's. But in the classroom, dopamine means the difference between the class learning and not learning, between them remembering what they learned and forgetting it before the bell goes, between them behaving and applying themselves or causing chaos. It is dopamine that even decides how well those critical first few minutes of lesson go.

If teaching is about creating the right neurochemical cocktail, then dopamine is the tequila in the twenty-first century teacher's margarita.

As you know, the brain 'works' by sending signals between brain cells. To do this the brain employs neurotransmitters that relay, amplify and modulate signals between a neuron and another cell. There are a range of such neurotransmitters such as noradrenaline and epinephrine which are linked to stress and 'fight or flight' response, melatonin[3] which promotes sleepiness and is known as the 'hormone of darkness' and serotonin which regulates mood among other things and is a key element in our fight against depression (hence the SSRI or 'selective serotonin reuptake inhibitor' family of antidepressant drugs such as Prozac).

Dopamine, or $C_6H_3(OH)_2\text{-}CH_2\text{-}CH_2\text{-}NH_2$ as it is known to people in the know, is a naturally occurring chemical in the brain that has an important role in our thinking, movement, motivation, reward, sleep, mood attention, physical growth, sexual development and learning. It even has a part to play in why bananas go brown.

Bananas aside, as they like to say on the Windward Isles, when just the right amount of dopamine is released at just the right time in just the right way the neurological consequence is learning. Dopamine is the principal 'synaptogenic' chemical in the brain, followed closely by glutamate, another key neurotransmitter linked to learning and memory. In other words, it is the number one chemical when it comes to laying down new pathways, building new templates and learning – and remembering – new things. As Dr Curran points out:

> In fact, if dopamine has been released with glutamate, your brain will learn whatever it is paying attention to at the time – and there is very little you can do about it.
>
> (Curran 2008)

So, create the environment where the right levels of dopamine are produced in their heads and they can't do anything but learn. And how do you do that? There are two good ways in which we can hit the dopamine production button in our heads, and one bad one, the use of which can do more harm than good. A quick and easy, yet wrong, way to produce dopamine in students' brains is through stress. Simply cultivate an environment of fear and anxiety and you will have the dopamine levels up in no time. The trouble is that dopamine produced in this way has the same effect on brain cells as painting by numbers using a bucket of paint. You simply flood the brain with this chemical in a way that can ultimately lead to a failure to produce dopamine leading to psycho-emotional conditions such as chronic fatigue syndrome. Such a high stress environment also generates high levels of the stress hormones leading to the sorts of harmful subconscious learning we talked about in chapter 10 and causes us to produce steroids that can kill off brain cells in the hippocampus, a part of our brain linked to the creation of memories and, hence, the neurological equivalent of sawing off the branch you are sitting on.

So, if high levels of stress as a way of producing dopamine are out, what does that leave? The 'good' two ways of producing this neurochemical are:

1   Reward
2   The anticipation of reward.

That's it. Simply (1) doing things they like doing or (2) knowing they are about to do the things they like doing, is enough to get just the right amount of dopamine being delivered to just the right places in their learning brains. In other words, you can create effective neurochemistry by ensuring they are enjoying your lesson, either through the nature of the work and the challenge itself and/or through the opportunities they have to experience enjoyment, opportunities that may or may not be linked directly to the subject matter they are learning but do have a direct impact on the process. These could be activities like telling a joke, having a laugh, doing physical exercise, working in groups or teams, having an element of surprise or novelty, listening to music in an appropriate way. In fact, you get the dopamine right by simply employing that old elusive perennial, having fun (more of which in the next chapter).

Such experiences in the classroom hit the 'reward' element of dopamine stimulation but what about the 'anticipation of reward' side of things? What this means is that if you get point one right – they enjoy your lesson – then point two will fall into place naturally. Just by walking into your classroom or seeing your face, their brain is receiving the message, 'This is where the good stuff happens' and the dopamine is starting to flow. You have created a virtuous circle of 4-(2-aminoethyl)benzene-1,2-diol-related learning just by being so damn good at what you do and the world will be eternally grateful.

What's more, and this is another reason why this particular chemical really is the teacher's friend, an appropriate surge in dopamine levels actually improves our memory for what was going on in the 15 to 20 minutes or so *prior to* that surge taking place. The brain likes doing what it likes doing. It is, in the words of Mihály Csíkszentmihályi in the seminal book *Flow: the Psychology of Optimal Experience*, 'genetically programmed to seek out pleasure' (Csíkszentmihályi 1990). It makes sense then that, when it finds itself in the throws of performing an act that is causing it to experience all the pleasurable feelings associated with dopamine, it does all it can to remember what brought about this experience so it can repeat it. Just by saying to the class, 'OK people, put your pens down, whose turn is it to play their favourite track today?' you may well be improving their memory for the 20 minutes of binomial fractions they were just working on.

The teenage brain is especially susceptible to dopamine and craves it and all the feel-good factors it brings. This means the teenage brain is also particularly susceptible to risk-taking, dangerous behaviours, falling in love and addictive substances. Research also shows that children with ADHD can become hyperactive as a way of self-medicating with dopamine.[4] What this all means in your classroom is that they will seek out dopamine either with your help or despite you. They will either get their fix by the way you present lessons and learning opportunities that engage positive emotions combined with novelty and engagement. Or they will mess around, take risks, challenge you because you stand for 'The Man!', push the boundaries and do anything else that can take them 'to the edge' (whilst pushing you over it).

Dopamine can be, then, the teacher's friend or the teacher's foe. Which one it ends up being is, as with so much in the twenty-first century classroom, down to you.

Chapter 15

The 'f-word'

If I had had a pound for every time the word 'fun' was mentioned during my teacher training I would have been a very rich student teacher and would have worn a better suit. (If I had had a pound for every time the word 'brain' was mentioned I would have had £3.50, and that was only because the scheduled lecturer did not turn up so someone stepped in at the last minute who had just read a book.)

Fun seemed to be the Holy Grail of good learning yet no-one in authority really seemed to be able to say why or even cared that much when the lessons were palpably not fun. There was certainly no space given over in the lesson planning sheets for 'Insert fun here' not to mention any of the other positive emotions we are capable of experiencing. A lesson without any positive emotions could still be deemed to be a good, solid lesson, despite what Plato said over 2,000 years ago – 'All learning has an emotional base' – and what neuroscience is telling us now – 'Learning (the building up of connections between nerve cells to form templates) is therefore largely directed and controlled by your emotional/limbic brain', in the words of the ubiquitous Dr Curran (2008).

By the way, in case you are worried about having fun when the inspectors come to call remember, you are not having fun, you are using positive emotions to access the limbic system to optimize dopamine secretion to facilitate autonomic learning.

It just looks like fun.

What Plato knew 2,000 years ago, a pioneering nineteenth century educationalist whom we will meet again in chapter 18, called Samuel Wilderspin knew 150 years ago:

> Accordingly, the utmost attention is given to the cheerfulness and happiness of those on whom (the system) acts. Instruction in reading, arithmetic, geometry, and various other things is made exceedingly amusing; smiling countenances and sparkling eyes are observable all

around when it is communicated; and what was dull and soporific, according to the old plan, is now insinuated so agreeably, that the child, while literally at play, is acquiring a large amount of valuable knowledge. At play he sees Nature's book, that world of beauties: he loves to look into it, there is no flogging to induce him to do it. All is enquiry and anxiety on his part. 'What is this?' 'What is that?' 'What is it for?' 'How did it come?' With numerous other questions of similar import. Oh, that we had teachers to teach more out of this divine book! Oh, that we had a public who would encourage and cherish them for so doing! What blessed results even have I seen, by one's being able to answer such enquiries!

(www.gutenberg.org/files/10985/10985-8.txt)

So, the question for the twenty-first century teacher is, are you specifically planning for the use of positive emotions during your lessons to make learning more effective all round?

Fun, of course, means different things to different people and whilst chopping up a pig's eyeball may get half of your class going it may have the opposite effect on the rest. Especially if you're using it to teach irregular verbs. Fun is also just a part of the picture. Here, according to Barbara Fredrickson, Kenan Distinguished Professor of Psychology at North Carolina and author of *Positivity: Groundbreaking Research Reveals How to Embrace the Hidden Strength of Positive Emotions, Overcome Negativity, and Thrive*, are the top ten scientifically accurate 'proven to make us feel good' list of positive emotions:

Joy
Gratitude
Serenity
Interest
Hope
Pride
Amusement
Inspiration
Awe
And, of course, at number one, Love.

(Fredrickson 2009)

What if you were to plan lessons that, rather than just focusing on what you wanted them to learn or the skills you wanted them to develop, also included how you wanted them to *feel* and what you were going to do to help them have the opportunity to do so? Could you plan a maths lesson that had opportunity for 'serenity' (although, maybe not too serene – remember, counting sheep can count as numeracy)? A DT lesson that has space for 'joy'? A PE theory lesson that had space for 'gratitude', and not just at the end?

Of course, there are no such things as positive, or indeed negative, emotions. There are just emotions and our individual responses to them. Like fun, they will mean different things to different people and one person's pride may be another person's arrogance. (The way to spot the difference, I was once told, between an arrogant person and a confident person is that the former makes you feel worse about yourself and the latter makes you feel better about yourself. Easy really.)

The emotions I recommend when I'm working with teachers usually include the following:[1]

Novelty: Remember, 'it's the brain stupid'. The human brain, 'kludge' that it is in David Linden's words, can't make its mind up for itself. While on the one hand the reptilian brain seeks routine, predictability and the sense of safety such sameness brings, higher parts of the brain crave novelty and unpredictability, especially in the young brain. The Von Restorff Effect[2] decrees that if something stands out as being novel and in stark contrast to what is around it in either time or place, it makes it more memorable. (Our friends at Wikipedia also refer to this as the 'isolation effect' and throw in the 'serial position effect', the 'humor effect' and the 'bizarreness effect' for good measure.)

Suspense: 'Coming up after the break … '. In broadcast terms this is called 'throwing forward' and it is a very clever way of holding people's attention and creating a sense of suspense. Similarly, setting the learning outcome as, 'Today we are going to learn the structure of the sonnet' would have a very different effect if you phrased it as, 'Today we are going to learn how to win the man or woman of your dreams in just 14 lines'.

Winning: Some of the most tedious moments of my life have been on a primary school playing field watching my children's non-competitive sports days. According to Judith Rich Harris, author of *No Two Alike: Human Nature and Human Individuality*, children use three different 'systems of the mind' for carrying out three main social tasks they are faced with during childhood, namely a 'relationship system' for getting on with people, a 'socialization system' for fitting in and a 'status system' for competing. 'Children want to conform *and* compete', she says (Rich Harris 2007). Winning and losing is part of life so get over it and learn how to compete[3] (as well as how to collaborate) and learn how to win and win graciously and positively whilst enjoying all the feel-good feelings that come with knowing you have achieved something special through your hard work and effort.

Losing: See above. If you don't know how to lose you don't know how to play.

Pathos: Although not every scientist agrees, there is a growing body of knowledge to show that we have 'mirror neurons', that the parts of our brain that we use to experience our own emotions such as happiness, sadness or disgust, are actually activated by watching someone else experience those emotions. Feeling sorry for someone may be one thing – sympathy – but helping young people fire up parts of the brain that will help them actually feel like what it is like to be someone else – empathy – takes their learning to a whole new level. Especially when you remember the key role that emotion plays in the learning brain. I once observed a history lesson on the capture, transportation, auctioning, torture, punishment and murder of Black African slaves. It was a perfectly satisfactory multisensory, fully VAK-ed lesson. Yet I left with a huge sense of unease and anger. How can you have a lesson where the torture and castration of human beings is treated in the same way as you would treat other historical 'facts' such as the dates of the Franco-Prussian War or factors surrounding American Independence? There was a whole emotional level to the learning that the teacher simply ignored, something I found pedagogically, not to mention morally, wrong.

Curiosity: In 2005, I led a three-month circumnavigation of the British Isles on the back of this one word.[4] We took our motivation from one of Proust's shorter sentences:

> The real voyage of discovery consists not in seeking new landscapes, but in having new eyes.

The project was essentially a voyage of discovery from A to A. The whole point was to try to show how being curious can change everything, if you let it. Especially when you consider that, as a word, 'curiosity' has the same origins as the word 'curator' which means to look after. Curiosity is a survival drive within us all. If teachers tap into it, the battle for motivation in the classroom is half won. Whether it's true or not I don't know, but it has been said that Einstein's mum used to ask him what questions he asked at school at the end of each day. I have repeatedly tried that with my three children over the years but they simply look at me gone out! School is the place where you go to be the passive recipient of other people's knowledge as far as their experience has shown them. Yet, research shows that three- to four-year-olds ask, on average, 3,000 to 4,000 questions in a year. What happens to the toddler's question-posing mania? Does it get knocked out of him or her by education's fact-giving mania? It doesn't have to be that way. This is one of the reasons I love messing with children's heads under the guise of *Philosophy for Children*.[5] For those of you who haven't come across it yet, *Philosophy for Children* or *P4C* started with an American professor of philosophy called Matthew Lipman who realized that his undergraduates at Columbia University could tell him what Socrates or Descartes thought but couldn't think for themselves. To do something to change this, Lipman put together a programme and a process, based around a number of children's storybooks he wrote of differing levels of complexity, starting with five-year-olds. The process involved creating a 'community of enquiry' with children seated in a circle, giving the community a stimulus such as one of his stories or a poem or a picture or a song or whatever you think is relevant, and then garnering the *children's own questions*. The group then address these questions in a careful and democratic way. It is a very powerful – albeit a little long-winded – process that creates some quite stunning insights into children's thinking and was the origin of my *Thunks*, of which more later. What it does do is tap into that most powerful of emotions, though, curiosity.

So, to what extent are you using emotions such as curiosity to get children thinking and learning in your classroom and *not as an optional extra*?

And then there's the whole idea of whether we should actually teach children how to be happy. Well, from a health and well-being perspective there seem to be lots of positive reasons for doing this, including research on longevity that found that happy nuns lived longer as did Oscar winning actors compared to those who were nominated but never made it.[6] Not to mention the fact that 'gelotologists' have found that laughing and generally being happy increases production of immune cells, drastically decreases levels of the stress hormone cortisol, decreases levels of epinephrine linked to hypertension and heart failure, releases natural opiates from the pituitary gland to help with pain relief, raises levels of antibodies in our saliva, produces the natural antibiotic enkelytin, helps combat pulmonary problems, eases respiratory tract infections, increases antibodies by 50 per cent after flu injections, increases quantities of 'killer cells' and accelerates the body's anticarcinogenic response.[7,8] There is even research that found mothers who laughed a few hours before breastfeeding released a chemical into their milk that helped reduce the baby's symptoms of eczema.[9] Laughter may also make you cleverer, as there is also research suggesting that its 'biological function is to make brain operations more efficient'.[10]

Some may argue that teaching happiness is covered within school anyway under a general PSHE 'health and well-being' banner, but in his book *Happiness: Lessons From a New Science*, economist Richard Layard, the government's so-called Happiness Tsar (or Baron Layard of Highgate as he is known to his New Labour friends) shows that he has more than an inkling of what goes on in the standard PSHE lesson:

> Regrettably, it is often taught by non-specialists even in secondary schools and its purpose is not radical enough – it should aim to produce a happier generation of adults than the current generation.
>
> (Layard 2005)

As has been widely reported, the teaching of happiness has been championed at Wellington College,[11] an independent school in Berkshire where headteacher Dr Anthony Seldon (who, the school's website points out, is also a biographer of Tony Blair) states:

> 'Happiness' is the contemporary buzzword. Every media outlet is discussing whether it should be an objective of government policy and whether it can be taught. It can be and must be, in our opinion.
>
> (www.wellingtoncollege.org.uk/page.aspx?id=2198)

The school has linked up with Cambridge University's Well-Being Institute[12] and designed lessons that address related issues such as the relationship between mind and body, between their conscious and subconscious and between their past, present, future and fantasy lives. I am inclined to agree with Dr Seldon. We need to teach children to take the time as well as tell the time. What's more, happiness is something you take, not something you find. It is like fruit, not air. Our children need to be taught this before they go through their entire lives waiting to be happy. Part of such happiness teaching is to help them understand that, despite adverts such as one I saw for a mobile phone eBay application headed 'Shop While You Shop', you can't buy your way to happiness (happiness by such events is the most transitory type, happiness through relationships is the next best and happiness through having a meaning in your life comes out on top). However, the UK's biggest teaching union is quick to bring its own particular brand of hard-done-by misery to the joyful proceedings with one of its leaders quoted on the BBC News website as saying:

> Our members recognize the diagnosis but will be concerned by the solution. If schools are going to spend more time on developing ethos

and encouraging pupils to be confident and happy then less time needs to be spent on lessons.

(http://news.bbc.co.uk/1/hi/education/6618431.stm)

Research quoted in the *Scientific American Mind* article entailed exposing students to a funny video clip after learning a list of words. The students who laughed after learning improved their recall by 20 per cent.

You've got to laugh ... .

Chapter 16

It might be touchy-feely but it's still the most important thing you do

One of the first groups I worked with using the *Philosophy for Children* approach I mentioned briefly in chapter 15 was a group of year nine students at a school somewhere just off the Watford Gap. The head of year had called me into her office one day during one of my visits to the school to ask my advice. She said that, as a school, they felt they knew what they were doing with their gifted and talented cohort and that the troublesome oiks also demanded and received a great deal of their time and energies. She was worried, though, about the ones in the middle. The 'lost boys and girls' as she called them. You may know them as the 'grey children'. Those students in the lesson who never seem to raise their heads above the parapet, who never appear on the teacher radar, who never do or say anything noticeable, the ones you need a photo of on parents evening, you know the ones … .

I recommended the *P4C* approach and we put together a programme that consisted of a few lessons each term for a year working with me, supported by a friendly and willing classroom teacher. I just felt that *P4C* had a way of getting quiet kids to talk. I was right.

Over the course of the year, these 'quiet' children started to run their own *P4C* club during lunchtimes, held philosophy lunches to which other students and staff were invited, led a whole school INSET session on why they wanted *P4C* approaches in all lessons, went into the feeder primary schools to deliver *P4C* lessons to the year sixes, spoke at a national conference, the first children to address this particular group of *P4C* practitioners, were featured on *Teacher's TV* and Radio Four's *Learning Curve* and put together a website about their experiences. What was at the heart of this transformation? I think it was quite simple:

My thoughts count therefore I count.

From a sociological ('Self-esteem, a person's positive or negative evaluation of him – or herself – has been recognized as a predictor of social problems in the recent research of psychological and social development'), psychological ('Past research studies have found direct links between low self-esteem and substance abuse, unprotected sex, criminal behaviors, particular personality disorders, depression, and suicide'[1]) and neurological ('Robust behavioral data indicated that the participants responded relatively rapidly in the congruent condition when associating self with positive items, supporting the hypothesis that most people have a positive attitude towards self. Scalp event-related brain potential analysis revealed that self items in the congruent condition elicited a more positive ERP deflection than those in the incongruent condition between 350 and 450 ms after the onset of the self items'[2]) point of view, self-esteem, 'The highest thing we can hope for', according to the philosopher Spinoza, is your bottom line. And I say that as a teacher, as a parent of three, as a husband, as a human being and as someone who has seen the best and the very worst of the effects of self-esteem. If we want adults who are healthy both physically and mentally, who are capable of making and sustaining meaningful relationships, who can deal with challenge and stress and failure and even success in the twenty-first century, we need you to send young people away from our schools with good self-esteem, no matter what it says on their bits of paper.

Before I give you the best definition we've come across of self-esteem, one I referred to in *Essential Motivation* and make no bones about referring to again, let me take you through two interesting and not a little controversial opinions about self-esteem.

One is that you can't raise someone's self-esteem above your own. What are you doing to look after yourself to be able to look after others? Teaching is a hugely giving profession and, because of that, you have to take in order to have something to give. This is especially true if you are a school leader, not only in terms of looking after yourself but also because you are such a powerful model to the people who work for you (even if all they are learning is how *not* to lead a school).

I tell headteachers of a true story I heard about from the States of a man who died at his desk at work, but no-one noticed for three days. Why? Because he was always the first one in each morning and always the last one to leave. People were so used to him being at his desk when they arrived and when they left that no-one thought to check he was still breathing. My question, then, for headteachers everywhere is this one:

Would your staff notice if you were dead?

The other curious idea about self-esteem is that you can't raise someone else's. It is not yours to raise. After all, it's *self*-esteem. It's not what I think about you, it's what *you* think about you. I can think you're a waste of space but as long as you don't agree then your self-esteem will be OK. Alternatively, I can think you're great but if you think you're a waste of space, then me simply disagreeing with you will not change anything. And trying to 'pump you up' by getting you to say positive things about yourself just makes matters worse. According to *The Economist*,[3] research shows that 'positive self-statements cause negative moods in people with low self-esteem because they conflict with those people's views of themselves'. What I can do, though, is to create the opportunities, the ethos, and the atmosphere in which you can start to see for yourself how great you can be.

This is what I believe was inadvertently happening with the 'lost boys and girls'. I didn't go in and give them some ra-ra tubthumping motivational speech. Far from it. We never touched on the issue of motivation or self-esteem or anything remotely psychological. I simply asked them questions like 'Is it ever right to bully a bully?' and 'If I stick a bunch of flowers in the back of a computer does it become a vase?'

(And so *Thunks* were born.)

To what extent, then, are the children in your care given the opportunity to raise their own self-esteem?

Which brings us to the best definition I have come across. Bear in mind that it is a two-part definition and what counts is that you *feel* these things, not that you *are* them. To have high self-esteem I must feel capable and I must feel loveable.

Simple really. Yet, you know people who feel capable but don't feel loveable don't you? For example, who said this?

> I have worked very hard all my life, and I have achieved a great deal – in the end to achieve nothing.

Any ideas? I'll give you a clue – he was voted the *Greatest Briton of the Twentieth Century*.[4]

Winston Churchill, who spoke the sad line above to his private secretary Anthony Montague Browne, was sent off to boarding school before he was eight whereupon he was effectively forgotten about by his parents. His sense of rejection and sadness haunted him all his life. In the book *Churchill's Black Dog*, psychiatrist Anthony Storr quotes Randolph Churchill as saying, 'The neglect and lack of interest in him shown by his parents were remarkable, even judged by the standards of late Victorian and Edwardian days' and cites his mother's failure to reply to his letters from school or visit him as a key reason for him feeling 'exceptionally lonely and abandoned'. Storr says:

> We are, I believe, entitled to assume that Winston Churchill was deprived by parental neglect of this inner source of self esteem upon

which most predominantly happy persons rely, and which serves to carry them through the inevitable disappointments and reverses of human existence.

(Storr 1989)

Churchill's last words before slipping into a coma in 1965? 'I am bored with it all.'

Which brings us to Karen Carpenter. In various sources relating to her life and death there are references to her relationship with her mother. I once heard a radio interview years ago where a friend of the family described how Karen Carpenter's mother 'never said she loved her'. Maybe it was the same friend, Frenda Franklin, who is quoted in the New York Times as saying:

> Karen's mother never told her she was a good singer.
> (www.nytimes.com/1996/10/06/magazine/karen-
> carpenter-s-second-life.html?pagewanted=1)

(When we work with parents, by the way, we always recommend three things they can do for their children each day: tell them you love them, praise them for at least one thing and, because we know incontrovertibly that appropriate physical contact helps the brain develop in a healthy way, hug them.)

Although there are arguments from a neurological point of view that the psychological flaws in an individual are laid down around the age of three[5] (researchers who looked at 1,000 children and then re-examined them at age 26 found that 'children's early-emerging behavioral styles can foretell their characteristic behaviors, thoughts, and feelings as adults, pointing to the foundations of the human personality in the early years of life'), it is claimed that self-esteem starts to fall into place between the ages of five and eight.[6] Before that, feeling capable and feeling loveable work independently of each other. At this stage, according to the research quoted by Flinders University in Australia, self-esteem can be seen to operate across five areas of a child's life – 'physical appearance, social acceptance, scholastic ability, athletic and artistic skills and behaviour'.

According to the turn of the century US sociologist Charles Cooley, we have what he called a 'looking glass self'.[7] Who we come to think of as who we are is just what we see reflected in the way others see us. And this is something that starts at an early age. Just who are these 'others'? In childhood, according to Jaana Juvonen and Kathryn R. Wentze in their fascinating book *Social Motivation: Understanding Children's School Adjustment*, they can be divided into four groups – peers, parents, teachers and an individual's best friend (Juvonen and Wentze 1996). And they are in this order in terms of their influence too, although the last one clearly lags behind the other three.

Parents may play a hugely important role in the development of a child's sense of self-worth and their self-esteem (and it would appear mothers especially so – there is even evidence of a correlation between a mother's low expectations of her daughter and that daughter's subsequent sense of having little control over her life[8]) but the teacher can and does make a significant difference too, for better or for worse. The authors of the study are at pains to point out that the teacher effect 'correlates significantly', even suggesting that their research may have not fully revealed the significance of the teacher effect:

> The correlation between teacher approval and self esteem may actually underestimate the influence of a given teacher in a child's life.

They also reveal – and this is telling for all those teachers everywhere who have asked me, as I described in chapter 10, if their influence is too little too late with some children from some families – that 'Evidence from our laboratory further reveals that teacher support may serve to compensate for low parent support ... higher teacher support resulted in higher levels of self esteem.'

Furthermore, OECD research found that being an avid and enthusiastic reader at school[9] was more of an advantage to a child than having educated and professional parents. In other words, do teachers make a difference to young people from troubled backgrounds who are battling to find their voice in the world? As sure as eggs are eggs and grandads carry Polos!

And then there's Robbie Williams. In the 2006 Emmy-award winning BBC documentary *The Secret Life of the Manic Depressive*,[10] Stephen Fry talked about his troubled school life and also interviewed other celebrities who have battled mental illness. One such interview was with former *Take That* singer Robbie Williams who has fought with mental illness, self-esteem issues and related drug and alcohol problems for a long time. For me, Williams was a prime example of someone who *felt* eminently capable but also, somehow, *felt* very unloveable. 'My career went like that,' he describes to Fry pointing upwards with one hand, 'and my self-esteem and my depression went like that,' as he points down with the other. Find someone in the staffroom with a copy of Williams's 1997 CD *Life Thru a Lens*, then fast-forward track 11 until you get to about 13-and-a-half minutes. You will then hear a very powerful and personal poem by Williams aimed at a former English teacher of his who told him that all he was good for was joining the army, entitled *Hello Sir, Remember Me?*[11] I have known schools that have based a whole day's INSET looking at self-esteem and emotional intelligence around this one poem that reveals the extent to which teachers have the power to harm – or to significantly enhance – the young people in their care.

Young people who are actually very talented but have a very low self-worth is something that I focus on especially when I am working with independent girls schools. I have met too many female teachers who tell me, once the unspoken subject is broached, how 'stupid' they felt at school but then, upon arriving at university where the population, although rarefied, was less so, realized that, actually, they were quite clever. You can see the look in their eyes that belies how angry and cheated they felt by the experience. Another female teacher I met told me how she had spent years teaching in the same school because she felt that if she moved, 'they would find her out'. In *Britain on the Couch*, psychologist Oliver James reports on research conducted on working class and middle class girls in Great Britain that bears this observation out fully:

> All the middle class girls, without exception, were considerably more anxious and stressed than the working class girls. Despite mostly having done very well academically, they felt they had not achieved enough. ... The majority of them (the middle class girls) went to schools where high performance was the norm and therefore high performance came to be regarded as average. A young woman who did well would not see herself as particularly outstanding because achievement was what was expected of her.
>
> (James 1998)

James goes on to quote the head of a particularly high-achieving Birmingham girls' school who says:

> Even our really clever girls do not realize how clever they are. All their friends are bright and intelligent and they do not realize everyone is not like that.
>
> (James 1998)

Of note is the fact that the subtitle for James's book is 'Treating a Low Serotonin Society'. Serotonin is a neurotransmitter, an imbalance of which is linked to clinical depression. Prozac works – and no-one is quite sure how – by raising levels of serotonin in the brain. In a 2008 report entitled *Adolescent School Failure Predicts Depression Among Girls*, the researchers found that there was a direct link between 'adolescent school failures' and depression in young adulthood in girls. (There were no such correlations in boys.) And, as James's work highlights, school failure isn't an absolute. It's relative and personal. If you think you are a failure, no matter what it says on the bits of paper, you are a failure. Bearing this in mind, the conclusion of the 2008 research is telling, giving the subject of this chapter:

> This study highlights the mutual interplay between school failure and psychological functioning. It is suggested that school adaptation in adolescence be considered a mental health issue.
>
> (McCarty *et al.* 2008)

So much for those who feel 'capable but don't feel loveable'. What of those, then, who feel 'loveable but not capable'? These are the types who are the life and soul of the party but ask them about their aspirations and expectations and they are full of the 'I didn't do well at school, I'm not very clever' justifications to explain away why they haven't achieved as well as others. Or rather, why they think they haven't. I went to a parents evening once for my seven-year-old daughter where the class teacher was at pains to point out how 'average' she was at literacy and numeracy but 'what a delightful girl she was to have in the class'. It was only at the end of the interview, when I broached the topic of subjects like art and dance that the teacher said, 'Oh yes, she's very good at them!' This is 'loveable but not capable' training in action.

In a similar vein, there is the story of one of the UK's most successful ever clothes designers, Sir Paul Smith. Smith left school in Beeston, Nottinghamshire at the age of 15 with no qualifications, partly because he didn't see the point and partly because of what was, at the time, undiagnosed dyslexia.[12] He wanted to be a professional cyclist until a serious accident put him in hospital for six months. A new circle of friends opened the door to him on a whole new world of fashion and design which he merged with his father's experience as a 'credit draper' making blazers for the likes of Brian Clough's Nottingham Forest Football Club. ('Cloughie was really clever because he realized that instead of all arriving in tracksuits, blazers would give you the edge on the other team because you looked like a team and you had a certain attitude,' says Smith.[13]) From cycling to work at a fabric warehouse in the Midlands to Fifth Avenue via Savile Row and Buckingham Palace to pick up his knighthood, you would think such achievements would be enough proof to anyone about how clever they are. But this is not the case with Smith. In an article in *The Observer* he says:

> Dyslexia had a big effect on me. ... My biggest regret is my lack of education ... I tend to feel inadequate if I'm at a dinner party and the

subject starts getting heavy. Then it's on with the court jester jacket I'm afraid.

(*Observer*, 25/09/05)

We all know people who have achieved a great deal but still carry around with them this burden of stupidity all their lives. But it is an unnecessary burden. What are you doing to make sure no child leaves your care with such a burden?

Although not actually part of the Hippocratic Oath as many believe, the phrase 'Primum non nocere' is one that all doctors are taught in medical school. It means 'First, do no harm'.[14] Maybe there should be something similar for teachers too. I know that the vast majority of us never deliberately set out to do harm but how many of us do so inadvertently? With a better understanding of the power that a teacher has, an understanding that draws on what is known in neuroscience, psychology, sociology and any other 'ology' you care to mention, the twenty-first century teacher begins to understand just what Spiderman's Uncle Ben meant when he said:

With great power comes great responsibility.

Chapter 17

What's the real point of school?

According to the writer John Mortimer:

> The main aim of education should be to send children out into the world with a reasonably sized anthology in their heads so that, while seated in the lavatory, waiting in doctors' surgeries, on stationary trains or watching interviews with politicians, they may have something interesting to think about.

I saw a colleague of mine put a task to a group of primary headteachers a while back. It was for them to answer the simple question, 'What is the point of education?' As you may expect from a group of primary headteachers, most of the answers came back as, 'To educate our children', 'To bring the best out of them', 'To help them fulfil their potential' … . While I am sure that such answers were the genuine reasons why *they* were in education none of them is the answer as to what the school system is for.

And when you understand that you can start to realize why it looks like it does and, importantly, what can be done to change things for the twenty-first century.

As we heard earlier, business guru Tom Peters feels that, 'education is economics and economics is education' (Peters 1994), and while we have seen there is more to it than simply churning out qualified people, Peters is making clear that being stupid is certainly not the way forward to economic success. Despite his business focus, Peters is passionate about education. 'I get very emotional about this topic,' he admits in his 2003 book, *Re-imagine!*, describing how he wrote a chapter on the topic in a 'rage against the knowing malevolence of the designers of our schools system'. He describes how legendary industrialist J.D. Rockefeller established the General Education Board in the US in 1906, an organization whose goal was that:

In our dreams, people yield themselves with perfect docility to our molding hands.

(Peters 2003)

As Peters says, 'How could so many people be so collectively stupid?'

Yet, at the time, that was what we wanted – an education system to do just that. What we in the UK had started with the Agricultural and Industrial Revolutions, Rockefeller was taking to its logical conclusion, followed shortly after by a man called Frederick W. Taylor[1] who would change the face of the world of work forever. A mechanical engineer from Pennsylvania, Taylor was driven by the need to make the working practices in the factories and elsewhere more efficient, to address what President Theodore Roosevelt had described as the 'larger question of increasing our national efficiency'. The answer, Taylor felt, lay not in individual achievement but in the system. 'No great man,' he states in his seminal 1911 publication *The Principles of Scientific Management*, 'can (with the old system of personal management) hope to compete with a number of ordinary men who have been properly organized so as efficiently to cooperate.'

Taylor promised greater efficiencies leading to higher productivity leading to shorter working hours and more money for all (although the latter two were often abused by certain less than scrupulous factory owners who saw it as a way of getting people to work more for less money while they made bigger profits). The trade-off for all this greater productivity and wealth was quite straightforward. It was vital that people didn't think for themselves. If they did, then they would mess up the system. As Taylor says:

In the past the man has been first; in the future the system must be first.

(Taylor 1911)

So, out went the artisans, the artists and the thinkers. 'Craftsmen had been thrown out of work by the machines' as Bertrand Russell wrote in 1952 in *The Impact of Science on Society*. Instead, in came Man's role as cogs in the apparatus, human and machine working together to produce. This was something parodied by Charlie Chaplin in his 1936 masterpiece *Modern Times*, a comment on the desperate times suffered by people during the Great Depression, something which he felt was created 'by the efficiencies of modern industrialization'.

In the early stages of the Industrial Revolution, children[2] were very much part of the industrial process but with the various Factory Acts[3] of the nineteenth century in the UK, children were not allowed to work in the factories until they reached the age of nine. For example, the Factory Act of 1802, also known as the *Health and Morals of Apprentices Act*, not only outlawed the use of children under nine in the textile mills but also legislated that:

> every such apprentice shall be instructed, in some part of every working day, for the first 4 years at least of his or her apprenticeship … in the usual hours of work, in reading, writing, and arithmetic, or either of them, according to the age and abilities of such apprentice, by some discreet and proper person, to be provided and paid by the master or mistress of such apprentice, in some room or place in such mill or factory to be set apart for that purpose.
>
> (www.umassd.edu/ir/resources/workingconditions/w1.doc)

Schools became a way, then, of keeping off the streets the children that the new Act meant were no longer in the factories with their parents whilst, at the same time, serving to equip young people with enough of the three Rs to be able to work in the factories when they were old enough and develop prerequisite respect for authority, willingness to die for your country and a love of (and fear of) God.

And what better model for a school than a factory? I was observing a history lesson once where a group of children in a dire and bleak inner-city school were being shown a video on life for children in the Victorian mills. Although they seemed oblivious to it, the irony was not lost on me of how the list of rules the Victorian children were subjected to – punishments for being late, for whistling, singing or talking, for opening a window, for swearing, for not immediately following instructions, for leaving the workplace untidy or for leaving it without permission – were pretty much identical to the rules these twentieth-century children were expected to follow at school.

In *The Unfinished Revolution* by John Abbott and Terry Ryan, a book that I have been urging teachers to read for years, they describe how, far from being designed as a process whereby we bring the best out of young minds, 'a primary aim of education became preparing workers for their place in rationally planned manufacturing' with formal education being used by successive governments 'to develop loyal, productive and socially contented citizens'. And for us, in class-ridden England, this was especially so:

> For England, probably more than for any other Western country, education of the masses was a form of social control totally separate from the education of the elite.
>
> (Abbot and Ryan 2000)

(By the way, before you dismiss such claims as 'socialist conspiracy theory propaganda' you may want to look at the profile of the man who wrote them, John Abbott,[4] head of the *21st Century Learning Initiative*,[5] public-school and Trinity College educated, ex-Geography teacher at Manchester Grammar School when it was 'the most highly selective grammar school in the UK' and a former grammar school headteacher. The sort of school that Peter Ustinov went to where they wrote on one of his reports, 'He shows great originality which must be curbed at all cost'.)

What's more, as Adam Smith pointed out in *The Wealth of Nations*, it became a vicious circle:

> The man whose whole life is spent in performing a few simple operations ... has no occasion to exert his understanding or to exercise his invention ... He naturally loses, therefore, the habit of such exertion and generally becomes as stupid and ignorant as it is possible for a human creature to become.
>
> (Smith 1776)

No wonder we are having such a battle to change the way we do things in schools. No wonder introducing areas such as thinking skills can be so challenging. Built into the very DNA of the whole concept of schools – even the buildings themselves if you still happen to be teaching in a Victorian school with its factory-like high windows and austere appearance – is the goal of getting young people *not* to think for themselves.

Chapter 18

An accidental school system

So, we have established that the early roots of what we have now as our national system of education in the UK were designed to create children who would respect authority (do what the teachers say), respect God (do what the Church says), obey the Monarch (do what the government says), be good unthinking workers (do what the boss says) and die for their country (do what the general says).

And if you don't believe me on this then surely you will trust the word of a Tory politician speaking in the House of Commons and recorded in Hansard in 1807:[1]

> Giving education to the labouring classes of the poor ... would teach them to despise their lot in life, instead of making them good servants in agriculture and other laborious employments to which their rank in society has destined them; instead of teaching them the virtue of subordination, it would render them factious and refactory ... it would enable them to read seditious pamphlets, vicious books and publications against Christianity.

> (Gillard 2007)

What about, then, the make-up of the school system with its classification and grouping of children according to age? Why did we start doing it like that and, more pressingly, why do we still persist in doing it that way across the vast majority of schools in the entire world?

Let's start our journey then in the obvious time and place – the seventeenth century and what is now the Czech Republic. Here you will find a man called Comenius[2,3] who is known both as the 'teacher of nations' and also, importantly for our story, as the father of modern education. Poor old Comenius, an orphan, chased out of several countries, spending years as a homeless refugee roaming Europe, was invited to England to open a new school but had to leave again when Civil War broke out, lived in caves, huts and even hollow trees, narrowly missed death on at least one occasion, had various manuscripts burned, lost one wife and two children to the plague, another wife to the stresses and strains of being constantly on the run and finally died at the age of 78 in Amsterdam in 1670.

During his hard life he was also a prolific scientist, writer and teacher and developed what was, for the age, the radical view that the education of children could be done in a way that didn't involve the traditional rote memorization of Latin texts followed by cold baths and a sound beating. He also firmly believed that education was the right of every child, not just the ones with the money and influence to appear to the world more clever than they really were.

'Not the children of the rich or of the powerful only, but of all alike, boys and girls, both noble and ignoble, rich and poor, in all cities and towns, villages and hamlets, should be sent to school,' he wrote.[4]

Although a profoundly religious man, for him God in the classroom was about opening children up to the world, not closing them down, and it is for these views that he has become synonymous with a European education ideal of equality and access for all children. Having an ideal and making it work, though, are two different things and anyone with one foot in the classroom and one hand on their heart will tell you, we're not there yet.

From seventeenth century Europe to nineteenth century Scotland, we see the earliest attempts at providing education for children as young as two, although the main reasons seemed ostensibly to be to allow the parents to continue their work in the cotton mills of New Lanark. Here, pioneer Robert Owen established an Infant School for children from the age of two and upwards whose instruction was to be 'whatever might be supposed useful that they could understand, and much attention was devoted to singing, dancing, and playing'. This model caught the eye of a group of Radicals and Whigs who transported the whole concept, teacher and all, to London in 1818. Here the concept was further developed by an English educational pioneer by the name of Samuel Wilderspin whom we met briefly in chapter 15 and who, in his book, *The Infant System for Developing the Intellectual and Moral Powers of all Children, from One to Seven years of Age*, noted that until that point:

> Schools for infants then existed, but what were they? Simply dame-schools, with the hornbook for boys and girls, and perhaps a little sewing for the latter. Their sign was 'Children taught to read and work here', and their furniture the cap and bells, the rod in pickle, and a corner for dunces.
>
> (www.gutenberg.org/files/10985/10985–8.txt)

Wilderspin put forward the idea that children would achieve 'a higher state of physical, mental, and moral health' if infant education followed four clear rules:

> First, to feed the child's faculties with suitable food; Second, to simplify and explain everything, so as to adapt it properly to those faculties; Third, not to overdo anything, either by giving too much instruction, or instruction beyond their years, and thus over-excite the brain, and injure the faculties; and, Fourth, ever to blend both exercise and amusement with instruction at due intervals, which is readily effected by a moderate amount of singing, alternating with the usual motions and evolutions in the schoolroom, and the unfettered freedom of the play-ground.
>
> (www.gutenberg.org/files/10985/10985–8.txt)

In fact, he is credited with the invention of the playground (and, showing a certain entrepreneurial bent, also ran a company providing play apparatus). Play was a cornerstone of his educational philosophy and he firmly believed that, 'Physical health is essential to mental vigour if it is to come to manhood.'

There was also a social aspect to his ideals, addressing a feeling of the time that a life of crime and malice was something that would be instilled in young children unless education did something to prevent it:

> If the physical, mental, moral, and spiritual constitution be properly acted upon, fed, and trained, it adds to the happiness of the child; but if this is not done, it becomes miserable, and as a consequence restless, troublesome, and mischievous.
>
> (www.gutenberg.org/files/10985/10985–8.txt)

There are two great themes in Wilderspin's work that have both influenced thinking and practice in early years education in the 150 years since they were propounded and been completely – and increasingly – disregarded at the same time. Firstly, his view on education as being something that didn't have to take place in a classroom:

> The absurd notion that children can only be taught in a room, must be exploded. I have done more in one hour in the garden, in the lanes, and in the fields, to cherish and satisfy the budding faculties of childhood, than could have been done in a room for months.
>
> (www.gutenberg.org/files/10985/10985–8.txt)

Anyone who has ever taken a group of children on a field trip or a nature walk will attest to this fact. Yet, according to a 2005 House of Commons Education and Skills Select Committee report quoted in *No Fear – Growing Up in a Risk Averse Society* published by the Calouste Gulbenkian Society there has been a general decline in both in the quality and the quantity of outdoor education experiences, the lack of which 'impoverishes students' learning and represents a missed opportunity for curricular enrichment'. We have a whole generation of children who will never know if they are agoraphobic or not. The report lays the blame fairly and squarely on the shoulders of the Elfin Safety,[5] pointing out that 'some schools and local authorities are demanding excessively lengthy risk assessments and we have found evidence of unnecessary duplications in the system', something the author of *No Fear*, Tim Gill describes as:

> A regime of secondary risk management ... in which the different agencies involved – school, local education authority, destination, Ofsted and government departments – appear to be more concerned to defend themselves against accusations of poor practice than to work together to support learning activities.
>
> (Gill 2007)

Gill also cites the example of the Thomas Deacon Academy in Peterborough, a stunning-looking educational building and a flagship of the academies programme but a school without a playground because, as the headteacher of the school is quoted as pointing out, 'I think what the public want is maximum learning.'

We couldn't do the three Rs in anything but a formal environment so we end up with, in the words of educational technology pioneer and student of Piaget, Seymour Papert from Massachusetts Institute of Technology, the classroom – 'an artificial and inefficient learning environment that society has been forced to invent' (Papert 1993). Remember, nothing like schools exist in nature. Unless you're a fish.

The second string to Wilderspin's pioneering bow was the need to teach children to think for themselves and from as young an age as possible:

> The error of the past system (for such I hope I may venture to call it) as to mental development was, that the inferior powers of the mind were called into activity, in preference to its higher faculties. The effort was to exercise the memory, and store it with information, which, owing to the inactivity of the understanding and the judgment, was seldom or never of use. To adopt the opinions of others was thought quite enough, without the child being troubled to think

for itself, and to form an opinion of its own. But this is not as it should be. Such a system is neither likely to produce great nor wise men; and is much better adapted to parrots than children. Hence, the first thing attempted in an infant school is, to set the children thinking, – to induce them to examine, compare, and judge, in reference to all those matters which their dawning intellects are capable of mastering. It is of no use to tell a child, in the first place, what it should think, – this is at once inducing mental indolence, which is but too generally prevalent among adults; owing to this erroneous method having been adopted by those who had the charge of their early years.
(www.gutenberg.org/files/10985/10985–8.txt)

Interestingly, and in a way that seems at odds with his ideals to our twenty-first century eyes, Wilderspin is also the inventor of the 'gallery' – the fixed rows of ascending seats, the youngest child at the bottom, whose purpose was 'to have the children altogether, so as better to attract their attention simultaneously' whilst the teacher was engaged not in rote learning exercises but in oral lessons and 'lessons on objects'. Think The Royal Institution Christmas Lectures or Johnny Ball in his heyday rather than Tom Brown's School Days.

While Wilderspin and others were trying to prepare the minds of the very young for thinking, those influencing policy on older children were settling on a less 'child-friendly' approach: the 'monitorial method'[6] developed independently by educationalists Dr Andrew Bell and Joseph Lancaster.[7] For the latter, the classroom, as described by an Australian educationalist and both an advocate and alumnus of the Lancastrian model, was:

a parallelogram, the length about twice the width. The windows were to be six feet from the floor. The floor should be inclined, rising one foot in 20 from the master's desk to the upper end of the room, where the highest class is situated. The master's desk is on the middle of a platform two to three feet high, erected at the lower end of the room. Forms and desks, fixed firmly to the ground, occupy the middle of the room, a passage being left between the ends of the forms and the wall, five or six feet broad, where the children form semicircles for reading.

Lancaster was not a fan of corporal punishment it is said; however, misbehaving boys could find themselves tied up in sacks or hoisted above their classmates in cages – something I'm sure I've seen in an episode of *The Simpsons* – but this is far from what Wilderspin was advocating at the time.

Bell's similar but competing model was also known as the Madras model[8] as it was based on the practices he saw as superintendent of an orphanage for the illegitimate and orphaned sons of officers in India in 1789. Bell's stated goal in his 1807 book, *An Analysis of the Experiment in Education, Made at Egmore, near Madras*, was 'to make good scholars, good Men and good Christians' although the subtitle of the book reveals other more utilitarian aims where he describes a system that is:

> alike fitted to reduce the expense of Tuition, abridge the labour of the Master, and expedite the progress of the Scholar.
>
> (Bell 1807)

To this, and remember our lessons from the Industrial Revolution from chapter 17, he also adds that his proposed system could be:

> a Scheme for the better administration of the Poor-laws, by converting Schools for the lower orders of youth into Schools of Industry.
>
> (Bell 1807)

The Madras-type school involved children being arranged into forms or classes where each would find his own academic level and be promoted up or moved down these academic rankings according to achievement. Not only did this mean that 'no Class is ever retarded in its progress by idle or dull boys', but also, Bell argued, such a system was more efficient. In the same amount of time it would have taken a teacher to instruct one boy or hear him read a lesson, he could now read to classes of 20 boys or 'hear them say a lesson, each a portion by rotation'.

Do you remember reading aloud and around the class when you were at school, the Sword of Damocles working its way from pupil to pupil? Do you still perpetrate it? Does it actually achieve anything? My belief is that, rather than take on board what is being read, those who are about to read are more concerned with when their time will come, those who are reading are more concerned with not stumbling over words and looking foolish in front of their classmates and those who have read are simply too filled with the relief of getting it over with to concentrate on anything at all. But, for Bell, this mythical sword was a great motivator:

> and the Scholar is continually stimulated to obtain pre-eminence in his Class, and even rise above it; and be promoted to a superior; and especially not sink below it, and be degraded to an inferior Class.
>
> (Bell 1807)

What both the Bell and the Lancaster models shared was the division of labour between the various layers of authority in any given classroom, with a great deal of instruction being carried out by students who had 'got it' to those who hadn't 'got it yet', all under the watchful eyes of a hierarchy of tutors, assistant teachers, teachers, sub-ushers, ushers, school masters, superintendents, trustees and visitors. In this way the Masters can have, in Bell's stately words, 'the hundred hands of Briareus, the hundred eyes of Argus, and the wings of Mercury', which I think should be part of the Qualified Teachers Status accreditation.

While the infant children were dividing their time between the gallery and the playground and the older children were trying to avoid being degraded or ending up suspended in a cage, there were plans afoot for the children in the middle. In 1847, a translation of a book published originally by an Inspector of the Academy of Strasbourg was printed in England in which it was stated that:

> Every school, in obedience to this principle, should be divided into two great classes – the one including children from 6 to 9 or 10, the other those from 10 to 14; and it would much subserve many important purposes, if these could be taught in separate rooms.

With it, the education system which was already splintered by class, sex and religion now became further divided by age. Wilderspin had argued that it was:

> a great error to separate children and cut them off from the advantage of all object-lessons, and gallery-teaching, because they are the youngest. They learn more through sympathy and communion with their five or six year elders, than the most clever adult can teach them ... and therefore the separation in many infant-schools of the children, invariably into two classes, sometimes in two rooms, is a great mistake, and can only arise from ignorance of the laws under which the young mind unfolds itself.
>
> (www.gutenberg.org/files/10985/10985–8.txt)

However, there was now a movement towards keeping little children away from the older ones, primarily so as not to disturb them. As decreed by the 1871 Committee of Council on Education in their *Rules to be Observed in Planning and Fitting Up Schools*, infants need to be taught in a different room 'as the noise and the training of the infants disturb and injuriously affect the discipline and instruction of the older children'.

This was matched in the early nineteenth century by a call to have children interacting with the educated mind of a qualified teacher rather than printed or regurgitated material, something that, as it necessitated a more pedagogical approach, further underlined the need to separate children by age. The main protagonist behind this was another Scotsman, David Stow[9] (someone to whom Samuel Wilderspin says, 'much credit is due, for having written useful books and performed useful works,' before adding rather pointedly, 'I am not the man to deprive him of this his just due, but I have such faith in the honour of his countrymen in general, that I believe the time is not far distant when some one of them will give to me that credit which is fairly and justly due to me with respect to the educational movements in Scotland'). Stow felt the key to educational improvement was in better teacher training matched by dividing children into age divisions of two or three to six, six to eight or nine and nine to fourteen. This was further developed by a Professor J. J. Findlay in his 1902 publication *Principles of Class Teaching*, where he called for the age divisions to be set as infancy (birth to around four years of age); early childhood (four to six); later childhood (seven to nine); boy or girlhood (ten plus). It was also Professor Findlay who called for a clear break in schooling at age 11 between primary and secondary (Findlay 1902).

And, as they say, the rest, as they say, is history.

So, that's how we ended up with the system we've got now, however the important question is does it work? Well, according to research I found for my foreword to Dave Harris's book on transition, *Dropping the Baton*:

- 40 per cent of children lose motivation and make no progress during the year after transition.[10]
- Children who were making steady progress in primary school actually go backwards in the first year of secondary school.[11]
- There is a discontinuity between the primary and secondary curriculum, and a lack of information passing between schools relating to pupils' abilities and existing achievements.[12]
- Teachers rarely identified children's individual abilities as making a difference to the transition process, focusing instead on institutional initiatives, an emphasis that carries the risk of creating a degree of helplessness for individual pupils (Zeedyk *et al.* 2003).

The answer, then, is could do better. Or, in the words of a primary headteacher I met in Rotherham once, 'Transition is like trying to mate a cat and dog!'

And what does the neuroscience tell us about separating children by age? Well, for starters, when we put adolescent males to work with younger children there is not only a reduction in testosterone levels but also a rise in prolactin[13] (a chemical associated with breastfeeding), children with the same birthday can have as much as a two- to three-year spread in terms of brain maturation (Jensen 1996) and the brains of boys and girls mature at different rates with girls entering the adolescent stage of brain maturation earlier than boys (de Bellis *et al.* 2001).

So, maybe it is time to start rethinking how we organize things in education. Doing it because we've always done it is one thing, but doing it because we sort of stumbled across it and it seemed like a good idea at the time and it seemed to stick even though we live in very different times now is something else altogether.

Chapter 19

Exams – so whose bright idea was that!?

In the China of 2,000 years ago, being a state official was a great privilege that brought with it access for you, your friends and families to power, prestige and the sort of wealth that government contracts could bring. Originally the only way you could be part of such an elite was, basically, already to be part of this elite. A system of relationships and recommendations known as 'Ta you guanxi' translated as 'He has some connections' was what determined who received the top jobs and who didn't. But then in AD 85 Emperor Zhang of Han[1] set out an annual quota of officials drawn from erudite Confucian scholars and this selection process began to involve not just who you knew but what you knew. This selection process now included a procedure called 'shece' or 'lot strip' in which candidates drew bamboo strips at random on which was written an examination question.[2]

It is the spirit of this combination of the testing of prior knowledge balanced with the pursuit of a fairer way of doing things that appealed to the educational pioneers who were looking to open up education to the burgeoning middle classes in mid-nineteenth century England. A growing demand for education meant a growing demand for quality education, the sort of education that would lead to university and a prestigious, high-earning career, but questions were being asked about the suitability and competence of schoolmasters. Good schools knew they needed an objective and independent way of assessing their worth (and in my experience, schools are always better than most teachers think but never as good as most heads say). Some were already seeking out reports on their competence by impartial 'people of consequence' (Gillham 1977), the forerunners of our lay inspectors today, where someone trained as a postman can tell a post-graduate professional with 20 years' experience if they are doing a good job or not.

These schools saw their opportunity for benefiting from the reflected glow from the halo of the indubitable auspices of the universities of Oxford and Cambridge. It was a way of guaranteeing the impartial and academically rigorous assessment of their quality following what was known as the 'Exeter Experiment' of 1857 (Fowler 1959). At the same time, according to one writer at least, these universities also saw the same circumstances as an opportunity to shake themselves from their 'academic torpor'.

The Exeter Experiment was a competitive public exam for local schoolboys set up at the behest of the Bath and West of England Society for the Encouragement of Agriculture, Arts, Manufacture and Commerce (a sort of Young Farmers meets Chamber of Commerce meets Rotary Club meets Local Operatic Society sort of group) and masterminded by two unlikely accomplices. Frederick Temple, a double first from Balliol College, Oxford, who had worked at the examinations department there and had gone on to become HM Inspector of Training Schools, and one Thomas Acland, a Tory MP for West Somerset and a gentleman farmer. Both were vexed by the question of providing a better quality education for the middle classes and the idea appealed to them of using the sleepy West Country city of Exeter as a test bed for trialling a new sort of public examination, under the auspices of Temple's connections back at Oxford University. This was the first time that Oxford had held examinations for 'candidates who are not members of the University' and the occasion merited a visit by the great and the good, complete with caps, gowns and hoods. In fact, in the early years of these 'local' exams, the chief examiner would travel in full academic regalia by train carrying a locked box with the exam papers inside.[3]

These weren't the first school exams, though, as there is evidence of diocesan visits in the sixteenth and seventeenth centuries to test children's attainment and to consult with the teaching staff about their practice in some schools, but the Exeter Experiment was a thrown gauntlet of educational assessment that was picked up by both Oxford and Cambridge in the years to come, followed by other universities such as the Northern ones with the forming of the Joint Matriculation Board in 1903. In fact, by 1917 the universities had a complete grip on the examination system in the UK (Lawton 1980).[4]

No-one seems to disagree with the idea of an independent verification of how well things are being taught and how well these things are being learned. Nor did there seem to be much discussion as to the nature of what an exam looked like, namely a printed set of questions to which the students replied in writing, in silence and behind closed doors. Yet six hundred years earlier, as described by Christopher Stray of Swansea University in a fascinating paper entitled *The Shift from Oral to Written Examination: Cambridge and Oxford 1700–1900*, in the Oxford and Cambridge of medieval times, examinations were 'public, oral and in Latin'. He quotes a writer named Rouse Ball who in 1889 said:

We are perhaps apt to think that an examination conducted by written papers is so natural that the custom is of long continuance. But I can find no record of any (in Europe) earlier than those introduced by Bentley at Trinity in 1702.

(Stray 2001)

For those of us who went to a comp, the 'Bentley' he is referring to is the controversial Master of that college, Richard Bentley,[5] appointed in 1700, 'Trinity' is Trinity College, Cambridge, and 'continuance' means going on for a bit.

Although Stray points out that he thinks Rouse Ball is wrong and that there is a case for written exams being part of the overall process dating back to 1560, what comes through is that the most widespread means of assessing an individual's learning was through a good old-fashioned heated debate between a number of learned people all at the same time and lasting for two hours or more. It was only towards the end of the eighteenth century that the piecemeal movement was made away from oral examinations to written ones, and it wasn't until 1828 that all papers were in printed form rather than being dictated. It was also around this time that the poor chap who came bottom of the heap when it came to the competitive system of degree honours, that is to say the one who received a third but only just, was rewarded with a special honour all of his own. As he was receiving his degree from the vice chancellor, a large wooden spoon was lowered from the gallery by his fellow students. Seventy-five years later, organized rugby came to Wales.

Despite differences in motivation for moving away from the oral exam and the *viva voce* approach, one factor was relevant for both institutions. The growth in the middle classes fed by the success of the Industrial Revolution and Great Britain's economic and academic expansion meant that there were simply too many students to be able to successfully run any sort of oral assessment and, in an echo of the industrial processes going on outside the hallowed halls, a system of sitting students down in large numbers in an 'exam factory' model made a great deal more sense from an efficiency point of view.

Which is great if you are from a wealthy family with a decent education behind you, but where does that leave students for whom the written word has not been their main means of communication? For example, maybe your school has a growing Somali population; after all, the UK is home to the largest Somali population in Europe with Cardiff having the single largest Somali population in the UK.[6] Estimates are that there are up to 250,000 Somalis living in the UK, a six-fold increase from 2001. But did you know that, despite a particularly strong poetic tradition, Somali culture is predominantly an oral one with no official written language until 1972 (Mcintyre-Brown 2001)?[7] Willy Russell, the Liverpool-born play-wright, was an English teacher for a while but felt that the working class students he was teaching were being unfairly penalized as the oral tradition of their backgrounds was ignored as they had to sit – and often fail – exams that were in purely written form. 'Schools fail most of the people most of the time,' he is quoted as saying in an interview with *The Guardian*, which is quite a broad generalization but has its roots in his own experience at school, leaving with just one O-level. He loves what he has called 'The poetry of common speech' using his time as a woman's hairdresser, his first job after leaving school, to listen to the wit and genuine wisdom of the ladies of Liverpool: 'working-class people who can talk about Jean-Paul Sartre. She might get elements of it wrong, but she knows her Thomas Hardy and she knows her Bernard Shaw', as he described these prototype 'Educating Ritas'.[8]

In recent years, there has been a considerable effort made in opening up the possibility of academic success without recourse to the written exam, especially with a pendulum that swung towards (the still written) course-work, but which seems to be swinging back again. A report in *The Guardian* in August 2009 described how boys overtook girls in one fell swoop in the GCSE maths exams, something they put down to the removal of course-work. I remember reading once that exams favoured the male-type brain, geared as it was to sudden bursts of activity followed by periods of inac-tivity sitting by the fire digesting what it had just caught, telling stories and passing wind, whereas the female-type brain was better suited to less intense but more sustained effort over time. Reflecting on my time during the exam seasons I endured at school and university, and given that I quite enjoyed the exam itself, if not the revision, and did well, I would tend to concur. But then my son has just got himself into Durham University with a BTEC qualification from a local college that was entirely coursework-based after rejecting a more academic exam-oriented sixth form college.

An exam treats all children *as if* they had received the best possible education in the best possible environment with the best possible pre-paration. But that simply isn't true. When I was a classroom teacher, I remember being struck by the fact that the French exam wasn't a measure of how good they were at French. After all, if I had been able to give them one-to-one tuition they would have done better. Rather, it was a flawed assessment of how well they have learned French in Northampton, in a class of 32, sitting next to Darren with the Tourette's, for three 50-minute periods a week, one of which is a Friday afternoon.

And before you tell me they are a necessary evil and there's nothing you can do about exams, consider the UK school that has rejected the exam factory model completely and still manages to get students into good universities. According to the BBC News website:

> A total of 45 pupils from the school have gained a university place without formal qualifications and of the 12 who have already graduated, all but two got a 2:1.
> (http://news.bbc.co.uk/2/hi/uk_news/education/8401133.stm)

We are happy to speak up against animal testing but what about child testing? Even *The Times*, conservative organ that it is, knows that enough is enough, referring to children in the UK as 'overexamined but under-educated'.[9] What does this mean for the twenty-first century teacher? The written exam is part of the 'tyranny of syntax' I mentioned in chapter 10, the idea that learning has to be written down neatly in sentence form to count. And spelled correctly. But this writing is a relatively modern invention and spelling all the more so.[10] (I like the fact that the final 'wheel' during the Trooping of the Colour is so complicated that it can't be written down and needs to be taught by old soldiers to young soldiers.) Nor does the written word suit everyone; although it obviously suited you otherwise you wouldn't be qualified to do the job you are doing now. You may well have to teach children to 'jump through the hoop' of the written exam – exam technique, how to revise, stress control, that sort of thing – but don't let the hoop take over. Ensure there are plenty of opportunities for exploring the 'oral traditions' of your students, wherever they are from, and do not be too sucked into the academic snobbery associated with the written exam hegemony. After all, Shirley Valentine may well have done better in pre-nineteenth century Oxford University than you.

Chapter 20

Educated is not enough

Who are you most proud of? One of your students came from a good family with their own business, did well at school and later went on to get not one but two doctorates, the first in anthropology, the second in medicine, as well as becoming an officer in the army. Another of your students in this imaginary class, a girl, was home taught on a farm for a while before joining school where she eventually dropped out to care for her ill mother and grandmother. She later worked as a seamstress and was once arrested for breaking the law.

Which one of these would be on a plaque in your school hall?

In case you don't know your biographies of famous – and infamous – people, the second one is Rosa Parks[1]; the first one is Dr Josef Mengele.[2]

Five hundred years ago the French writer Rabelais wrote, 'Science without conscience is the ruin of the soul', and that is as true now as it was then. Maybe more so. The bankers whose greed was at least partly to blame for the global economic downturn were qualified and educated people. Some of them have even apologized for their actions (which is more than Mengele ever did). In the summer of 2009, the chief executive of Goldman Sachs, one of the world's most lucrative companies, announced:

> While we regret that we participated in the market euphoria and failed to raise a responsible voice, we are proud of the way our firm managed the risk it assumed on behalf of our client before and during the financial crisis.[3]
>
> (http://dealbook.blogs.nytimes.com/2009/06/16/goldman-regrets-market-euphoria-that-led-to-crisis/)

The 'market euphoria' he was referring to was the sub-prime mortgage market in the US where billions of dollars were loaned to people who couldn't really pay and whose debts were then wrapped up and hidden away in financial deals so complex that most of the people who ended up owning the debt, often big pension and insurance companies around the world, didn't know where the debt came from in the first place. That is, until it all came tumbling down. Goldman Sachs, for their part, underwrote $76.5 billion of the overall mortgage-securities market or 7 per cent according to Matt Taibbi, a journalist and blogger with *True/Slant*, an online 'original content news network' and a great example of Web 2.0 in action, bypassing traditional print media for news.[4] Of that figure, $29.3 billion was sub-prime – people who probably couldn't pay – but there was also a further $29.8 billion that were what was called 'Alt-A' mortgages, a new class of definition somewhere between 'prime' and 'sub-prime', which Taibbi describes as 'characterized, mainly, by crappy documentation and lack of equity: no income verification, no asset verification, little-to-no cash down'. In other words, clever, educated people whose only goal was to generate wealth for themselves and their clients, were behind giving mortgages to people who couldn't afford them and whose homes were subsequently repossessed (the number of homeless families went up in 2008 in the US with a growth in the number of families who were not previously seen as 'at risk'[5] and there is also the threat of worse to come) and selling the newly hidden and repackaged debt onto people like, in Taibbi's words, 'some Dutch teacher's union' that had prior to that been investing in safe government bonds.

As part of their 'apology' Goldman Sachs has apparently set aside $500 million a year for five years to help 10,000 small businesses according to *The Economist* who added that 'Some were left unimpressed.' Across the second and third quarters in 2009, the bank made over $100 million a day on a staggering 82 separate days and is already sitting on $16.7 billion for 'pay and compensation'.

One of the reasons I like working with young people in the whole *Philosophy for Children* area is that it allows us to explore issues to do with ethics and morality in a way that otherwise may not happen. I'm not teaching them what to think, nor preaching to them some religious edict of 'Thou shalts' and 'Thou shall nots', rather I am encouraging them to dig deeper than the simple, 'If I do that, I'll get this' mechanistic view of the world, whether the 'this' is exam success, a new pair of Nikes or world domination.

As philosopher Ayn Rand put it in *The Fountainhead*:

> Integrity is the ability to stand by an idea. That presupposes the ability to think.[6]

> (Rand 1961)

Mengele said, towards the end of his life, that he didn't do anything wrong. The 'apology' from Goldman Sachs is matched by its 'but didn't we do well' tone. Is your job to teach children to pass exams? Or is it to teach children to think and, from there, grow as morally sound and decent people who are educated to know right from wrong and use their education accordingly?

Your answer to that question will determine what sort of society your grandchildren grow up in.

Chapter 21

Is yours a teaching school or a learning school?

'Is yours a teaching school or a learning school?' is a question I have been putting to teachers for many years now.

And it is a question you need to be able to answer.

I know I can teach for a week without anyone necessarily learning anything. I also know that not everything I teach gets learned nor is everything that gets learned what I've taught. But when you make that shift from teaching to learning it changes everything. Your job isn't to teach them. Your job is that they learn. As German philosopher Heidegger once wrote, 'Teaching is more difficult than learning because what teaching calls for is this: to let learn.'[1] Now, combine that shift in emphasis with some of the other innovations and insights I have been trying to share with you in this book and I hope you will be able to see a real opportunity to change the nature of teaching and learning in the twenty-first century.

For many years, the deal in the classroom, broadly speaking, was, I will teach you and the extent to which you either 'get' or 'don't get' it, that, then, is the measure of your academic ability. I have fulfilled my part of the bargain in teaching you. Learning what I taught you was your part of the bargain. For me, this is like the doctor giving me one medicine in order to try and heal me and, if it doesn't work, blaming me as she had 'done her bit'. It's what Howard Gardner of multiple intelligences theory, calls 'single-chance education' (Gardner 1983). You have just the one fleeting opportunity to jump on the knowledge train as it passes through the room and all must enter through the same door.

When you shift your purpose in the classroom from teaching to making sure the child learns, you realize that this is no longer adequate. Your doctor's job is not to give you medicine, it is to make you better. You would go back to the doctor and ask for an alternative drug if the symptoms persisted. Equally you now need to offer your children an alternative means for learning what needs to be learned.

And by that I don't mean just teaching things the same way but louder. Or slower. Or more often.

What this new model calls for is 'multiple-chance education' (Gardner 1993) where students can access the information in a variety of ways that will allow them the opportunity to play to their strengths and, also, work on their weaknesses. Such variety of approach – and the watchword here genuinely is 'variety'; after all, it's hard to hit every student all of the time – cuts across not just how you offer opportunities for learning in your classroom but the nature of the classroom and even the school day as we shall see in chapter 22.

What's more, as part of being a 'learning school', it is important that you teach children *how* to learn. This will sound self-evident to many of the teachers reading this book, but it wasn't always the case. The whole idea of 'Learn to Learn' seems to be a relatively new phenomenon, at least on a widespread scale. (In the past, on the rare occasions where there was some form of teaching children how to learn work going on in the odd isolated school, it was usually carried out by an odd and isolated teacher.) That the idea of actually teaching children how to do the thing we expect them to do every day of their school careers is self-evident is, even now, not always the case and I still do get asked in schools whether I think it is a good idea. It is a question that even now I am unsure how to respond to since 'Well duh!' never seems that professional.

In 2001, a four-year research project looking at the nature of 'learning to learn' in schools in the UK was launched by a team that linked King's College in London, the Institute of Learning, the University of Reading, the Open University and 40 primary and secondary schools across five education authorities around the country.[2] The project was under the auspices of a better-eight-hundred-years-late-than-never Cambridge University.

Part of their findings was that learning to learn was not a single discrete skill but rather 'a family of learning *practices* that enable learning to happen'. They then plumped for the accurate but less catchy LHTL over L2L adding, 'the HOW word seems important'. This is something echoed by think-tank Demos[3] in their 2004 report entitled *About Learning* and commissioned by the then minister for schools standards, David Milliband. Exactly what the members of this 'family' are, the report doesn't make clear, but Demos quotes from the Royal Society of Arts' *Opening Minds* project where there is a detailed range of 'competencies' including:

- Understanding how to learn, taking account of one's preferred learning styles, and understanding the need to, and how to, manage one's own learning throughout life
- Learning, systematically, to think

- Exploring and reaching an understanding of one's own creative talents, and how to make best use of them
- Learning to enjoy and love learning for its own sake and as part of understanding oneself.

This idea of a 'competency curriculum' is one that has gained good ground in schools across the UK in recent years, transmogrifying into the important but difficult to pronounce acronym PLTS or 'personal, learning and thinking skills'.[4] (Notice it is 'personal, learning and thinking skills' and not, as some have read it, 'personal learning and thinking skills'.) That said, as I write these words there has just been an election in the UK and with the change of government we could be back to drawing reeds with exam questions written on them again soon.

According to the RSA, the *Opening Minds* project[5] was developed because they felt that 'the way young students were being educated was becoming increasingly detached from their needs as citizens of the 21st century'. The feeling was that developing 'real world skills or competencies' was the way forward in schools, not just the teaching of facts and it is a project that is proving to be both popular, successful and terrifying in equal measure. One of the fears is that schools are being asked to focus on skills at the expense of knowledge, in particular 'subject knowledge', the great untouchable of the educational elite.

The battle lines between the teachers of subjects and the teachers of children were drawn up well before recent innovations such as the PLTS framework or the *Rose Review* into primary education. As long ago as 2002, Prince Charles had waded into the fray, arguing that:

> Many of those who leave school with good qualifications nevertheless have an education which is somewhat shallow-rooted.
> (http://news.bbc.co.uk/2/hi/uk_news/education/2301259.stm)

In particular, and if you were to be cynical you may say unsurprisingly, he was concerned that British children were not taught enough British history. 'They lack valuable and essential knowledge and understanding about their national history and heritage' (to which another cynic might add, 'You learn about my family and I'll learn about yours').

Since then Prince Charles has established *The Prince's Teaching Institute*,[6] the aim of which is, among other things, 'to promote the idea that subject knowledge, subject rigour and the enthusiasm for communicating them are essential requirements for effective teaching'.

As you would expect, then, the late, lamented *Rose Review*,[7] where 13 stand-alone subjects would have become merged into six 'areas of learning' including 'historical, geographical and social understanding' and 'scientific and technological understanding', had both the Prince and the *Daily Mail* in apoplexy.[8] 'Children to learn about blogging and climate change as Government reforms relegate history in curriculum' is how that venerable organ summed up what would have been the biggest shake-up in primary education since the *Plowden Report* in 1967. 'The Prince believes rigorous teaching in traditional subjects was the basis of a good education', according to Bernice McCabe, power-dressing co-director of the Prince's institute, quoted in the article, which also decreed that 'critics of the approach warn it smacks of 1970s-style teaching methods', presumably the same methods that helped me to achieve A grades in my A-levels and qualify for Durham University, with the same nameless 'critics' fearing 'pupils would leave primary school ill-equipped for GCSE and A-level study, where teaching is subject-based'. Interestingly, the 2006 *Nuffield Review Higher Education Focus Groups* found that young people starting university these days needed a year's remedial work to develop the skills needed to succeed at university anyway. In the words of the report:

> narrow accountability based on exam success and league tables needs to be avoided. This leads to spoon feeding rather than the fostering of independence and critical engagement with subject material. Learners who may have achieved academic success by such means at A Level, it was felt, are increasingly coming into HE expecting to be told the answers.
>
> (www.nuffield14–19review.org.uk/files/news44–2.pdf)

As E. M. Forster said, 'Spoon-feeding in the long run teaches us nothing but the shape of the spoon.'

One of the pioneers of the 'skills-based' curriculum work has been my friend and colleague, Jackie Beere, who was involved with the RSA project as a headteacher of a secondary school in Northamptonshire and was also involved in the Demos report mentioned above. She also received an OBE for her pioneering work as an Advanced Skills Teacher, although given her divergence of views with the Prince that is as far as her honours will probably go. I invited Jackie to bring her expertise in the 'competency curriculum' approach to the QCA project we had been asked to undertake and that I mentioned in chapter 3.

One of the findings which we reported back to the QCA I put under the heading of 'The B-Word' – 'B' standing for 'Boredom' – and stated in my report that:

> We are boring the motivation out of our children. Disaffection means 'to cause to lose affection or loyalty'. We are the cause. We dis-affect

children. We talk about motivation but we need to have a serious conversation about de-motivation.

Both online and in our one-to-one interviews it was the word 'boring' that was used most often to explain lack of student motivation. You know that phrase about the Sixties, 'If you can remember it you weren't there'? I've been in science lessons like that. The second most common word used was what appears to be the B-word's antidote, 'practical'. Which is where approaches like the 'competency curriculum' can play a very powerful part. To test this we sent Jackie into the three schools to work with teachers and children on delivering a lesson that was based around a set of skills. Note that the students were not using skills in isolation. They were still learning 'stuff'. They just happened to prioritize the development of a range of skills employed in the learning of the 'stuff'. 'Skills' then 'stuff', not 'stuff' and then, maybe, 'skills'.

Feedback from both students and staff in terms of motivation were, although not without their challenges, very positive, as summed up by these comments from one of the geography teachers involved:

> Both of my Year 8 classes are working through it at the moment and really enjoying it. The class that we filmed are working particularly well – they have some excellent plans for their 'own tasks' and most lessons they have come straight in and got on without me prompting them. They are working well in their groups and taking on responsibility for their own tasks – they are also doing a lot of extra work in their spare time. They are also able to recognize the competencies better now and have the confidence to judge their own performance.
>
> The other class I taught had a much less successful launch – they are a very weak group and work badly in teams – and I actually had to abandon the launch lesson half way through because they were so awful which was a shame. However at the end of that lesson I explained the project fully to them and said that they could have another chance next lesson if they worked well. They did – and are now really into the project too – although they do need a bit more support.

One of the interesting aspects of such a project was that a similar intervention in each of the three schools threw up a range of different findings, which I summarized as follows:

School One in the Midlands

1 The changes to the curriculum mean that we do have a great opportunity to make things different. If we don't grasp this chance then there could be dire consequences for our society. But there is a great pressure on schools to be 'traditional', focus on the 'basics' and do it like they've always done it.

2 The better the lesson is planned, the more opportunity the teacher has to do very little during the lesson. 'Lazy teachers' are the ones who will step back and let children sort things for themselves, help children find the knowledge but not drip-feed them with it and allow children to learn more by teaching less.

3 The ability to work in teams of different abilities and strengths brings with it a variety of experience that will allow more children to succeed, contribute and learn.

School Two in the West of England

1 The opportunity to plan in a cross-curricular way is very beneficial, helping to break down barriers between subject areas, helps develop much-needed confidence and is motivating for staff.

2 Working in this way has positive implications for transition with the primary schools and has clear benefits in terms of employability (and not just, do well at school and you'll get a good job).

3 These lessons explicitly help to develop emotional intelligence in the learners including aspects such as resilience and awareness of self and others.

School Three in the East of England

1 Students can 'do well' at school academically by sitting and copying passively but we do them a great disservice if we allow that to continue and claim we are a 'good' school. These lessons help develop active learning.

2 The content of the lessons is important (the need to know 'stuff') but the skill and competences that are developed are the *most* important. The lesson structure is governed by the competences to be developed, not by the subject matter. The lesson objectives move from 'What I will learn … ' to 'What I will learn to be … '.

3 Having the support both of the 'knowledgeable expert' as well as the opportunity to work across boundaries and plan in a team are all vital elements of the process of helping teachers build the confidence to learn to work in this way.

Overall, the attributes developed in the 'learning', as opposed to 'teaching', classroom experience I was able to sum up in nine separate headings:

1   Choice
2   Responsibility
3   Trust
4   Practical nature of the work
5   Development of competences
6   Fun
7   Multiply-intelligent working
8   Independence
9   Team working.

As I wrote in my final report:

> None of the above is surprising or rocket science. We know what to do. We need now to work out *how* to do what to do.

Which, again, is where you come in. One of the findings from the Cambridge University *Learning How to Learn* research was that a key element of the success of any learning-focused classroom was the set of beliefs that the teacher carried into the room. Teachers may well have been given a series of strategies about, for example, *Assessment for Learning*, but this was done 'without considering what they already believe about learning in the first place'. In the report by project director Professor Mary James of the Institute of Education, she compares and contrasts two separate year eight English lessons, A and B, highlighting the differences in terms of quality of independent thinking and learning that was achieved. Lesson B outshone a perfectly acceptable lesson A. Why?[9]

According to the report:

> Underpinning lesson B ... was the teacher's strongly held conviction that her job was to make her classes less passively dependent on her and more dependent on themselves and each other. Unlike the teacher in lesson A, her beliefs about learning all centred around a move towards the greater independence of her pupils.

Which brings me back to where I started this chapter. Do you believe your job is to teach children or help them to learn? Do you believe your school is – or should be – a teaching school or a learning school?

Your answer changes everything.

Chapter 22

Things that get in the way of the learning that are nothing to do with the teaching

Although I wouldn't like to argue with Dr Andrew Curran when he says that the most important thing in the classroom is the teacher, there are plenty of factors that can interfere with students' ability to learn that have got very little do with you. Although, once you are aware of them, you can start to accommodate them in the way you plan not only your lessons but also your classroom and even your entire day.

Lighting is one of my favourite examples. As I stated in *Essential Motivation*, on the subject of fluorescent strip lighting:

> Apart from not containing the full light spectrum that our brains need, they also flash on and off around 100 times a second, inducing in us 'stress type' levels of the hormones cortisol and ACTH ... In a relaxed state the brain is processing information at about five to ten times per second, which can be multiplied by 20 during prolonged exposure to fluorescent lights.
>
> (Gilbert 2002)

According to one website[1] I have found since writing these words, the range of hazards that fluorescent lights expose us to include:

> Headache, eyestrain, eye irritation, fatigue, difficulty in concentration, increased rate of 'misjudgments' and accidents, malaise and irritability caused by noise, glare and flicker from fluorescent lighting, increased stress (which may in turn lead to heart disease), changes in hormone production, allergic skin reactions and dermatitis, 'cutaneous light sensitivity', increased risk of seizure in epilepsy sufferers, higher incidence of miscarriage and the speeding up the aging of the retina.

Although it's probably worth pointing out that the website in question belongs to the *Natural Lighting Company* in Glendale, Arizona, it does resonate with findings I have come across elsewhere.

It's not just the type of lighting that is at question though, it is also the nature of the lighting, according to seminal research by Dr Rita and Dr Kenneth Dunn and detailed in their book *Teaching Students Through Their Individual Learning Styles.* (I know there is a great deal of controversy thrown up by the idea of 'learning styles' but think of it rather as what I call a 'learning mix' – the variety of factors that will ensure we learn as best as we can at any given time.) The best way to think about this learning mix is to consider it from your own perspective as a learner. So, starting with lighting, are you a one little lamp above your desk with the rest of the room in darkness sort of learner or a whole house lit up while you do your marking type? Or maybe you prefer natural lighting anyway? What about candlelight in your classroom? I know the Elfin Safety has a seizure when you use the words 'candle' and 'classroom' in the same breath but there is a world of difference between reading, for example, *The Canterbury Ghost* in candlelight with the blinds drawn and reading it under the uncompromising glare of a bank of fluorescent lights. I know because some schools do it that way.

And what about being outside to learn? Do you remember the 'environment of evolutionary adaptedness' from chapter 8? The idea that we are like we are because of the millions of years we've spent doing other things. Well, we've spent millions of years under (a) full spectrum, (b) natural lighting in (c) a green environment. That's what we are 'designed' for. Classrooms usually fall down on all three counts. On the subject of the green environment, there is plenty of research about how beneficial that is to us too. In a report entitled 'Nearby Nature: A Buffer of Life Stress Among Rural Children', the researchers found that having access to green environments reduced stress levels for children, regardless of what the stress was, compared to those who didn't have access to such environments. Further research from the Landscape and Human Health Laboratory at University of Illinois at Urbana-Champaign has found a remarkable range of benefits of proximity to green environments including the discoveries that working in a green environment reduces symptoms in children with ADHD, that girls living in apartments with 'greener, more natural views' had higher self-esteem scores compared to those living in 'more barren but otherwise identical housing', that women who live in apartment buildings 'with trees and greenery immediately outside report greater effectiveness and less procrastination in dealing with their major life issues than those living in barren but otherwise identical buildings', that there were 48 per cent fewer instances of crime against property and 56 per cent fewer instances of violent crime in apartment buildings bordered by trees and greenery than in identical apartments nearby surrounded by 'barren land', that the greenness of the surroundings correlated in inverse proportion with the number of crimes, in other words that more trees = less crime, that women living in apartment buildings with trees and greenery 'immediately outside' committed fewer 'aggressive and violent acts against their partners' than those in 'barren but otherwise identical buildings' and that the women living in the green surroundings used a 'smaller range of aggressive tactics during their lifetime against their partner'.[2] Green spaces have also been associated with quicker post-operative recovery periods and, if you leave work stressed, you are more likely to be less stressed when you arrive back home if you have travelled through a green environment than if you have headed home though a built-up environment.

I bet the Local Authority didn't think about that when it sold off your school fields.

One teacher told me how she had a group of boys in her class who were behaving in typical 'boy-like' ways so as an experiment she moved all of the boys closer to the window for several lessons. To her surprise their behaviour improved, only to deteriorate when she moved them back to their original places a few weeks later. Another lady, a special needs teacher, once told me about a boy she had been working with outside a classroom and who was working well. On his return to the classroom things only started to deteriorate when the teacher switched the classroom lights on at which point the special needs teacher had to practically drag the boy from the classroom. When she asked him why his behaviour had changed so abruptly his reply was, 'Those lights, Miss! They do my head in.' I also once read an article claiming that raised levels of cortisol caused by these lights lead to weight gain and diabetes under the title, 'Fluorescent Lights Make You Fat'!

What opportunities then do you have in your classroom to experiment with the quality of the lighting? To have lights off more often or, maybe, half the lights on or half the lights off? Or even go outside to learn, heaven forbid?! And never underestimate the powerful effect light can have on our overall state. To quote the great Italian film director Frederico Fellini:

> Light is everything; substance, dreams, feelings, style, colour, tone, depth, atmosphere, narrative, ideology. Light is life.
>
> (www.iguzzini.com)

Another factor from the Dunn and Dunn learning mix is eating and/or drinking whilst learning. When you are at home working on your own do you make sure, before you start, you've got your cup of coffee or glass of wine? Some people are 'nibblers', eating and drinking whilst learning. Others would rather save their intake for the breaks, even using the promise of a cup of tea and a Hobnob as motivation to keep going for that extra

20 minutes of effort. Regardless of your school rules, eating and drinking in the classroom or not *will* have an effect on your students' learning.

Or what about how you position yourself when you are working? Do you sit at a desk or table or do you regularly lie on the floor to work? Maybe you sprawl half on a settee, half on the floor but all over the place? Maybe you will vary the position you take depending on the nature of the work you are about to undertake?

In most classrooms, however, the rules are 'sit at your desk to read', 'sit at your desk to listen', 'sit at your desk to write', 'sit at your desk to think', interspersed with the occasional 'stand behind your desk to feign respect'. Does it have to be that way? One of the things I have picked up during my time observing lessons is that chairs and tables are often used in the classroom for crowd-control purposes, acting like groynes to stop the long-shore drift of children to the windows. Sometimes it is the layout of the room that causes the restlessness in the children in the first place. I remember observing a class of inner-city year ten students in a drama lesson and then, immediately after, in a history lesson. In the former the children were impeccably behaved as they wandered the dark spaces of the drama studio, sometimes sitting on the floor, sometimes in a semi-circle of chairs. In the latter, squashed into a small room made smaller by heavy classroom tables and chairs and the equally cumbersome attitude of the teacher, they were listless and troublesome. Even when a teacher does want to offer a little variety in the way they teach, they often feel that the bulky classroom tables mitigate against it, although it does seem odd to let the furniture determine the pedagogy. It really doesn't take that long for 30 children to move 15 tables to the sides of the rooms and make a circle of 30 chairs. My best time has been 58 seconds. And then the same amount of time to put things back how they were at the end of the lesson.

Would, then, you be prepared to allow, *in a managed and professional way*, children to lie on the floor to work in your classroom? One teacher I talked to about this said that in her class she had a couple of boys who refused to read until she offered them the chance to read whilst sitting under the table. Or what about allowing children to walk up and down as they read? I came across research many years back that found that children who were allowed to walk around as they read, learned better than if they had been sitting down to read. Remember the role that the cerebellum plays in both movement and reading? Or what about allowing your students to simply stand up to work? Ernest Hemmingway, Virginia Woolf, Winston Churchill, Vladimir Nabokov, Thomas Wolfe, Leonardo da Vinci, Benjamin Franklin, Thomas Jefferson, Napoleon, William Gladstone and Donald Rumsfeld all wrote standing up.[3] But then, why should we be so surprised? We've been standing or lying for millions of years. Sitting down at a table and desk is a very new phenomenon that restricts our ability to take the sort of deep breaths we need to take to fire our brain with the oxygen it needs to create the 20 Watts or so of electricity it runs on and involves most of our body weight resting on about four square inches of bone for extended periods of time.[4] No wonder it is called a SAT. Remember what I said about Darwin and his 'thinking walks' in chapter 11. In *Re-Imagine*, Tom Peters quotes the designer Niels Diffrient, when he says:

> My ideal office wouldn't have a chair. You would do two things: stand up or lie down. These are the body's most natural positions.[5]
>
> (Peters 2003)

So, what variety is available to your students when it comes to how they position themselves for learning in your classroom? And what about your own position in the classroom? According to an article on the '360-degree classroom' in *The Observer*, 'Consigning the teacher to a desk at the front is thought to stop him or her thinking freely.'[6]

Another factor identified by Dunn and Dunn is the time of day. Are you an early bird or a night owl? Do you fire on all four cylinders best during period one or period six? Are you at your most creative at midday or midnight? Your answer to these questions will reveal what is known as your genetically determined 'chronotype' and it is worth pointing out at this stage, for purposes of your own safety, that working contrary to your chronotype can kill you. Literally. Research found that early birds working nights, for example, had particularly high incidents of serious illnesses, including cancer. On a different, but still important, note it has been suggested that teachers on average have a preference for mornings whereas children, certainly at adolescent stage, have a preference for afternoons. There has also been shown to be a 12-hour spread in the population's 'chronotype' meaning that one person's early breakfast is another person's light supper. What's more, this 'social jet lag',[7] as it has been called, even seems to lead to an increased risk of taking up smoking with all the associated dangers that brings.

Do you work to your chronotype or theirs? Research at the University of Toronto has shown people can drop on average six or seven points in intelligence tests if they sit the test at what is, for them at least, the 'wrong' time of the day.[8] Do you cover that really important topic during period one on Tuesday rather than period four on Thursday because it is when *you* are awake? What might happen if you swapped it around ... ?

Temperature is another one of Dunn and Dunn's findings, and again, in my experience, in any group at any time there will be a definite split between those who feel the temperature is just right, those who feel it is too hot and those who feel it is too cold. Which brings me to the boiling of frogs. It is said that if you put a frog into hot water it will jump out because, essentially, it's not stupid, it's a frog. However, if you really want to do the job properly, the knack is to put it into cold water and then heat it *slowly*. The frog does not have a part of the brain that notices slow incremental change. Nor do we. Have you ever gone to walk into a colleague's classroom on a summer's day and as soon as you open the door a wall of heat hits you, yet all the windows are closed, half of the class is asleep and the TA is sitting in the corner wearing just a towel? It wasn't that hot when everyone walked in, it just became that hot slowly over the course of the lesson and no-one noticed it happening. So, be alert to the classroom temperature and remember that the optimum temperature is a different one for different people. There is even research claiming a six-degree difference between the optimal learning temperature for boys and girls, with a preference of 69 degrees Fahrenheit for boys and 75 degrees for girls (Sax 2006). Maybe opening a window and moving that girl from it and that boy to it might be just what is needed to help everyone learn better.

Sound is another factor that can split a group with all the severity of the Berlin Wall. For some people, they have to have some form of background noise when they are working to help them stay focused and prevent them from losing the will to live. For others, they are utterly convinced that in order for anyone to concentrate then they must be working in complete silence. We call these people, 'parents'. For some people, complete silence can be actually either stressful or distracting or both. I once read that the legendary science fiction writer Isaac Asimov[9] used to take his typewriter to busy shopping malls to write, tapping into the energy from the noise around him.

(And if you want information about music in the classroom – what to use and how to use it – I can only refer you to my colleague Nina Jackson's *Little Book of Music for the Classroom*.)

Another factor identified by the Dunns is what they call 'mobility'. When you are working on your own do you stay put until you finish a particular task or do you move around quite often, finding any excuse to get up and move? Again, ask a group of people this question and you will see the group divided into two camps. And, again, in the classroom we tend to allow for just the one camp – stay there until you finish the work. Yet, consider the Zeigarnik Effect,[10] that our memory for tasks is improved if the tasks remain incomplete, at least for a while. Students who interrupted their learning to do something unrelated remembered better what they had been learning than those who completed the task without stopping.

It may seem nice and neat to get your students to work through a task before they go onto something different, both for you and them, but, as Eric Jensen says in *Super Teaching*, a wonderful book I'll come back to later, 'Learning is messy' (Jensen 1995).

One teacher told me about what she called her 'group from hell', a year ten inner-city school IT group, in which one particular boy was a right little, er, nemesis. However, when she profiled the class using the Dunn and Dunn criteria what came up with this lad was that mobility was high up in his 'learning mix'. Not only that, but also he liked working with an adult. This is another of the factors that the Dunns identified – some people learn best on their own. Create a little 'cocoon of learning' and they will be the first to go to it to work in a solitary way. I know I would. Another friend and colleague, Simon Cooper-Hind, did such a thing when he was leading an 'estate' primary school on the outskirts of Southampton. He and his staff brought in patio umbrellas with ribbons trailing down to the floor 'into' which children could go to work on their own when they wanted to. Some children, however, like working in pairs; some like working in teams – think competitive male-type brains; some like working in groups – think collaborative female-type brains; some like working with an adult; some like a bit of all of the above. However, back to nemesis boy and the IT teacher. She found that *as soon as* she adapted her way of dealing with him to suit his learning preferences, that is to say she became a great deal more relaxed about letting him have a bit of a wander and encouraged him to come and show his work to her more often, she not only won him over *immediately* but also went on to achieve a good set of GCSE results from a group that were in danger of all failing completely. For me, this is a great example of the old adage:

> If they don't learn the way I teach them, then I'll have to teach them the way they learn.

Something that, if you put it into Greek, would and should be the equivalent of the Hippocratic oath for the twenty-first century learning school teacher.

Chapter 23

What do you use when you don't know what to do?

My all time favourite educational quote is from the great Swiss psychologist Jean Piaget. Apart from putting forward a view on children's development ('sensorimotor' stage from birth to two; 'preoperational' stage from two to seven; 'concrete operational' stage from seven to twelve and 'formal operational' stage from twelve upwards) that the neuroscience has finally caught up with, he is also quoted as saying:

> Intelligence is what you use when you don't know what to do.
> (http://en.wikipedia.org/wiki/Jean_Piaget)

Yet this seems the complete reverse of what we are expected to do in the classroom. The way we are taught to teach is to introduce a topic in such a way that everyone knows exactly what to do, check with them that they are clear about what they are supposed to do and then give them a worksheet with 30 questions on it for them to prove that they know what to do, the unspoken implication being that the quickest one to finish is the cleverest. And if they do get stuck, they are to put up their hand and suspend all effort until you are able to come round and unstick them.

In other words, in the classroom, intelligence is what you use when you know exactly what to do. If so, do you really know how clever your intelligent students are? I'm not sure about you, but I think I prefer Piaget's model.

Sometimes, then, we need to say, 'Everybody clear? No? Fantastic! You have seven minutes, in pairs. See if you can work out *for yourselves* what this poem is about or what this equation means or what this experiment will prove or what this French text is all about … '.

(By the way, giving such a task a deadline is a self-esteem thing. If they don't finish it's not because they weren't clever enough but because they ran out of time.)

To what extent do the children in your care have the opportunity to develop the Piagetian definition of intelligence? How do you set things up in such a way that they are learning to think for themselves?

Because I so like the Piaget quote, this is why I so enjoy doing *Philosophy for Children* with young people and, in particular, 'Thunks'. 'Thunks' are deceptively tricky little questions that 'make your brain go ouch!' and came about through my work trying to launch *P4C* in a number of schools across the UK in a way that was quick and effective.

The right and proper way of 'doing *P4C*' with children as put forward by Matthew Lipman whom we met in chapter 15 and drilled into you by SAPERE in the UK is essentially:

1 Sit them in a circle, the 'community of enquiry'
2 Give them a stimulus such as a picture or a text that you had sourced, photocopied and distributed
3 Spend time reading the text around the circle
4 Giving the group time in silence to come up with questions about the stimulus
5 Elicit their questions about the stimulus which you record on the board with their name next to it
6 Decide as a group how you are going to decide as a group which question to start with
7 Decide which question to start with
8 Bounce that question back to the child who asked it
9 Start.

This system works and works well so I'm not knocking it. It's just that often I had about 30 minutes to work with a completely unknown group, observed by a cynical panel of staff, to try and produce some sort of result that showed just what great thinking these children were capable of.

So, like some paramilitary splinter group, I had to come up with a way of doing things where I could go in, have an impact and be back in my car and onto the next one before anybody really knew what was happening. A sort of 'shock and awe and wonder' strategy. I didn't have the luxury of the nine-step opening gambit and, to be frank, I'm too lazy to spend time sourcing documents and photocopying them unless I really have to. It was as a result of this that 'Thunks' were born, as I found that philosophically-contentious questions could cut out the middle seven steps above and I could cut straight to the chase, namely making children's brains hurt.

The way I do these sessions now involves the following process:

1 Sit them in a circle, the 'community of enquiry'.

As King Arthur and the person behind kaizen know, a circle is a powerful, egalitarian, non-hierarchical, all-inclusive way of bringing a group together to work.

2   Tell them that in this session they can't be wrong.

Although that may also imply that they can't be right either ... . Every time I say this to them they look at me like they don't believe me, as if they know I'm still going to be playing the 'guess what's in the teacher's head' game, regardless of what I might be telling them, that I'm still going to try and catch them out and show them how clever I am and how not clever they are. This is why step four is so important.

3   Tell them that my target for the session is to make their brains hurt. Can't have a lesson without a target ... .

4   Warm up their brains with some Possibly Impossible Questions.

These are creative thinking questions that serve the double purpose of warming up the brain for a bit of mental exercise and also reassuring them that, seriously, there are no right answers and so, honestly, you can't be wrong. My favourite question is 'What colour is Tuesday?' although you could have 'Which is heavier, rich or poor?' or 'What is there more of in the world, light or dark?' or 'Which is more like a bird – a dog or a tree?' or 'What would change if pigs ruled the world?' You get the idea ... . (I once heard the poet John Hegley describe how he asked a group of children similar sorts of questions. In response to the question, 'What's the difference between a dog and a deckchair?' one child answered, 'Deckchairs can't fly!' I also like the question from a year eight girl relayed to me by her teacher, 'Can a cat climb higher than a dog can bark?')

For more possibly Impossible Questions have a look at the Independent Thinking website.[1]

5   Start with a 'Thunk'.

My three favourite 'Thunks' are 'Is a broken down car parked?', 'Is black a colour?' and 'If you read a newspaper in the newsagents without paying for it, is it stealing?'. (For more 'Thunks' have a look, again, at the Independent Thinking website[2]; at www.thunks.co.uk, where you can add your own or respond online to other people's such as these that came in recently – 'If you send a slinky down an escalator will it ever reach the bottom?' and 'Is the Hokey Cokey *really* what it's all about?'; or check out my *Little Book of Thunks*, a book Amazon recommended to me when it first came out. You'll be pleased to know I declined to review it.)

One SEN teacher I met once referred to such questions as 'thought hand grenades', as she would sit her group in a circle and toss in such a question and then stand well back. 'Thunks' have even achieved notoriety in *The Observer* in an article entitled 'Drop GCSEs. We should be teaching our children to think'[3] and on BBC Radio 4's *Today* programme during UNESCO's *World Philosophy Day*[4] where I was asked to write a few 'Thunks' especially for them and their website. These are what I suggested:[5]

1　Is certainty the same as truth?
2　Do all Polos taste the same?
3　Is the Hokey Cokey really what it's all about?
4　Can you photograph a wink?
5　Is my God your God?
6　Is there a difference between an 'exit' and a 'way out'?
7　Could God be an atheist?
8　Is Monday not Tuesday as much as Wednesday isn't?
9　Are two all-you-can-eat breakfasts twice as big as one?
10　Is it OK to let someone in the queue behind you?
11　Does having plans help you become the sort of person you used to want to be?
12　Can you be proud of someone you've never met?
13　Just because we can, should we?
14　Should you trust everyone once?
15　Is a hole a thing?
16　Does your house weigh more when the bath is full?
17　Is saying 'I don't know' better than guessing?
18　Can a good person choose not to go to heaven (should it exist)?
19　Is refusing to be weak the same as being strong?
20　Could a nun disguise herself as a nun?

I also spoke at a recent *TEDx* conference in Dubai where 'Thunks' went down very well with a very mixed audience.[6] I do not share all this 'Thunking' with you to blow my own pedagogical trumpet but to underline just how much interest there is in having children think for themselves, how much controversy it causes, how simple it is to achieve, how much fun can be had doing it and, above all, to urge you to have a go with any group of children and see what happens.

One thing I can guarantee will happen is that they will not respond how you think they will. Every time I have worked in this way – and I mean *every* time – there is a child who, during the session, is brilliant. They are eloquent, they are forceful, they are persuasive, they are intelligent, they are creative, they are confident. It is only afterwards, when the teachers who have been observing feed back to me, that I discover that that child never normally speaks in lessons. It is a phenomenon that other teachers have witnessed for themselves on countless occasions when they play around with *P4C* themselves. I think one of the big reasons it happens in this way so consistently is to do with the nature of the 'rules of engage-ment' as set up in step two above – you can't be wrong. By taking out the threat of failure that exists whenever thoughts are either 'right' or 'wrong', what you are left with is just 'thoughts'. *And everyone has thoughts.* It makes me wonder how many children go through their entire school careers not joining in for fear of getting it wrong? What's more, taking right or wrong out of the picture is a lot more effective than simply telling a group to 'have a go, it doesn't matter if you get it wrong'. Getting it wrong in front of their peers is as world-endingly embarrassing for them as it is for you.

On the subject of 'joining in' something else to bear in mind when working this way is that participants don't have to speak to participate. It's about 'thinking skills' not about 'talking skills'. (Talking skills are improved, but only as a sideline to the main event. Research in Scotland also shows that *P4C* improved IQ scores of a group of five- to eleven-year-olds by 6.5 points and that this improvement was maintained into their secondary education, despite the fact that they were no longer doing it.[7] The most surprising aspect is that it continued after the lessons stopped at secondary school. The saddest aspect is that the lessons stopped at secondary school.) One of the shy girls from one group I was working with (and for more information on *P4C* and self-esteem see chapter 16) was telling me after-wards that she wanted to be a barrister and that she felt that developing her thinking in this way was really useful. When I asked her about whether being quiet during the sessions was an issue she said categorically that it wasn't. She did join in, just not out loud. What she liked to do was sit there and listen to other people's points of view and reflect on them internally. Having to speak would actually get in the way of her own thinking. What I also find, and I'm thinking of certain boys here in parti-cular, those who talk the most are usually the ones who think the least. This is where the *P4C* technique of always ending a session by going around the circle and asking each member to come up with one sentence to sum up what's been going through their head, is useful. It is here where you are met with the 'My brain hurts' responses, although another one that often crops up relates to the surprise many children experience at realizing that people have different opinions from each other.

My favourite response, though, in all the years I have been doing this, and a line that is testimony to the power of the process, was from a nine-year-old boy who summed up a session with me by saying:

I've just realized how big life is.

Something to remember when trying to encourage thinking with your students, whether it is in a specific thinking skills lesson or even in a traditional subject-based session, relates to the power of silence. Often the teacher response, when a question they have posed is met with silence, is to panic. The widely quoted average 'wait time'[8] – the pause between asking a question and then diving in with the answer (or another question, which means they've got two to answer now) is between 0.7 and 1.4 seconds. As someone once pointed out to me, the only person who can answer a question that quickly is the one who posed it! I used to encourage teachers to put their hands behind their back once they had asked a question and count on their fingers to ten as a way of stopping themselves from jumping in, but maybe I was being overgenerous. Researcher Mary Budd Rowe who pioneered the concept of 'wait time' found that by waiting for just three seconds there was a dramatic increase in the quality of the student responses including an increase in the length of the response, an increase in the likelihood of the response being correct, an overall decrease in the number of 'I don't know' or non responses, an increase in the number of people attempting to answer the question from across the class and, in US research, an increase in SAT scores.

Neurologically speaking, some people are 'fast processors' and some are 'slow processors' based on the way that electricity cycles through their brains. The fast processors can process quite a few chunks of information in a short period of time and quickly come up with an answer. The slow processors can process fewer chunks in a set period of time and therefore it takes them longer to respond. On the whole, they are just as clever. They are just not as quick. But, in a classroom situation, we tend to equate quick with clever, the two even being synonymous in many a school report. The message we unintentionally send to children when we work like this is, 'He's quicker than me, therefore he's cleverer than me, therefore I'm not very clever, therefore I'm stupid' and then we hit the slippery slope of self-esteem road before veering across the off-ramp of self-fulfilling prophecies. What's more, if you are a quick thinker, the danger is that you only end up ever thinking quickly. One of the cleverest people I know, a former aid to Stephen Hawking, is one of the slowest thinkers I have ever met, no good in a pub quiz but great at brewing the beer.

It has also been remarked that you can split fast and slow responders along sex lines, especially when they are younger. So often in primary schools it will be boys who have their hands up first, before they've had sufficient time to even think about the answer, often before you've had time to ask the question. They don't so much care about accuracy as being first. Girls, on the other hand, are happy to share an answer with everybody once they have had the time to work out if it is the right answer. They don't want to be first, they want to look good.

Another benefit of the waiting for an answer approach is that it sends a message to the students – it is your job to answer this question not mine! Too often when confronted with any situation which involves asking a student to think, they know that if they look pathetic enough, stick their hand up and say in a whiney voice, 'What have we got to do, Miss?' that you will sort them out and do the thinking for them. Eventually this becomes the set response to everything, especially if, when they do have a go, they feel they always fail. A well-known phenomenon in the classroom is the way in which children – girls in particular according to some research – can develop what is called 'learned helplessness',[9] where their response to a new challenge is predicted by their failures in previous challenges and they simply don't try in order to obviate yet more feelings of inadequacy. In a fascinating online article entitled 'Learned Helplessness and School Failure'[10] by Robert Gordon and Myrna Gordon, they refer to it as 'a conditioned response to failure that creates cognitive, motivational, and emotional deficits in our children' and, unchecked, it can lead not only to school failure and disaffection but also mental illness such as depression.[11] This is particularly the case, according to research by Paul Gilbert from the Mental Health Research Unit[12] in Derby (Gilbert 1984), (following the original research by Martin Seligman[13] that involved some quite unpleasant experiments on dogs and rats), when the following criteria are met – 'the individual is aware of uncontrollable factors in their environment, the individual views the situation as unchangeable and they blame themselves for their helplessness'.

(By the way, the flip side to learned helplessness is what we seem to allow to develop in our Gifted and Talented children which is an inability to deal with failure because they have never experienced it. What do you do when you don't know what to do? They don't know, they've never been in that situation before. The biggest disservice we do our G & T children is not letting them fail every now and again. Ten out of ten consistently with the same child is not good enough.)

The Gordons argue convincingly that 'learned helplessness' needs to be addressed using a 'three-legged stool' approach which (1) confronts the reasons why the child has developed such a response, (2) seeks to understand the nature of the 'root beliefs and distorted perceptions' that the child carries and (3) that gives the child 'the tools to change'. In other words, as a teacher once told me, 'Don't ride the bike for them!'

A primary school in Bootle shared with me their 'Four-B' strategy for helping children think for themselves. Whenever a child became stuck, rather than resorting to a state of learned helplessness they, instead, went through the four Bs of, and in this order, Brain – Book – Buddy – Boss ('Boss' being the teacher). In other words, when they felt they were stuck they had to spend some time thinking about it for themselves. Then, if they were still stuck they were to consult their books or the board. If, after that, they still felt stuck they could go to one of their peers. This could be 'informal', going to a friend and seeking help, or 'formal' where the role of the child in the 'Expert Chair' was to help those who had reached the third B. Be reassured that these 'buddies' will also be learning. You can't really know whether you have learned anything until you can put it into your own words and teach it for yourself to someone else. As Virgil said, 'As you teach so you shall learn, as you learn so shall you teach.' (Insert *Thunderbirds* joke here – you know you want to.) The fourth B is when the child comes to you for help, something you should only give if they can prove they have exhausted the other three Bs first. Another version of this I have heard of is 'Three before me' or 'Four before me', where the child can only go to the teacher for help if they can demonstrate they have attempted three or four different strategies for trying to think for themselves first. In other words, in a managed, structured and supportive way, you are actually teaching children how to think for themselves.

So, in the interests of encouraging children to think, and for themselves, it is worth moving away from the 'put your hand up if you're stuck' approach in the classroom. What's more, it is also worth moving away from the 'put your hand up if you know the answer' game too. This is especially apparent when you observe a 'hands up question and answer' session in a classroom and see the 80:20 Rule in action. Also known as the Pareto Principle after the turn-of-the-century Italian economist who noticed that 80 per cent of the land was owned by 20 per cent of the people, this rule describes nicely how 80 per cent of the responses come from 20 per cent of the children, the same 20 per cent. Which means that large groups of children can sit there for extended periods doing absolutely nothing and, because every time you ask a question you receive the sort of answer you were looking for, you think the lesson is going well.

What's more, if you do pick on a child who isn't answering, if he or she looks dumb enough for long enough you have to move on anyway.

Some schools have banned the 'hands up' approach altogether,[14] such as the Jo Richardson Comprehensive in London claiming that 'the ban on putting hands up has improved attention levels'.

Another benefit of eschewing the 'hands up to respond' scenario is that it helps you avoid having to say, 'Don't shout out!' 100 times a day, especially important when you think that often when we say don't shout out, what the child hears is, 'Will you stop being so enthusiastic with your right answers. Your learning's getting in the way of my teaching, now stop it!' Sometimes you can do a 'shout out' activity; sometimes you can do a 'shout in' activity where they have to say the answer but only so they can hear or else turn to a partner and tell them the answer as soon as they think they know. Or else you could get them to work in groups and give them 30 seconds or so to answer your question, something that actively involves the whole class and also gets talking those who would otherwise be loath to talk in front of the whole class.

Which brings us back to 'Thunks'.

Sometimes when you are working with a child in a *P4C* session and especially if they are at the more academically able end of the spectrum of classroom achievement, and you ask them a question like, 'Is there more future or past?' their response is, 'I don't know.' And they are quite right. They don't know. No-one knows. But you are not asking them what they know, you are asking them what they think. And they are separate things. For me, knowing is clever, wanting to know is intelligence. Helping children who know so much (that is to say, have good memories and a subscription to the *Discovery Channel*) and are always first with the 'right answer' to be comfortable with not knowing an answer but putting forward a suggestion of their own thinking is a hugely important task for any teacher. Think of it, if you like, from a scientific perspective. Here you start with a thought, a hypothesis, which you then have to try and turn into something that you know. For this reason alone we need to have our academically gifted children comfortable with thinking but not knowing. On top of that, something else I have noticed is that it is the more academically able children (and adults for that matter) who are less able to take on board new information and change their minds. I like *P4C* because it opens up chinks of uncertainty to allow the truth to get in. So, go on, change your mind, prove you've got one, as they say.

I once heard thinking skills advocate of long standing Robert Fisher[15] tell a group of headteachers of the Oxford admissions tutor who was asked the question, 'With so many A grade students in front of you, now more than ever, how do you separate the intelligent ones from the ones who have been well schooled and who have a good memory?' The response was that, actually, it was very easy, just as it is for Richard Lambert, Director of the CBI, when he said, 'For employers, differentiating between pupils who have straight As is not a problem'. How? According to the admissions tutor, 'I just ask them a question no-one's asked them before.' I think Piaget would approve.

Chapter 24

A short word on thinking about thinking

There are many ways to fail a test.

You can not know the answer because you forgot to revise. You can not know the answer because you chose not to revise. You can not know the answer because you didn't get around to revising that particular bit. You can not know the answer because you were away during that particular lesson. You can not know the answer because you just didn't 'get' that particular aspect of the curriculum. You can have got things wrong and revised the wrong thing. You can have revised well but just forgot it in the exam. You can have run out of time to answer the question even though you knew the answer. You can have misread the question and answered it wrong. You can have revised it but that particular bit just didn't stick. You can have tried to revise it but your notes just didn't make sense. You can have revised it, memorized it and regurgitated it well but had it down wrong in your book in the first place ... .

And there are as many ways to get ten out of ten as there are to get zero out of ten.

Lifting the lid on children's brains, peering in and asking, 'How did you get what you got?' is what metacognition is all about and it is a vital cog in the 'learning school' machine. What's more, research has shown a link between metacognition and intelligence.[1] Yet it is often overlooked in the headlong rush towards covering the curriculum (although I once came across a lady from New Zealand who had been a 'metacognitive teacher', whose job was to help children genuinely think about what they were seeing when they visited an art gallery).

Helping children develop effective metacognition can be broken down into two important areas, as identified by the man who coined the word, Stanford psychologist John Flavell.[2] These are 'metacognitive knowledge' and 'metacognitive strategies'. With metacognitive knowledge, students learn about, for example, their preferences in the learning mix we described in Chapter 22. Do they work best in the evenings, on their own, in quiet, etc. ... ? In other words, as the ancient Greeks put it at the Temple of Apollo at Delphi, 'Know thyself'. Encouraging learners to reflect, in advance, on their learning can be useful, with questions like, 'What will be the best way for me to approach this challenge?', 'What are the likely obstacles to me doing well?', 'What needs to happen for me stay motivated to do this task?' and 'How will I benefit from doing well in this task – what's in it for me?'

When it comes to metacognitive strategies, also known as 'metacognitive regulation', it becomes a question of helping the student reflect on the thinking processes that they may use to address the challenge. These could include questions like, 'What do I already know about this area?', 'Have I faced challenges like this before?' and 'If so, what did I do to address them?' Once the work is underway, metacognition continues with questions like, 'Am I on target with this task?', 'Do I understand what I am doing?' 'What can I do to help myself better understand this?' and 'How will I remember these key pieces of information?' (For more on metacognition and memory see the next chapter.)

As a teacher, you can encourage children to develop these metacognitive practices by questioning them and encouraging them to question themselves in this way. Constantly asking, 'How did you get that?', is a powerful way to encourage such reflection in the classroom and far more useful than leaping in with a 'Not good enough' or even a well-intentioned 'Well done'.

Metacognition has a key part to play in the process of goal setting, as we constantly ask ourselves whether we are on course towards our chosen goal or not. So, an important step as a teacher is to make sure you align your goals for them with their goals for themselves. For example, a tutor once told me about one of the students in her class at a sixth form college who was a talented student orally and a great speller but who was not achieving the grades he was capable of in his written work. This was because he kept using 'odd words' in his essays and she couldn't fathom why. So I asked him. He knew exactly why and was able to give me a perfectly straightforward reason. He started off by telling me that his spelling was atrocious and, when I pointed out to him that his tutor had told me that his spelling was good, he replied by telling me that it was not true but, because he had a good vocabulary, if ever he came across a word he couldn't spell, he just put in a word he could spell. When I asked him why, he told me that, when he had been at secondary school, every time he had an essay handed back to him it was covered with red pen! In other words his goal for a piece of work was not 'highest grade' as the tutor had assumed, but 'least red'. The quality of the work was further down his list than his desire to avoid getting things wrong.

Maybe the goal of that least achieving, most disruptive boy in your class is to be the least achieving, most disruptive boy in your class, something he achieves each and every lesson. You, on the other hand, whose goal it is to have all your students working at level six, fail.

A personal example, if I may, relates to my son. When he entered secondary school I knew he was more than capable of achieving A grades in his work, so I began the process of pushing him to achieve these, abetted by his class teachers. But then I stopped myself. I realized that A grades are good for parents and good for teachers but actually weren't good for him. He had a different goal, namely to not be a 'boff'. In other words, his number one goal for his school day was to have a circle of friends, something that doing well at school would mitigate against in his view. It wasn't that he didn't want to do well, it just wasn't number one on his list. The deal I struck with him, then, as he approached his GCSEs was one we called the 'B-Boy' strategy. In other words, the goal he was to achieve was 'B grades and a life'. Not 'all life and no qualifications' or 'A grades and no life'. Just Bs and a life. His minimum expected grades, I remember, were Bs right down the line (apart from RE which, in his irrefutable words and given the quality of the teacher I tend to agree with, 'doesn't count'). We had simply aligned goals, although when he was awarded an A star in his chemistry coursework I grounded him for a week. His actual GCSEs did include a number of As but they were there because he wanted them to be, not because I wanted them there.

By the way, I'm not setting myself up as the world greatest parent, far from it, but I have children so I may as well experiment.

I mentioned this to a group of teachers in Cornwall and it caused a great deal of heated debate and controversy amongst what was a high-achieving academic staff. In the break a lady came up to me, though, and said to me, 'I was pushed to get A grades but wished I'd got Bs and a life. I won't be 16 again.'

I was observing a year ten PE theory lesson a while back and, at the beginning of the lesson, the teacher handed back to the students a modular test they had sat the previous lesson and that he had subsequently marked. As is always the case the students looked at their own mark, looked at their friends' marks and then the teacher said, 'OK class, put them away now. Let's get on with today's lesson'. What he missed was the metacognitive opportunity to say, 'OK, who got question three right? Who got it wrong? If you got it wrong you've got two minutes to go and find someone who got it right and tell you, not the right answer, but *how* they got the answer right.' In other words, *how* did they remember the difference between an ectomorph and a mesomorph or whatever it was? That way, more students would have been able to pass the test next time around.

The logical extension, then, is that we should be encouraging our students to copy, not preventing them. This, of course, is not cheating because that way, as it says in the Teachers' Guide to Classroom Clichés, you are only cheating yourself. Rather it is what in Neuro-Linguistic Programming circles is known as 'modelling'.

There has been a great deal written about the use of NLP[3] in schools, some of it very positive, some if it quite scathing. For my part I am very much pro-NLP and have found it an invaluable, but not inviolate, tool in my work with young people and teachers as well as in my own personal development. It grew out of the work that linguist John Grinder and undergraduate psychology student Richard Bandler undertook in the 1970s at the University of California. Those words 'undergraduate', 'California' and '1970s' have been enough to put many academics off the whole NLP idea, but all I would suggest, if you have not done so already, is to find out more about it and work out for yourself what you can take from it. In case you didn't know, the whole idea of VAK in the classroom, that we have a preferred way of taking information on board during learning, a preferred 'modality' that is either visual, auditory or kinesthetic, comes from NLP. This is, as academics are quick to point out, neither rocket science nor strictly accurate,[4] yet it is, in my experience, a really useful way of helping young people get past specific learning blocks and helping teachers make sure they teach outside their own preferred way of learning. (For example, many of the maths classes I have observed have been delivered in a predominantly auditory way, the information coming to the students through their ears. Yet I, and many of the students in the classes I speak to, have a visual preference when it comes to maths and what made no sense in auditory form makes complete sense when presented visually. As a student I had often wished I had been clever enough to understand my maths teachers. Now I was.)

Bandler and Grinder's early work involved looking at patterns of language and behaviour, in particular effective hypnosis and therapy to understand the 'difference that makes a difference'. What do people who are successful in their field do to achieve that and how can that then be shared with others to achieve similar success? This works at a very broad level too. If you want to be a great teacher simply act like 'a great teacher', if you want to think like a great entrepreneur approach each challenge as if you were Richard Branson. It can also work at a far more subtle level, too, where you examine the patterns of language the 'great' practitioner uses, the tonality and submodalities of their speech, their facial expressions, their entire body language, even their eye movements. Observing other people in such detail – and such acuity is a big part of success in NLP – and then applying it to yourself or teaching it to others is what is referred to as modelling and this is the sort of 'copying' I advocate in the classroom. Find a student who has done well in a given aspect of a subject and not only find out how but help them to find out how too. Once the meta-cognitive 'secrets of their success' are better understood they can be better transmitted to other students in the class too.

I have not yet come across a school that brings together a 'focus group' of students who did well in their exams and ones who didn't and really pick their brains about what went right and what went wrong. By learning the metacognitive secrets of the highest achieving students and teaching others to use their strategies, you are not only teaching children to pass their exams, you are also teaching them *how* to pass their exams. Not only that, as we will see in the next chapter, you could also be teaching them to *remember* to pass their exams.

Chapter 25

Remember to succeed

We have fantastic memories. You do (although it does deteriorate with age). Your students do. The reason they forget what you think you have taught them is not because they have poor memories, although many students think that is the case and grow up into adults who feel they have lousy memories too. They forget because the learning was not *memorable*. We spend a great deal of time teaching children things but never seem to spend any time helping them to remember what we have taught them. Yet memorizing key information is one of the easiest parts of the learning cycle and can be one of the most fun if you take rote learning out of the equation (although not altogether because it does work).

To what extent, if at all, are you helping young people remember what you have been teaching them? To what extent have you addressed the 'hidden question' I mentioned in *Essential Motivation* that is there every time you say to a group, 'Now go away and learn this and I'll test you tomorrow', which is '*How* shall I go away and learn this so you can test me tomorrow?' Yet I see it time and time again – teach a child how to remember the information, then test them and that child will perform well.

What's more, there are two big benefits from teaching children memory strategies. One is that, obviously, it improves their memory. The second is that it has a direct impact on their self-esteem. Remember in chapter 16 I said that you can't raise someone's self-esteem? What you can do, however, is set up the opportunities that allow people's self-esteem to grow. If I say to an individual or a class, especially a bottom set group, 'Guess what, you all have great memories', then they not only won't believe me, they will also have the data to back up their refutation of my claim. All they would need to do is to show me their test results for the last however many years of school. However, if I simply teach them a strategy, test them and allow them to get ten out of ten they will see for themselves what they are capable of. And, in my experience, they often soon see the bigger picture of, 'If I can do that what else can I do ... ?' Research has found that learning new things actually helps strengthen your brain and that this is all the more effective if you *believe* you can learn new things. People who have what is known as a 'growth mindset'[1] have higher levels of brain plasticity. In other words, by reassuring children that they can learn and proving to them how powerful their brains really are, we actually help grow their brains.

Some people have said, me included, that we remember every little thing that ever happened to us, that it all goes in and stays there somewhere, but we have trouble getting it out when we need it. Research is now showing, though, that our memory isn't quite as eidetic as that, as pointed out in a fascinating paper entitled the *Seven Sins of Memory* by memory researcher Daniel Schacter. He describes seven ways in which our memories can let us down, the first three – 'transience' where memories slip over time and with age; 'absent-mindedness' where you forget where you put the scissors and go looking for them where you had them last and then forget what you were looking for and so go back to the room where you started and remember that this was about scissors and then you go to where you think you last saw them making scissor movements with your fingers; and, thirdly, 'blocking', an example of which is the tip of the tongue syndrome you experience at parents evening with the name of that child whose parents are sitting expectantly in front of you – being 'sins of omission' (Schacter 1999). The last four – 'suggestibility' where you can be tricked into registering false memories through things like leading questions; 'bias' where the way you feel now can alter the way you remember events from the past (remember how wonderful and free teaching used to be under the Tories?); 'persistence' as seen in the recurring unwanted memories experienced in post-traumatic stress disorder; and 'misattribution' where you 'remember' experiencing something that didn't happen (remember how wonderful and free teaching used to be under the Tories?) – are 'sins of commission'.

So, although our memories are fallible, they are still good enough to *never* be the problem when it comes to passing exams. In other words, forgetting to remember to pass the exam is an unforgivable way to fail given all that we know about remembering.

One of the most useful ways to look at memory is with the following equation:

RRR+R

At the risk of making you sound like a pirate if you happen to be reading this book out loud, our first three Rs are:

Registration – taking the information on board in the first place
Retention – hanging onto it when it is in there
Recall – bringing it back out, preferably as and when you need it.

For the purposes of the classroom, and the 'seven sins' notwithstanding, we can assume that the middle 'R' is not a problem and our learners are capable of retaining what they have learned. In a nutshell, then, the secret of having great recall, to be able to pluck from inside your own head the information you need as and when you want it, is based on the strength of the first 'R'. In other words, the better the registration, the better the recall. And the secret of effective registration?

If you can see it, you can remember it.

On the whole, and this is especially true for children, we have lousy memories for abstract concepts. As St Thomas Aquinas said, 'Man's mind cannot understand thoughts without the image of them.' But when we 'concretize' things, turn them into something we can see, even if only in our heads, then it makes them far more memorable. To what extent, then, do you expect your learners to remember things that they cannot see and how can you take these invisible ideas, ideas such as 'regular verbs', 'policy of appeasement' and 'sodium permanganate' (which I know is a 'thing' but try telling that to a dyslexic 11-year-old), and turn them into pictures in a child's head?

Once you have made the abstract concrete, you can then work not only to make the concepts memorable but also unforgettable. For example, if you make sure they are seeing the images in colour, this has been shown to improve our memories (Wichman, F. *et al.* 2002). Remember too, we have a better memory for colours than we do for words. Not only that, but when we colour coordinate memories it improves our ability to recall those memories.[2] Add to that the research that, when we picture things, if we include movement in that picture it makes it easier to recall. Similarly, if we include ourselves in this colourful moving image then that, too, improves recall. And then the fun really starts. Sex not only sells, it also aids recall. Introduce an element of sex or at least sexiness into the imagery (and remember, no-one needs to share their images with anyone else) then recall rates will soar, as will fun, although that is no coincidence either if you remember our brain lesson from chapter 15 – the part of our brain that deals with long-term memories is very closely linked to the part of our brain that deals with emotions in our limbic system. You remember your first time. And it doesn't have to be just sex, as the actress said to the bishop. Things that are extreme make ideas unforgettable too, not to mention when things are weird, bizarre, funny and yucky. You remember your first time.

When I was learning to become a language teacher, during my PGCE I became aware that I was learning to teach not 'French' but 'rubbish'. Lumps of sound. What I called 'phonic blobs'. Groups of phonemes that meant nothing to anyone who had never been to France, met a French person or who had any experience of Frenchness. If I told a group that the French for 'chair' is 'chaise' I may well have been saying that French for chair is 'flub' or 'snerch' or 'ffffafaflaf'! They are all just strange sounds the teacher is making, made all the more nonsensical if she is at the front waving around a flash card. Then I came across the *Linkword* system developed by a Dr Michael Gruneberg[3] when he was at the University of Swansea. Think of learning new things a little like the game of Scatch, where you have a ball and a Velcro glove (catch for people who can't catch – you know who you are ...). For the new things to stick you need to hook them into existing learning. It's one of the reasons why pre-exposure to learning is effective (Kalla *et al.* 2001). But with foreign words, as with the learning of many new concepts, there is no prior knowledge to hook the new learning onto so it becomes like throwing a ball against a wall instead. How much of your teaching comes bouncing back at you because there is nothing to hook it into? The *Linkword* system, then, addresses this and combines it with the other aspects of enhancing memory I have mentioned above, namely we have a great memory for images, especially if they are weird, yucky, etc. ... .

So, for example, what is the French for 'map'? If I say to a group of children that it is 'la carte' then for most of them, apart from the boy sitting at the front with his French–English dictionary sitting neatly on his desk along with his neat collection of pens who is able to tell me that the word 'carte' is etymologically linked to 'cartography' and hence maps, I am just spitting out a guttural phonic blob. And, then to make matters worse, I tell them that it is a feminine word. I then expect them to remember all of this when I test them tomorrow, along with nine other equally nonsensical phonic blobs of one gender or another. However, when I use the *Linkword* system (and remember this is not *the* way to learn a language, just *a* way) I can get them to imagine an old rickety wooden cart piled high full of maps that they are trying to drag out of the mud. What's more, to help them remember the gender I get them to imagine pouring perfume over the maps. (According to the system, you should associate feminine words with 'perfume', masculine words with a 'boxer'. If you find this a little sexist then replace with two other notions that you are happy with that clearly demark 'male' and 'female' in your world, such as 'guns' and 'flowers' or 'beer' and 'Shake 'n' Vac'.) So, imagine pouring perfume over this pile of maps and they are all slipping and slithering about and the whole scene stinks. Or get them to imagine holding a budgie over a lit candle (la bougie – candle) and spraying it with highly flammable perfume (feminine) or sticking a clove of garlic in your eye (ail – garlic) and hammering it home with a boxing glove (masculine). You get the idea. I haven't got round yet to telling a group of children that the French for seal is 'phoque'. And it involves a boxer … .

In this way it is so easy and so much fun to learn, to remember, even to be unable to forget, key vocabulary that otherwise would take hours of slog, assuming that the learner did have the motivation for it in the first place.

Remember I said that memory strategies could have a positive effect on self-esteem? I introduced the *Linkword* system to one of my bottom set groups when I was a real teacher and their test results went from one out of ten, two out of ten or 'What test?!' to ten out of ten. Some of these young people had never had ten out of ten in anything before, ever. They felt great. So did I. (It's allowed.)

The *Linkword* system for languages is just one example of the application of what we know about how to make learning memorable but there are plenty more and, once you understand the principles of making the 'registration' element of the learning process more effective, you can make your own up.

My colleagues Roy Leighton and Dave Keeling came up with a simple little acronym of their own for summing up the many aspects that make learning memorable. It is that learning should RING. In other words, it should be 'Relevant' (in *Essential Motivation* I quoted neuroscientist Rita Carter as saying, 'Items of interest … are retained better than those that are not. So personal and meaningful memories can be held in their brilliance while dry facts learned at school may soon fade away' (Carter 1988); I still feel resentment when I think about how, if I had spent more time learning to play the piano as a child and less time learning algebra, I would be spending more time playing the piano, as an adult, than I do using algebra); 'Interesting' (I repeat, 'dry facts learned at school may soon fade away'!); 'Naughty' (What's the French for seal?) and a 'Giggle' (remember positive emotions and the limbic system).

To what extent do your lessons RING?

I was doing some work, once, with an A-level psychology teacher who was about to deliver a revision lesson and was probing me for ideas. I asked him what were the sorts of things that, if his students could memorize them and then regurgitate them in the exam hall, would help them to remember to pass their exam. Aspects of the course that, as soon as the examiner said 'Pick up your pens and start', they could scribble down on their papers and it would be the equivalent of having their books in front of them. With the lessons minutes away he showed me the revision guide he had produced and in it there was a section on 'Methodological Issues' listing eight factors to take into account. (They were, however, just listed, not numbered. Yet numbering things serves to improve our memories too.) The list was, from memory even though it was about eight years ago, as follows:

Ecological validity
Sampling
Ethics
Generalization
Strengths and weaknesses
Quantitative and qualitative assessment
Psychometric testing
Reliability.

All of these are abstract concepts and, therefore, hard to memorize, entailing about 20 minutes of rote learning in a repetitive way. Yet turn them into a story (another strategy that helps – we have great memories for stories, especially as they link things together in a linear way, something else that helps) and you're onto something. So, in about 20 seconds and under the heading 'EMI' for 'Eight Methodological Issues', the list above became:

> I was getting my library card validated when an eco-warrior (ecological validity) came in and started urinating (sampling) on the library books. Then a vicar came in (ethics) followed by a general (generalization) whereupon they started arm wrestling (strengths and weaknesses) trying to force the other's hand down onto sharpened 'Q's pointing up (quantitative and qualitative). Suddenly a psychopath (psychometric testing) came in, chopped their heads off and drove off in a Robin Reliant (reliability).

Now, if that happened to you, you *would* remember it!

I employed a similar strategy to help my son *remember to pass* his English GCSE. So, the list of factors to consider when analysing a piece of text or poetry:

Irony
Metaphor
Oxymoron
Alliteration
Onomatopoeia

Repetition
Syllables
Imagery
Theme

Quickly transmogrified into:

> I was ironing (irony) a horse (metaphor) when a stupid person came
> in on an ox (oxymoron) being chased by an alligator (alliteration) so I
> hit the alligator over the head with an encyclopaedia (onomatopoeia)
> again and again (repetition) and, when it was dead, lay it out on a slab
> (syllables), took a photo (imagery) and the moral of the story is …
> (theme).

And yes, he got his 'B' target in English.

Effective registration is not entirely limited to whacky pictures though.
If you think about memory from a VAK perspective, that we have memories for pictures, memories for sounds and a physical memory too, our
muscle memory, and that these memories are stored in different places in
our heads, you will start to understand the importance of VAK-ing our
memories too. If all I use is one channel for remembering then I only have
one channel for recalling. Yet if I use all three channels then I have three
times the chance of remembering the learning when I need it.

For example, I have worked with History teachers where we took the
'Five Most Important Reasons People Went From the Countryside to the
Towns in the Industrial Revolution' (a superlative is always useful to generate
interest and improve memory I find), namely money, industry, education,
quality of life and housing, and 'anchored' each in turn to one of the fingers on my left hand. For example, my ring finger becomes 'money'
because of the link to gold, my middle finger (the one I drive with) I
imagine as all oily and greasy or maybe even missing thanks to some hor-
rible industrial accident; my pointy finger I put on my bottom lip and say
the internationally recognized phrase for stupidity, 'duh!'; my little finger I
raise as I drink my pretend cup of tea out of a china cup to signify quality
of life and I stick my thumb up happily and say, in a cod-West Country
accent, 'Oi live in a brick 'ouse now, marvellous!'

Does rote learning work? Yes, absolutely. Repetition reinforces connections between brain cells leading to better myelination and the creation of
what can be lasting long-term memories. There are two significant down
sides, though. One, it is as boring as hell and demands high degrees of
motivation of learners, self control and the sort of boredom threshold you
would associate with train spotting or reality TV. Two, despite being

effective it is not *efficient*. You may be achieving the results you want to achieve with your classes, so you are working effectively, but are you working efficiently? Could you, by using different memory strategies and techniques, achieve the same results by working less? Could you even achieve better results by working less?

I have used the finger technique for 'The Five Pillars of Islam' just as successfully as I have used it for remembering the purpose of the skeletal system. I even used it with a group of language teachers when I asked them to describe to me the difference between a D grade and a C grade sentence. I felt that sometimes students simply forget to get a C rather than simply being incapable of it. (Although that presupposes that the student knows the difference too. Do your students know *exactly* what level each bit of work they produce is, why it is so and what they need to do to improve on it – basic *Assessment for Learning* stuff these days I think?) The French teachers came up with five factors that separated Ds from Cs, things like adding a connective, expressing an opinion, using different tenses, 'jazzing it up' with a 'C'est super choutte' type phrase. Nothing too demanding. I then drew around my left hand and 'anchored' each of these factors onto a finger, the idea being that, sitting in an exam and writing with my right hand, I could look at my left hand and remember what was needed to ensure that I was working at C grade level. The teachers then not only put poster versions of this around the room, they also had the students create their own version in the front of their books.

Anyway, you get the idea – muscle memory is a powerful ally to help children remember to pass exams so, have a think about what aspect of what you teach can be memorized in such a way. Or better still, teach your learners the strategy and let them come up with their own versions. After all, you don't have to do all the work. Homework then becomes not simply 'Go away and learn this and we'll see how many out of ten you get tomorrow' but 'Go away and work out how you are going to get ten out of ten and then tomorrow share that with the rest of the class.'

Before I close this chapter, those of you who are paying attention will know that we have an 'R' dangling, the fourth in our memory equation. This is the 'R' that research proves can help us improve our memories by, according to some claims, a staggering 400 per cent. It is the 'R' that was highlighted in the research of German psychologist Hermann Ebbinghaus[4] over a century ago but that we still ignore in the classroom. And it is the research that led to the writing of the classic 1988 paper *The Spacing Effect; A Case Study in the Failure to Apply the Results of Psychological Research* by University of Nevada researcher Dr Frank Dempster.

This 'R' stand for review.

What Ebbinghaus proved – and Dempster proves we ignore – is that because our memories decay very quickly over time, the majority of what was supposedly learned disappearing within days, reviewing the knowledge in a systematic and periodic way will prevent us from forgetting the material. This is something called 'spaced learning' and simply involves revisiting the learning for a few minutes after a day, a week, two weeks, a month and then six months. It is a phenomenon used in a number of language learning software programmes, including a remarkable one called *SuperMemo*[5] developed by Pietr Wozniak from Poland and featured in a fascinating *Wired* magazine article entitled *Want to Remember Everything You'll Ever Learn? Surrender to This Algorithm*. Wozniak realized that the spaced effect worked best if the material was reviewed at the right time, namely just at the point where you were about to forget it. He realized that if he could identify that and turn it into an algorithm, he could design a computer programme that would help people vastly improve their memories when it came to learning a foreign language.

So, to improve your memory, go back over what has been learned in a set and spaced fashion. Not rocket science, is it? But, as Dempster points out the spacing effect is 'one of the most dependable and replicable phenomena in experimental psychology', is shown to be twice as effective as what he calls 'massed presentations' or cramming and 'truly ubiquitous in scope', that is to say wherever it is observed, it works. Yet:

> With all of these characteristics in its favor, the spacing effect would seem to have considerable potential for improving classroom learning. However, there is little evidence that this potential has been realized.
>
> (Dempster 1988)

Another example of the way laboratory facts fly in the face of, and are subsequently[5] ignored by, educational practitioners, uncovered by the *Wired* article relates to the research of Robert and Elizabeth Bjork from UCLA in the US. They identified that the harder things are to learn, the better your chances are of remembering them. In other words, by making learning 'easy' as, for example, many language-learning courses promise to do, they actually make it far more difficult to remember the material than it could otherwise have been. As the *Wired* correspondent goes on to state:

> Precisely those things that seem to signal we're learning well – easy performance on drills, fluency during a lesson, even the subjective

feeling that we know something – are misleading when it comes to predicting whether we will remember it in the future.

In the twenty-first century, are we – are you – using what is scientifically known about the nature not simply of memory but of learning as a whole to ensure that every one of the children in your care is working as well as they possibly can be? Dempster is not so sure, concluding as he does that, 'nor is there much evidence that the next generation of educators is being better informed'.

But now you've read this chapter you have no excuse. Don't let another hundred years go by without using insights such as the 'spacing effect' to help children in our classrooms. As I said at the opening of this chapter, there are many ways to fail an exam. Don't let neglecting to teach your students to remember to pass be one of them.

Chapter 26

How are you smart?

Of all the ideas to come out of a university and into classrooms over the last 30 years, surely the one that has produced the most debate, the most controversy, the greatest amount of printed material and spoken words has to be the theory of Multiple Intelligences as put forward by Harvard professor Howard Gardner in 1983.

And rightly so in my book (which this is).

Although there are many detractors from his theory, some of whom I am convinced are driven more by academic jealousy over Gardner's 'academic rock star' status than anything else, I have seen nothing to rival the theory's ability to open up learning to huge numbers of otherwise disenfranchised people, people for whom the narrow IQ view of intelligence would otherwise have consigned them to a life of ignorant thick-ness! When it comes to democratizing learning – the 'dumbing up' I mentioned in chapter 10 – the effective understanding and use of MI theory has no equal.

One of the ways of muddying the waters over MI is in the actual definition of both what is intelligence and also what is *an* intelligence? Gardner admits that 'this is not as simple a matter as I'd like it to be', adding that proponents of his MI theory 'have used the term "intelligence" in a variety of ways and I myself have added to the confusion'. In his 1993 book *Multiple Intelligences: The Theory in Practice* he tries to clarify matters and defines an intelligence as what he calls 'a biophysical potential', something he goes on to describe as follows:

> All members of the species have the potential to exercise a set of intellectual faculties of which the species is capable.
>
> (Gardner 1993)

In other words, we are all born with – and can further develop – a range of potential abilities, a range that includes verbal, physical, social, intrapersonal, visual, logical, musical and naturalistic intelligences.

So, the question isn't 'How smart are you?' – the singular, convergent, IQ-related, what's your 'g', old-fashioned question. Rather it is, 'How are you smart?' – the optimistic, divergent, learning democratized, twenty-first century question. If I were to go up to any child in your classroom and ask them that question would they all have an answer? If I pointed out a child in your class and asked you the question, 'This child, how is she smart?' would you have an answer?

One way to think about the concept of multiple intelligences is to think of human intelligence like a cake. We all have a cake and we all have eight slices of cake. Of course, our slices are of different shapes and sizes from each other but, and this should be written up on a wall in your staffroom, we all have the full cake. It is worth remembering too that, if you are working within a department or faculty in a secondary school setting, you and your immediate colleagues will have been pre-selected for your cake slice size by dint of the fact that you are qualified in languages or art or PE or maths or science. If you are sitting in your faculty staffroom reading this then take a look around you at your colleagues. You are as much a cross-section of society as a football team or the London Philharmonic or the cast of *Hi De Hi*. (And beware, because being in a team of like-minded people can make you dumb. In the words of James Surowiecki in *The Wisdom of Crowds*, 'Homogenous groups are great at doing what they do well, but they tend to become progressively less able to investigate alternatives' (Surowiecki 2004).) Your students, on the other hand, especially the young ones who have not yet had to make a choice over their GCSE options, are very much a cross-section, thrown together by chance and united only by their age and their postcode.

So, over the course of a term or a topic, to what extent do you roll that cake? Over, say, a four-week period, do you ensure that at least once, logical mathematical intelligence comes to the top, at least once musical intelligence comes to the top, at least once intrapersonal intelligence comes to the top? That, over that period, everyone has the chance to (a) play to their strengths and (b) work on their weaknesses? And notice, too, that we are talking about *their* strengths and weaknesses, not yours. I once took a maths teacher through an MI planning session, focusing specifically on 'probability'. Under 'musical intelligence' I suggested the idea of a probability rap, something he dismissed because he didn't think he was able to do such a thing. But, as I pointed out to him, I'm not asking you do to it; I'm asking them to do it. If we prevent them doing something just because we are not able to do it, then we are limiting them by our own limitations. The logical extension of which, by the way, is 'I don't want anyone cleverer than me in my classroom' (more of which in chapter 30). But we have to have children cleverer than us or else, as we have seen, the world will end! Are you planning lessons for people like you? Are the children in your class doing things you can't do? If not, why not, especially if they struggle doing the things you can do? One tip here is to have a month without using the word 'poster' when it comes to setting a task for students to do. There are so many alternatives you could offer to this old perennial chestnut. And anyway, children are rubbish at posters. Next time offer them the chance to show they have learned the material by producing a t-shirt or a badge or a web page or a screensaver or an advertising jingle or a press ad or a storyboard or a CD cover or a credit card or a shopping bag or a phone app or a video game or a football hoarding or an online advert or … .

For me, this is right at the heart of the 'dumbing up' process. Giving more people access to – and then the opportunity to use – knowledge, as part of the process of democratizing learning. As Dylan Thomas once said when describing how he didn't want to 'write down' to the workers, 'The thing to do is to bring the workers up to what one is writing' (Lycett 2004). If that student doesn't 'get it' by writing an essay (linguistic) then maybe he or she will 'get it' by being allowed to build a model (physical-kinesthetic) or representing it as a learning 'map' using pictures and colour (visual) or turning it into a rap (musical). As I said in chapter 21, the doctor doesn't just give you one chance at getting better. She will do whatever it takes until she finds what works for you. And, given what I have just been saying about letting children learn in ways you can't, she doesn't treat you for the ailments she's got either. It is the same for the twenty-first century teacher who has such a variety of learning styles and strategies at her disposal.

It is not in the nature of this particular book to give you a stack of activities and exercises relating to MI in the classroom. There are plenty of other books entirely dedicated to such an endeavour. My preferred way of using it for lesson planning is something that I also shared in *Essential Motivation* so I refer you there too. One strategy that I will share with you, though, as it is as simple as it is powerful, is an idea I developed I call *8Way Thinking*. This 'polycognitive curiosity engine', as I could call it, combines an all-encompassing MI approach to the world with the sorts of question-generating used in *P4C*.

It came to me waiting for a bank manager in Ipswich, looking out from a soulless office block to one of the several derelict churches strewn across the town, this one beached in the middle of a roundabout surrounded by busy traffic and the odd tractor, what with this being Ipswich. I had had a conversation a few weeks prior to this with Gifted and Talented guru Dr David George in the back of a car travelling around the TT circuit on the Isle of Man and he explained how he used MI theory with group of G

& T children to help them think about, for example, trees. He got them writing about trees, drawing trees, even listening to trees with a stethoscope. Generally, using all eight intelligences to explore what was around them. *8Way Thinking* grew out of thinking about David's work, combined with my *P4C* experience mixed with the boredom of waiting for a bank manager in Suffolk.

The way it works is embarrassingly simple yet how well it works is not to be sniffed at.

I took Gardner's eight intelligences and simplified them as follows:

logical-mathematical	numbers
musical	sounds
spatial	sights
bodily-kinesthetic	actions
interpersonal	people
intrapersonal	feelings
naturalistic	nature
linguistic	words

By the way, remember when I said that you all have the full cake, however you do have slices of varying sizes. I can only think of one living person who has all eight of these intelligences in a major way. In other words, a man with a very big cake. This is a man who, starting at the bottom of the list above, has written nine books and a number of linguistically rich and tongue-twistingly challenging songs, whose animal TV programme lasted for 19 series and was voted 'Most Popular Factual Entertainment Show' at the *National TV Awards* not once but five times, who the Daily Mail review of his autobiography[1] described as 'a man of enormous emotional warmth', who has performed at Glastonbury in front of tens of thousands of adoring if rather stunned people on four separate occasions, who was a junior national backstroke champion, whose paintings sell for tens of thousands of pounds and whose portrait of the Queen was voted the third favourite by *Radio Times* readers, whose musical career has included backing Kate Bush, being backed by the Beatles and releasing many chart singles including the 1969 Christmas number one, who has an honorary doctorate from the University of East London and arrived in the UK in 1952 with a plan of what he wanted to achieve and £297 in savings.[2]

Can you tell who it is yet?[3]

Anyway, back at the bank, I then looked at the old, empty church and asked myself eight questions about it through the spectrum of each of the intelligences. For example:

Numbers	Why did it close and when?
Sounds	What bells were there and what could they play?
Sights	What different geometric patterns are there in the structure of the tower?
Actions	Where are the bricks from and how was it made?
People	Who was the first vicar and who was the last?
Feelings	How does it feel to stand in such a place?
Nature	What wildlife lives in the old churchyard?
Words	What was its name and how did it get it?

It didn't matter that I didn't know the answers to these questions. That wasn't the point. The thinking usually stops when the answers start anyway. As an Australian rabbi once said, 'I'm not looking for answers that make the questions go away.' The questions were the starting point.

Imagine, now, these key words arranged in an octagon around a central theme. This theme can be anything you like – 'Love', 'To Kill a Mocking Bird', 'Myself', 'Vodka', you name it … . All you have to do, then, is to think of a question about whatever the central theme is but through each of the *8Way* 'angles' in turn. So, for example, not long after coming up with this idea my daughter had to do a presentation on London as part of her literacy work at primary school. She was expected to go away and research 'London' and then prepare a four-minute presentation on what she had discovered. While the words 'research', 'prepare' and 'presentation' may seem little things to us, to a nine-year-old girl with undiagnosed dyslexia this was quite a daunting task for which she was not properly equipped. However, using the *8Way Thinking* model we put the word 'London' in the middle of the *8Way* octagon and I encouraged her to think of a question or two for each angle, questions we then wrote in the octagon, radiating out from the middle. She had questions like, 'How many people live in London?' for 'Numbers', 'Where does the word "London" come from?' for 'Words' and 'What are the main sights in London?' for, obviously, 'Sights'. Radiating out from the questions she then started to add her answers until she had a page full of 'research' that she could read by spinning the paper around. For her presentation, she simply took in that piece of paper and chose three or four of the 'angles' and talked about the question she had posed and the answer she had come up with.

And that, as they say, is all there is to it.

To what extent do you use the Theory of Multiple Intelligences in your classroom to help give access to learning to all your learners? To what extent do you help those learners learn in a way that, at least some of the time, allows them to play to their strengths even though they may not be your strengths? Remember, giving the dyslexic child a wordsearch[4] because they have trouble reading the text is one form of differentiation. Giving that child the opportunity to learn but using a learning map with fewer words anyway is another. To what extent do you participate in the 'dumbing up' of your class and the democratization of learning?

Chapter 27

Muchos pocos hacen un mucho

Imagine if you could raise the test scores of young black people instantly and with barely any effort whatsoever. What if you could improve the performance of girls in a subject like maths where traditionally they have not done as well as boys? Well, research quoted in the *New Scientist* article 'The Curse of Being Different'[1] showed how to achieve just that. The researchers felt that something so simple as ticking a box to indicate your race or gender before an exam, as students were expected to do, could, at a subconscious level, serve to reinforce the negative views and stereotypes that society held about your race or gender, views such as 'Black kids don't do well at school' or 'Girls are no good at maths'. In one experiment, researchers staged a 15-minute session at the beginning of term with a group of African-American 12- and 13-year-olds, during which the students wrote about values that were important to them. This one simple activity reduced the achievement gap between the group and their white peers by an impressive 40 per cent. In another, one group of girls were asked to read a passage about the 'fixed' gender differences in numeracy ability just before they sat a maths test. A different group were given a passage to read that talked about how ability was modifiable, not fixed. This second group increased their achievement in the maths test by a staggering *50 per cent*.

Little things can make a big difference.

Sometimes I see schools that have been classed as 'good' in Ofsted-speak try to get to 'outstanding' by being, basically, 'gooder'. They simply try and do more of whatever it was that Ofsted picked up on. Yet, outstanding isn't about being 'more good'. It often involves doing things that are totally different from those that were deemed 'good'. But these things can be little things. What's more, apart from bearing in mind that little things can have a huge impact as we have seen, it is important to remember this – you cannot fail. Your classroom is a laboratory, each lesson is an experiment and, as any good scientist knows, experiments can't go wrong. You may not get the result you were expecting, or even wanted, but you still come out with a result, some form of feedback that you can use to tweak things further in the next lesson.

Gandhi entitled his autobiography, *The Story of My Experiments with Truth*, so you could maybe take that as an inspiration for such a way of working.

When I was a real teacher I used to plan lessons in great detail as per my training and then, in the classroom, explain in precise detail what I expected the students to do. There would always be one student, though, who listened diligently and attentively and then totally misread the instructions and went off and did something completely different. The interesting thing was that often what they stumbled across was better than what I had planned anyway. I learned quite quickly to set tasks that were both vague and focused at the same time. A clarity of outcome – what was to be learned – but a haziness in the process – exactly how they did it was up to them – was a far more effective way of setting up an activity in the classroom. What's more, working like this was much less stressful, as I didn't spend the lesson trying to bend the class to my will, as it were; involved less work in the planning stages for me which has to be a good thing; and produced better results in the classroom anyway.

If you approach a lesson, however, as 'this must work well or else I will have failed' – and heaven knows there is enough pressure on you to think this way – then you are setting yourself up for a constant and all-consuming sense of failure. And that can't be good for anyone.

One teacher I worked with was determined to 'get it right' all the time. He believed that he could 'get the job done' by the end of every day and go home with a clear conscience. But it is not that sort of job. Despite always being the first one in each morning and the last one to leave, he was never able to 'get the job done' and he was becoming a nervous wreck. What I realized at that point was that all teachers need a 'Fu*k it! switch'. This is the point at the end of the day where, for the sake of their family, their health and their overall general well being, they say, 'Fu*k it!', pack their bags, switch off the lights and go home. Tomorrow is always another day. One of the greatest acts of kindness I have witnessed by a member of a leadership team was when I saw him suddenly spring up from his chair, open a window and yell at someone in the car park at the end of the day to go home. I thought it must be a student hanging around the teachers' cars but it turned out to be an NQT who had a young family and was suffering the effects of balancing a first year in teaching with demands from home.

The job will always be bigger than you are. You will never keep on top of it and, like building a wall out of cats, just when you think you have it all sorted you will have to start again. It's the same in your lessons themselves. No matter how well you plan, it will not always go well.

I once heard comedian Phil Jupitus being interviewed about how he felt on those occasions when he simply bombed in front of an audience, unable to raise a laugh or the smallest titter. He simply replied that he found it fascinating, that he was able to stand back from himself on the stage and look at the situation and ask himself, 'I wonder why they are not laughing?'[2] This ability to distance yourself from what is going on – good or bad – and look at it with the objective curiosity of the scientist is a useful ability to have. Another comedian, Tony Hawks, was satisfying a bet by pulling a fridge around Ireland, something that you know, if you've ever tried it, does not always go to plan. However, he soon realized that rather than getting stressed about the setbacks, the very fact that he was writing a book about the whole experience meant the more there were, the better the book would be. After all, 'Went to Currys, caught the bus, went round Ireland, had some Guinness, came home' is not much of a book. As he says in *Round Ireland with a Fridge*, 'When you're writing a book, when things go wrong you just think – that'll make a good chapter. The more things go wrong, the better the book' (Hawks 1999). So – and in NLP circles this would be called 'reframing' – on a bad day, pretend you have a book to write. I know I do.

Remember, too, to do things *with* children and not *to* them in your classroom laboratory. Open up the debate about their preferred learning mix by asking them about what they think. Talk to them about why you are going to try using music in the lesson or get them up after every 30 minutes to do some physical exercise or allow them to record their homework as a rap or a radio jingle. Encourage them to take an active part not only in the teaching of the lesson but also in the planning of the lesson itself. The more you can open up what has been called the 'secret garden' of teaching to the learners the better, as it helps develop interested, responsible, self-motivated, independent learners. Not only that, by helping them understand the variety of ways in which people can learn, not to mention the range of 'biopsychological potentials' there are, it helps them form a variety of metacognitive strategies when it comes to approaching their own learning not only in your classroom but also outside, both now and throughout their lives.

One art teacher did just that with a *Doodle Day*[3] idea she had. She set things up in her school so that all teachers would let children doodle for the day during lessons and then got feedback from them about whether it helped with student learning. She was amazed at the 100 per cent positive feedback from her colleagues with a whole list of benefits including a calm atmosphere, engaged students, creativity and expression, cross-curricular learning, positive relationships, concentration, listening skills and confidence.[4]

When it comes to making changes in your classroom practice, it is also worth remembering that you should think in terms of 'little things'. Don't try and change everything straightaway or try every new technique you've just heard about in one all-singing all-dancing Braingym-ed, Mindmapped, fully VAK-ed and multiply intelligent 50-minute period that leaves the students gasping for breath and praying for budget cuts that will prevent you from going out on any more courses. Sometimes when I lead a lesson planning exercise on the use of Multiple Intelligences, I see teachers become all excited when they talk about preparing something along the lines of 'Repeal of the Corn Laws – The Musical!' If ever you find yourself contemplating how to represent the Periodic Table as a dance routine remember the adage 'Little Things'. In a similar vein, one thing I say to teachers when we are doing the MI planning activity is that if the word 'laminate' crops up then they are trying too hard! Ease back! Get a life! I really, really don't want you to work hard. Far from it, as we shall see in chapter 29. As the Eskimo saying goes, 'If you sweat, you die.' I want you to work less hard because the less work you do the better their learning, if you plan things well enough. As I have said, what I want is more efficient working from teachers. Work less but achieve the same, or even better results.

I was observing an English lesson one Tuesday morning where the teacher had been up all night cutting and pasting and sticking into envelopes for a 'kinesthetic learning activity' he was planning to use as a starter activity in the lesson. Within minutes of him handing out his carefully prepared envelopes, though, the class were messing about with them, skidding the laminated cards around or blowing them off the tables and generally causing havoc. Not only did he then have classroom control issues but they were compounded by the fact that he had carried into the classroom all the 'I've been up all night preparing that … !' emotional baggage. If, however, he had approached his planning from the point of view of 'What's the least amount of preparation I can put into this lesson to get the learning outcomes I want?', then things could have been very different. Maybe he could have used Post-It pads, given the students a page each and got them to write down the keywords he had on his cards, for example. That way they would have had a sense of ownership of the lesson, there would be a sense of curiosity as the lesson was unfolding before them (something that helps with motivation), you can't blow Post-Its off the table and he wouldn't have wasted his time and his lamination budget and built up resentment in the process.

So, for this book as for any other book you read with ideas for your teaching practice, think 'little things' and build on them from there.

And remember, start small but, above all, start.

Chapter 28

Your classroom is not just an environment in which you can show how clever you are

One of the best ways in which you can be an inspirational teacher is to give the children in your care the opportunity to be inspirational themselves. So says my Independent Thinking Associate and friend Will Ryan, pioneer of *Inside Out Leadership* – the idea that you lead a school from your own moral purpose, not from what the latest government directive tells you to do. How often, though, have I seen the classroom as the place not so much where children shine but where teachers perform.

But, let me reiterate – in a learning school your job isn't to teach the stuff, your job is to ensure that your children learn the stuff.

I was once working with – or at least trying to work with – a group of A-level psychology students but every time I put a question to them, their class teacher answered it. And in great detail. Her classroom was her domain and no-one would know more, contribute more or speak more than she would. She taught A-level psychology but I'm not sure what her students learned. They certainly didn't learn to find their own voice as independent learners. But, as Lord Chesterfield wrote in one of his famous letters to his son in the eighteenth century:

> If, therefore, you would avoid the accusation of pedantry on one hand, or the suspicion of ignorance on the other, abstain from learned ostentation. Speak the language of the company that you are in; speak it purely, and unlarded with any other. Never seem wiser, nor more learned, than the people you are with. Wear your learning, like your watch, in a private pocket: and do not pull it out and strike it; merely to show that you have one. If you are asked what o'clock it is, tell it; but do not proclaim it hourly and unasked, like the watchman.
>
> (The Project Gutenberg EBook of Quotes and Images From Chesterfield's Letters to His Son, by The Earl of Chesterfield. Available at: www.gutenberg.org/files/7539/7539-h/7539-h.htm)

One of the most inspiring books on teaching and learning that I have ever read is *Super Teaching* by American educationalist Eric Jensen. In it he describes a range of approaches to teaching by the 'high ego' teacher. The list includes:

• Wanting to let students know when they make a mistake
• Wanting students to remember you at the end of the year
• Wanting to be right about something in debate or discussion
• Hoping students will like you and think highly of you
• Having it be important to look smart, witty or charming
• Making students wrong for forgetting something
• Keeping things the same, protecting status quo.

(Jensen 1995)

How many of the above are you guilty of? I can see a few that strike a chord with me I must say! There are, of course, times where you need to be up at the front, rallying the troops as it were, but learning to grab their attention is one thing. Knowing when to let it go again is another. Psychologists have a phrase for the way our attention works. They call it 'in-out listening'. You can't be outside your head, listening to the pearls of wisdom from a teacher and inside your head trying to make sense of them at the same time. You are in one place or another. This is why we advocate 'not teaching' as an important strategy for helping children learn. Sometimes there is so much teaching going on there is no space for them to learn anything. One of my favourite teaching strategies was shared with me by a friend who taught in an FE college in Cornwall. He used to set his group up with a task and then nip to the loo for ten minutes with a good book!

How much do you talk in your lessons, for example? Remember, you don't get any extra points for talking when the whistle goes. Play the game where you ask the students to time your 'teacher talk' and then see how your guess at how long you think you spoke for matches with the actual length of time you did speak. You will be surprised. Another colleague of mine, Jim Smith, author of *The Lazy Teacher's Handbook*, describes how he plays a game with his sixth formers where he limits his initial teacher talk time at the beginning of a lesson to a set number of minutes or a set number of words. His students then monitor what he is saying to ensure that he doesn't go over his time or word quota. This way the baton is soon passed to the students to get on with the learning and they pay a great deal more attention to what he is saying at the beginning of each lesson (than they ordinarily would).

Another benefit from filling less of the lesson with your input is that it means you have less time to stray into that dark and barren pedagogical wasteland where the teacher clichés lurk. I have observed too many lessons where the only effect of the teacher cliché has been that of undermining the teacher using it. If you really want your class to respect you, then these clichés are to be avoided 'like the plague'. Here, according to an online forum, is a list of the ones that most people remember or, in the words of the World Wide Web resident who set the website up, 'This is where we post all of the stupid hackneyed things teachers say to kids in class.'[1] Here is my top ten from the list:

1 It's your own time you're wasting!
2 The bell is a signal for me, not for you.
3 You're only cheating yourself.
4 You think this is funny, do you?
5 (Following a student's yawn) 'I'm sorry, am I BORING you?'
6 I can stay here all day!
7 I'm sure your parents will find it equally amusing when they read my letter about why you have failed your exam.
8 If you spent a little more time working, and a little less time yapping, maybe we could see some results.
9 Would you [insert crime here] at home?

And my favourite, ever since I heard the joke about the inflatable boy who took a knife into his inflatable school and was summoned to see his inflatable headteacher:

10 You've let the school down, you've let me down, you've let your friends down but, most importantly, you've let yourself down.

You have been warned.

Remember through all of this, though, that downplaying your presence in the classroom is not in any way to do with downplaying your role in their learning. You are the most important element in the classroom and, as we have learned, you can and do make the difference between a child having a wonderful and fulfilled life or not. Think of yourself like a vase. The bit in the middle that isn't vase, the space, is as important as the bit around the edges that is vase.

In *Super Teaching* Jensen quotes from a book called the *Tao of Leadership* by John Heider (2005), adapting it to relate to teaching. Drawing on wisdom that goes back over 2,500 years, this is Jensen's view on teachers:

> A wise teacher lets others have the floor. A good teacher is better than a spectacular teacher. Otherwise the teacher outshines the teachings.

Be a mid-wife to learning – facilitate what is happening rather th. what you think ought to be happening. Silence says more than words, pay much attention to it. ... Let go of your ego, and you will receive what you need. Give away credit and you get more. ... The less you make of yourself the more you are ... Trying to appear brilliant is not enlightened. The gift of a great teacher is creating an awareness of greatness in others. Because the teacher can see clearly, light is shed on others ... .

(Jensen 1995)

So, then, are you a vase or a brick?

Brave heads and lazy teachers!

I believe that these two factors will significantly improve the quality of education in this country.

When I refer to 'brave heads' I am referring to headteachers who are, like some of the very best ones I've seen in my time in education, strong enough to stand up to the external pressures coming at them. Their unremitting message is:

> This is the way we do things here because this is what we know our children need from us most. Colleagues – teach the way we have agreed to do it. If the inspectors/parents/government don't like it then they will have me to deal with, not you. The buck stops with me not you so don't be scared to teach in the way we know is right.

Many teachers I meet feel scared and inhibited to try new things because of what others might say, yet those in a school with such a head enjoy a far greater freedom to innovate and experiment.

When Simon Cooper-Hind was a headteacher he used to rally his staff before an inspection with the reminder that, if Ofsted asked them why they were using a particular strategy, they were simply to reply, 'It's for the kids.' As he told me once, 'That way it can't be wrong. It could be better, but it can never be wrong.' Another head I met described how he asked himself three questions at the end of each day:

Am I acting in the best interests of the children?
Am I being professional?
Am I doing my best?

If he could answer yes to all three, he could go home with a clear conscience. In a report in *The Times* in 2008 entitled 'School Systems Let Down Our Children' the newspaper pointed out that:

Schools seeing most improvement seem to be those with determined headteachers not afraid to innovate.

(*The Times*, 29/09/08)

(Not forgetting the brave deputies there are out there too. After all, I have noticed that heads make things happen, but deputies make *sure* things happen.)

In *The Telegraph* in 2005 under the banner headline, 'The secret of our success? Ignore Government advice – The primary school that tops today's league tables says it did so by ignoring much of what the Government told it to do', it describes how headteacher Barbara Jones of Combe Church of England School in Oxfordshire:

> did not implement the national literacy and numeracy strategies imposed in 1998. After scanning them for useful advice and tips, she consigned them to a top shelf and continued with the tried and tested methods that have made the school the most successful in England.
> (www.telegraph.co.uk/news/uknews/1504532/The-secret-of-our-success-Ignore-Government-advice.html)

In my experience, the heads who care most are the ones who just don't give a damn.

Compare that with the headteacher I met in Essex who ruminated over lunch with me during a training day, 'I've changed nothing in 14 years.'

Does the phrase, 'Quit while you're a head' mean nothing … ?

So much for the heads, what then about the 'lazy teachers'? This is my way of suggesting that we need teachers who are prepared to step back just a little bit more from the teaching and help the children get on a whole lot more with the learning.

In many ways, this chapter is the corollary to the previous one. I am suggesting that as teachers we can step out of the limelight a little more to allow the learners to step into it and take their place as confident independent learners, empowered by a teacher to experiment and innovate in the way the teacher has been empowered to do by their leader.

Why are you planning the lesson when they could? Why are you leading the warm-up activity when they could? Why are you setting out the learning objectives when they could? Or maybe you could involve your Teaching Assistant in the process? Why are you dividing the class into groups, organizing the furniture, watching the clock and handing out the resources when they could? They probably did it for themselves at primary school anyway. Why are you setting and then marking the test when they could as part of the *Assessment for Learning* process? And why, oh why, are you still setting the sort of homework[1] that involves taking in 30 books to mark and thus robbing you of a Sunday afternoon spent with your family (unless, of course, your motivation is to avoid a Sunday afternoon spent with your family)?

LaoTsu in the *Tao Te Ching*, the ancient Chinese text that is central to the Taoism that we met in the previous chapter, said:

> A leader is best when people barely know he exists, when his work is done, his aim fulfilled, they will say: we did it ourselves.

I like that in a classroom. It's good for them, not to mention the benefits it brings to you. Not only will you get your Sundays back (and for more on the subject have a look at Jim Smith's *The Lazy Teacher's Handbook*) but it might be better for your health too. According to the Government's School Workforce statistics, three million working days were lost to stress in 2007, an increase on the previous year and something the *Daily Mail* reported as '15,000 Teachers Go Sick EVERY day (and it's Blamed on Stress and Ministerial Meddling)'.[2] With remarkable predictability this story was commented on online by a 'Foster, Leeds' with the remarks:

> Lets [sic] face it, a great proportion of teachers are whinging, moaning leftwing layabouts. They could'nt [sic] survive in the real world where your last week's figures or results depend on you keeping your job. If you don't like the heat get out of the kitchen! And [sic] try working for a living.

It's enough to make you. [sic]

Back in the real world, the benefits of teaching less can even go as far as your voice. Research from the National Center for Voice and Speech[3] in the US 'tracked' the voices of 57 male and female teachers, not only in their classrooms but until ten o'clock at night too and at weekends.[4] The researchers' main concern was your 'vocal folds tissue', which is on the end of the vibrations from your speech in the same way your hand is on the end of vibrations from a 'jackhammer'. Just how much they can safely withstand is what the researchers were trying to understand in order to identify 'safety criteria based on genetic disposition to vocal injury, degree of training in economic voice use, accumulated dose of vibration in a typical work day, and the amount of recovery available at night and on weekends'.

In looking at the speech patterns of the volunteers they did not assess *what* was spoken, but *how*, using a special voice 'dosimeter' to record and analyse features such as the pitch, tone and loudness of the teacher's voice.

This was something they were able to do a staggering 33 times per second over a 14-day period. This produced a 'voice dosimetry databank' of 20 million samples, the analysis of which threw up some interesting (how dare you say unsurprising!?) facts. For example, did you know that female teachers speak more than their male counterparts? Not only did they use their voices 10 per cent more when teaching, they used them 7 per cent more when *not* teaching. (I suppose one argument is, if we had done what they told us to do the first time they wouldn't have to.) The research also showed that female teachers speak louder at work than the male teachers. 'These results may indicate an underlying reason for female teachers' increased voice problems', according to Eric Hunter, deputy director of the NCVS (and bear in mind that teachers as a whole are 32 times more likely to experience voice problems than non-teachers according to one study).[5]

Joking apart, the neuroscience points to the female propensity for language both from an evolutionary point of view, where the neurological imperative in the young female brain is to build a community network through language, and also from a health and well-being point of view. In the words of Louann Brizendine, author of *The Female Brain*:

> Connecting through talking activates the pleasure side in a girl's brain ... a major dopamine and oxytocin rush which is the biggest, fattest neurological reward you can get outside of an orgasm.
>
> (Louann Brizendine, *The London Paper*, 13/09/06)

What the research showed too was that, sex differences apart, teachers are a fairly verbose group and they're not particularly quiet about it. Not only did all teachers speak about 50 per cent more when they were at work than elsewhere, what they said was louder and in a pitch that was 'trending upwards throughout the day'. And when they got home they continued talking for what the researchers describe as 'significant amounts of time'.

To save our 'vocal folds tissue' and everyone else's ears, perhaps it is worth trying our best to adhere to six language rules suggested by George Orwell in *Politics and the English Language*, (especially rule number one which sounds very much like a 'no cliché' rule to me):

Never use a metaphor, simile or other figure of speech which you are used to seeing in print.
Never use a long word when a short one will do.
If it is possible to cut a word out, always cut it out.
Never use the passive when you can use the active.
Never use a foreign phrase, a scientific word or a jargon word if you can think of an everyday English equivalent.

Break any of these rules sooner than say anything outright barbarous.

(Orwell 2000)

I went on a course once led by NLP founder Richard Bandler and hypnotist Paul McKenna where they described the way in which your speech
'bathed people in sound'. This is a nice way of thinking about it as you
consider the effects your voice may be having on yourself and others.
Remember, your voice is a tool, not just simply a means of getting across a
message, but a way to change people's thinking and their behaviours. Use
it wisely. Talking of which, here is a question for you:

Q: Why do teachers shout at children?
A: Because they can.

This is a thought that struck me during my teacher training when I
observed a teacher shouting loudly, inches from the face of a year eight
boy on the way into assembly one morning. Why do we do it to ourselves,
let alone them? Research from Canada on nearly 400 children over a
seven-year period starting in kindergarten, found that for some children,
'verbal abuse by the teacher is significantly related to subsequent delin-
quent behavior and academic difficulties in early adolescence'. Troublesome children, especially boys, as you may perhaps expect, were most
likely to be shouted at, with 'children who are relatively well adjusted' at
the lowest risk of being verbally abused, however, as the research tellingly
points out:

These children are the most vulnerable to subsequent developmental
difficulties.

(Brendgen *et al.* 2006)[6]

Shouting at children, unless either they or something near them is on fire,
is demeaning to them and to the nature of a postgraduate profession,
causes too much 'collateral damage' as the whole class starts to feel bad
and what you want to achieve you can achieve in other ways anyway. Just
find the teachers in your school who never shout and 'model' what they
do. Strategies I use include starting an interesting sentence loudly – 'The
thing that is fascinating is … ' – and then stopping expectantly, or starting
loudly but then quickly bringing my voice down (leading to the classic
line, 'Don't make me have to whisper!'). In my first few days as a 'proper'
teacher after that particular sobering experience as a student teacher, I
vowed never to shout at children. They had given me a bottom set group,
the sort with several notches in their rulers signifying the teachers they had

'disposed of' over the last year. The last one was a 'nervous breakdown' they told me proudly. However, the mental stress tables were turned when I refused to shout at them as they went through their repertoire. 'Why don't you shout at us?', they asked me in all seriousness. 'I don't shout,' was my straightforward reply and I stuck to my guns. (Not real guns, although that would be a way to avoid having to shout.) In fact the only time I can remember losing it with a child, one of my tutor group, where I stood him outside and then lambasted him in true teacher style, I then apologized to him at the end of the lesson whereupon he apologized to me for pushing me as far as he did and congratulated me on my 'technique'.

When it comes to attracting the attention of a noisy class, various effective strategies I have seen include the Brownie leader's favourite of putting your finger on your lips and standing with an expectant air, starting a slow handclap that soon gets taken up by the entire class or, and this is one I've seen used to good effect in an arena full of about 3,000 noisy people, simply raising your hand and waiting. When I first tried this with a class when I was doing a spot of supply teaching, I suddenly ended up with a group of children all with their hands in the air looking at me expectantly. Unsure what to do next, I raised my other hand which they all did too. We then swayed once to the left, once to the right, clapped our hands three times and got on with the lesson.

Another way of communicating with children in a non-verbal and definitely non-shouty way is the 'Hot Spot' idea. The Hot Spot is a part of your classroom you never normally go to and that you only go into in order to administer some sort of verbal discipline or to voice your displeasure at something the class has done. Never teach from there and never discipline the class from anywhere but there. It doesn't take very long before the class realize that if you are standing at the front then all is well but if you are standing in the Hot Spot they had better watch out! Before long, all you need to do is to start walking over to the Hot Spot and this is picked up at a subconscious level by the class and the noise starts to go down without anyone really noticing why.

I was once explaining this to an art teacher who had been having issues with a particular year ten group. We were planning a lesson that he was then going to deliver with me observing one Friday afternoon. I asked him what areas he was going to cover in the lesson and he mentioned the fact that he had to talk to them about the poor quality of their homework and that he was going to do this, as I have seen many teachers do, first thing. For me, the beginnings and ends of lessons are sacrosanct. Lessons are like sticks in this way, the bit in the middle is necessary but less important. Because we remember more from the ends than from the middle, it is important to make sure the children will remember positive experiences, not negative ones. What's more, we memorize through association. In other words, someone's memories for a particular event are linked to the environment in which the event took place. It's what you experience when you revisit somewhere you haven't been to for many years and your long-buried memories come flooding back to you. Or when parents come back into a school for a parents evening and you can see the colour drain from their faces. If you want your children to come into your classroom feeling positive then it is important that you send them out feeling positive. Just by coming into your classroom – or even seeing your face – the memories of the previous experiences with you come back to them and you have the power to determine what those memories are. What's more, research on people having colonoscopies showed that if the last few minutes of the procedure were bearable, they had a better overall recollection of the entire event, and were more able to forget or overlook how awful the experience was. However, if the last few minutes were bad, their memory of the entire procedure was a negative one.[7]

The beginning of a lesson is of vital importance too, not just because recall levels are highest for the early part of a period of learning, but also because, like the opening sequence of a Bond film, it sets the tone for what is to come. I have seen so many lessons get off to a dire start because the teacher used that time to do battle with the class over hats, earphones, their behaviour as they entered and 'Will you be quiet while I do the register – it should only be my voice I can hear, 10G!'. There are many ways of taking a register that don't involve taking a register. Getting the children to 'sign in' when they arrive, asking one of the children to register their peers when they arrive, taking it quietly a few minutes into the lesson, incorporating the taking of the register into a warm-up activity where the child has to give an answer when their name is called. This is especially effective when the activity is of a more general creative thinking-type one rather than a knowledge or memory exercise. One teacher I observed used to set tasks like, 'If you were a home appliance which one would you be and why?' and have the children sharing their response with the class as their name was called out. Another one was, 'Why is a history lesson like a ... (insert name of animal here)?' In such a way she had the class's attention, the register was completed, she had them in the right state for learning and had their brains 'warmed up' to ensure they worked well and knew why history was like a camel, all in the first few minutes of a lesson. What she never did, like her colleague was threatening to do, was start the lesson with a verbal roasting. Apparently, there are great similarities between the symptoms of ADHD, bipolar disorder and fear according to Dorothy Rowe, author of *Beyond Fear, Not Mad or Bad, Just Scared*. Speaking in *New Scientist* she said:

Like adults, children fear many things, but one thing all children fear is adults … If a child continues being afraid, she or he won't function normally, learn or be happy. The people responsible for that child's welfare won't be doing their job properly if they don't reassure them.

(*New Scientist*, 16/06/07)

What are you doing, then, to consciously and deliberately reassure children that 'it's OK'?

What we planned instead for the Friday afternoon art lesson was a starter that involved music from the Schwarzenegger film *Conan the Barbarian* accompanied by the teacher dropping the occasional plastic drawer on the floor whilst the class drew whatever these sounds inspired in them under the heading 'War'. After three minutes of this, the teacher pulled the class together and explained the objectives for the lesson in a quiet but excited tone (as if the objectives did actually matter) before telling them in a very matter-of-fact way that he would have to speak to them about their homework in 20 minutes and could one of the students keep an eye on his watch to remind him when that time came. Once the students were engaged in the main part of the lesson, the art teacher drew in poster paint squeezed from a bottle, a 'target' symbol of concentric rings on the floor in one part of his classroom. After 20 minutes he attracted the attention of what had become a comparatively diligent class and, from the centre of his target, in a serious but again very matter-of-fact way, had a go at them about their homework. When he finished he vacated his 'Discipline Hot Spot', put the smile back on his face and went back to his 'Teaching Hot Spot' as if nothing had happened. He never raised his voice throughout the entire lesson and the students left the lesson commenting on how much more calm, productive and enjoyable the whole experience had been.

Julie Duckworth, another Independent Thinking friend and colleague, a headteacher and author of *The Little Book of Values*, has one Golden Rule in her school – and it is a challenging school, not one in a leafy suburb. It is 'No shouting'. It is something that she is passionate about. 'Try getting your point across without losing your temper and your poise. No one hears the screaming anyway' is how she describes it in her *Little Book of Values* (Duckworth 2009).

So, for everybody's sake, talk less, talk more calmly and don't shout.

Even when you're not shouting there is evidence that your words may not be having the effect you wanted. Research quoted in the *Cambridge Encyclopedia of Language* examined classroom dialogues between teachers and children. One of the things they discovered was the way in which the single biggest obstacle to children understanding what we are trying to teach them is the language we use trying to teach it to them in the first place:

The teacher teaches within his frame of reference; the pupils learn in theirs, taking in his words which 'mean' something different to them, and struggling to incorporate this meaning into their own frame of reference. The language which is an essential instrument to him is a barrier to them.

> (D. Barnes, 1969, pp. 29–30, quoted in Crystal 1987)

This is what is being highlighted when you hear the child say, 'I used to understand it until the teacher explained it to me.'[8]

Asking children to teach each other as we found out in chapter 23 is a useful way around this. Or, when you have given a crystal clear explanation of a particular task and just before you unleash your class on it, to give them one minute to turn to a partner and describe to them what they think the task actually is can be useful too.

One of the biggest obstacles to becoming the 'lazy teacher', though is the fact that so many teachers are self-confessed control freaks. Do they enter the profession because they are control freaks or do they become control freaks once they have entered the profession? Until someone does some serious research on such a question, we will never know the answer. Yet the fact that they indubitably are so remains. So often I see classrooms set up in such a way that the one and only conduit for learning is the teacher, who then works hard to ensure that if any questions are going to be asked they will come *from* the teacher and if there are any answers going to be given they are to be given *to* the teacher. But one person's 'conduit' is another person's 'bottle neck' and this approach can slow down and often block the possibility of children learning anything in your classroom. Control is like respect. You get it through giving it. I have so often seen the situation where classes who consistently posed serious behavioural issues changed overnight when the teacher stopped battling with them for control and simply gave them a great deal more if it.

Remember, you can't control students. You can control yourself and influence your students. What's more, your influence is greater than your power. Don't be a control freak, be an influence freak.

Being a 'lazy teacher' is all about giving the learners as much control as possible over their own learning and letting go a whole lot more yourself, from planning lessons to communicating tasks to being the one main source of learning in the classroom. Which is where technology and, yes, Google comes in.

Chapter 30

Enthusiasm and the sort of 7 per cent rule

What you say, as a teacher, can have far-reaching consequences in terms of both a child's academic success and their overall well-being now and in the future.

Not only that, but also what you do says far more than what you say.

In 1967, two researchers named Albert Mehrabian and Susan Ferris produced a small piece of research with a large name and an even larger impact on our thoughts about the nature of communication. In their study, *Inference of Attitude from Nonverbal Communication in Two Channels*, Mehrabian and Ferris state that:

> the combined effect of simultaneous verbal, vocal and facial attitude communications is a weighted sum of their independent effects – with the coefficients of .07, .38 and .55 respectively.
>
> (Mehrabian and Ferris 1967 quoted in Lapakko 1997)

And with this, the idea that, in all communications, 7 per cent is words, 38 per cent is tone of voice and 55 per cent is the look on our faces, was born. Although the research has since been shown to be flawed from an academic point of view and such a conclusion is not exactly what the researchers were actually saying ('My findings are often misquoted ... Suppose I tell you that the eraser you are looking for is in the second right-hand drawer of my desk in my third floor office. How could anyone contend that the verbal part of this message is only 7 per cent of the message?', as Mehrabian pointed out nearly 30 years later) it has still become one of the most frequently cited pieces of research ever (including by this author on many occasions both in print and verbally; as writer and critic Neville Cardus once said, 'It is a dreadful pity when a beautifully spacious generalization is upset by one or two simple facts').

Whatever the overall proportions are, the fact that communication can be broken down into various elements only one of which is the words that are being used, remains indubitable. And the fact that great teachers use this to their advantage is equally so.

The word 'enthusiasm', as I mentioned in *Essential Motivation*, comes from the Greek word 'entheos' meaning, literally, 'the God within'. It is, as all good teachers know, contagious. Lack of enthusiasm, as the less good teachers sometimes seem to overlook, is also contagious. We talk of motivation but, here again, we need to be aware of de-motivation. Children who come to the lesson ready and willing to learn but become switched off by our behaviours and attitudes.

The way that we contaminate or infect others with our own emotional state, known as 'emotional contagion', has been the cause of a great deal of interest and study for centuries. In their fascinating and scholarly book *Emotional Contagion*, Professors Hatfield, Cacioppo and Rapson cite this definition of the phenomenon:

> the tendency to automatically mimic and synchronize facial expressions, vocalizations, postures, and movements with those of another person and, consequently, to converge emotionally.
> (Hatfield *et al.*, 1992, pp. 153–54, quoted in Hatfield *et al.* 1994)

In other words, your state helps create their state. But your baggage is not their baggage and it should be left at the door. Similarly, their state can influence yours and neither is their baggage your baggage. What, then, can you all do to ensure that the beginning of each lesson starts with a clean emotional slate for all concerned? One technique I came across is to start the lesson with a 'Brain Dump', a process by which all the destructive and stressful flotsam and jetsam are 'dumped' from the brain by spending two minutes scribbling them all down on a piece of paper and then throwing the piece of paper away. It's a bit like a performance review action-planning sheet in that way.

Another simple strategy I have been encouraging teachers to do at the start of each lesson is simply to smile. Not only does smiling have a positive effect on others, especially if it is a full Duchenne smile where the eyes 'smile' too as opposed to just the mouth (research shows that the difference between the two can be observed strongly in the look on the faces of Olympic gold medal winners compared to their silver medal-winning counterparts;[1] elsewhere, research (Seligman 2003) has shown that bronze medal winners are actually happier than silver medallists) but it can also improve your mood. Research from the University of California in 1990 proved, by training volunteers to mimic 'muscle by muscle' (and we have 44 facial muscles capable of making 5,000 different expressions) the facial expressions associated with emotions like happiness, anger and disgust, that 'voluntary facial activity produced significant levels of subjective experience of the associated emotion' (Levenson *et al.* 1990).

So, if you want to *feel* happy, *act* happy. Like a lot of the neuroscience, it's not rocket science.

If, then, the way we look communicates at least as much as, if not more than, the things we say, maybe we have to be careful in the things we are communicating? Especially when we combine that with the fact that we are all very quick to pick up what this non-verbal communication is saying. In *Emotional Contagion*, the authors suggest that:

> It doesn't take much in people's expressions, voices or actions for others to pick up on what they are feeling. Researchers have found that teacher expectancies and affect toward students can be determined from brief clips of teacher behavior.
>
> (Hatfield *et al.* 1994)

The research the authors are referring to is a study reported in the *Journal of Personality and Social Psychology* that showed, regardless of whether they had a year's teaching with a professor or saw just 30 seconds of video of a professor teaching, *with the sound turned off*, students could still consistently tell who the good teachers were (Ambady and Rosenthal 1993).

Because so much communication is non-verbal it can get to us without our realizing it too, influencing us in a subconscious way. The authors cite the famous example of the ABC newscaster who was inadvertently more positive in the manner in which he delivered the news on Ronald Reagan's 1986 presidential campaign compared to his counterparts on NBC and CBS. A follow-up telephone survey by the researchers found that Reagan was more likely to be voted for by the viewers of ABC News.

Time well spent is to observe a colleague in their classroom with a particular group and watch not *what* they say but *how* they say it. What are the subtle differences in the tone of voice, the look on the face, their body language as a whole in their interactions between different sorts of children? Remember, the differences can be very subtle from the movement of the eyebrows when being asked a question to the 'texture' of the voice being used in the response.

The question I put to teachers is what is the look on your face as a particular class enters the classroom? Is it a happy face welcoming them in that looks like you are pleased to see them? If not it should be, or at least the resemblance of one. So often I have seen teachers whose words, tone and looks convey the message, 'I don't want to be here and I don't want you to be here!' But we have a moral, ethical and professional duty not to look like that. We need to, at least, look like we *want* to be there. They *have* to be there, but we *choose* to be there. We're even paid to be there. What, too, is the look on your face as the class leaves the classroom? ('This is the time when I usually smile!', as some teachers point out to me, only half joking … .) Remember that I pointed out in the previous chapter that we learn through association. If they go out happy they are far more likely to come back in happy. Don't make me requote the research about the endoscopy … .

Not only does your enthusiasm beget theirs, it also has positive effects both on their behaviour in the lesson and on how well they actually remember what they learned. In one piece of research, a cohort of new teachers was split into two, with one group given 'enthusiasm training'.[2] By analysing video footage of their lessons over an extended period of time, the researchers were able to determine that the pupils who were taught by the teachers who had had enthusiasm training exhibited greater levels of 'on-task behaviour' than the control group. Also an intriguing paper entitled 'Audience recall as a function of speaker dynamism' published in 1966 showed that there was a 'significant and strong' relationship between the enthusiasm of the speaker, something they called 'speaker dynamism' and the immediate recall of what was said. 'It is concluded that audiences remember more from a dynamic lecture than from a static lecture' (Coats and Smidchens 1966), the researchers conclude, prompting one of those 'Well duh!' moments in the reader.

What intrigues me about this research, apart from the fact that anyone could be surprised by the results, is the idea of 'enthusiasm training', something I certainly never received at teacher training college. Maybe we should reserve our 'Well, duh!'s for the fact that, despite what we know about the efficacy of dynamic teachers, 'enthusiasm training' is not part and parcel of teacher training. So, just what is 'teacher enthusiasm'?

A paper published in 1978 in *The Journal of Teacher Education* entitled 'Effects of Enthusiasm Training on Preservice Elementary Teachers' identified eight overall component factors. As you go through this list have a think about great teachers you have either experienced as a student or that you work with now and think about not *what* they said but *how* they said it. *The Journal of Teacher Education* list is as follows (and notice the no cliché rule coming through in yet another guise in point six):

1   Vocal Delivery – e.g. changes in tone, pitch, speed etc …
2   Eyes – 'dancing, snapping, shining … ' etc
3   Gestures – to include the 'body, head, arms, hands and face'
4   Movements – e.g. 'large body movements'
5   Facial Expression – e.g. expressing emotions through changes in facial expressions
6   Word Selection – e.g. colour and variety of words used

7   Acceptance of Ideas and Feelings – e.g. praise, non-threatening responses, open to ideas …

8   Overall Energy – 'explosive, exuberant, high degree of vitality, drive and spirit throughout the lesson'.

(Collins 1978)

If we gave each of the eight factors a score of one to ten, where would you score on the scale? What could you do to raise your score or help others raise theirs? Have you heard or watched yourself teach? Daunting though the prospect of having a lesson videotaped can be to many teachers, it can be very useful as a way of highlighting small changes you can implement to increase your 'enthusiasm' rating.

Maybe as a training day exercise you could get yourself a copy of a Lee Evans video and, with the sound down so as not to upset staff sensibilities, deconstruct what 'dynamic' looks like by way of delivery. I'm not asking you to be Lee Evans in your lessons, and Lord knows I have seen a few teachers try and fail badly, but there is no harm in picking up a few tips from a masterclass such as his, regardless of whether you find a sweaty man playing an imaginary piano funny or not.

I observed a history lesson once where the teacher stood at the front of the class and with the most gentle of New Zealand accents and, without variation in tone, pitch or volume whilst rocking gently on his heels, read quietly from the textbook for an extended period in such a way that no-one could help but feel drowsy. No learning disturbed the tranquillity of this lesson. It was a classic exercise in group hypnosis. The only thing that kept me going was waiting for him to suddenly click his fingers and tell us that we were all now 'back in the room'. In fact the only thing that did unsettle the serenity of this lesson was when a girl sitting near me at the back of the class had obviously and understandably had enough and started to mess around. She was promptly, fiercely and with a good dose of sarcasm, rounded on by the teacher and sat there sullenly for the rest of the lesson. My heart went out to her. Quietly. Remember what I said about watching out for de-motivation as well as motivation?

Remember too, the research we conducted for the QCA in 2008 and the 'The B–Word'. Of all the higher-achieving children we either spoke to or who filled in our online survey, *many* of them said that they did not find their lessons interesting and of the ones who saw themselves as performing badly at school, *all* were as unanimous in how 'boring' their lessons were. As I wrote in the report:

There seems to be no excuse for boring the futures out of our children. Lessons do not have to be consistently boring. The subject is not boring. Any subject can be made interesting if 'to make it interesting' is on the list of criteria in the lesson plan.

(Gilbert 2008)

Yes, I know children are children and can spend hours discussing the merits of groundbait or mascara but express boredom within seconds of being shown the Pyrenees or St Paul's Cathedral[3] but I also know what I see in classrooms around the country. Enthusiastic, dynamic teachers – and by that I don't mean those engaged in a song and dance routine for 50 minutes but ones who take the professional time to actually think about engaging their learners in what they need to learn – and, at the other end of the spectrum, teachers who feel that going through the act counts as teaching. Maybe it does. But it doesn't count as learning in my book. Which, as I have said before, this is.

To what extent then do you plan for engagement of your learners? Are you an enthusiastic teacher and can you learn to be more so? Are you switched on by a certain topic or your particular subject area? Do you contaminate your learners with your passions, if I can use such a phrase? Is 'to make the lesson interesting' one of your lesson planning criteria? Does your love of your job, of your chosen craft and métier, come through in your lessons – rainy days, Mondays and Ofsted visits notwithstanding? Does not only your love of teaching come through but also your love of learning? And do you look like you actually *like* children, not like the FE lecturer I was told about who, when a colleague asked him why he was standing outside his classroom looking at his watch, replied that there was still another 50 seconds before he had to be 'in there' teaching his class.

Wherever else your God may be, when you are teaching, ensure you have one inside too.

Chapter 31

Everyone remembers ...

It is a fact of life that everyone remembers their best teacher. It's also true, as conversation will reveal at a dinner party where you happen to let slip that you are a teacher, that everyone also remembers their worst. As a teacher you have an inordinate amount of power and influence over young people, a force that exerts itself upon them throughout their entire lives.

Churchill once said that, 'Headmasters have powers at their disposal with which Prime Ministers have never yet been invested' (Churchill 1930) and it is true. The government can only control what goes on in classrooms by fooling us into thinking it can. In other words, if we let it. It is powerless though, and necessarily so. Try as politicians might to exert some form of gravitational pull over what goes on in the classroom, at the end of the day, the direct impact on those children is created by you and you alone.

And it is an impact that has a direct effect on who and what they are and who and what they become, an influence that extends, as we have seen, even as far as the very physical architecture of their brains.

The influence you have over the future of the world – and the overwhelming global economic need for you to do your job well – led top business consultancy McKinsey and Co (the company where Tom Peters worked when he wrote *In Search of Excellence*) to undertake a major global research project on just what it was, exactly, that made good school systems good. Co-authored by erstwhile chief advisor to Tony Blair, Michael Barber, the 2007 paper, entitled *How the World's Best Performing School Systems Come Out on Top*, created headlines around the world.

According to the report, governments worldwide spent US$2 trillion on education in 2006, yet 'the performance of many school systems has barely improved in decades' (Barber and Mourshed 2007). (We are not immune to this fact in the UK. The report quotes a 1996 study published by the *National Foundation for Educational Research* that showed that 'despite 50 years of reform, there had been no measurable improvement in standards of literacy and numeracy in English primary schools' (NFER 1997).) They wanted to try to identify what made the difference in the systems that were not only performing well but also improving quickly.

The main source of information they drew on for assessing the quality of an educational system was the OECD's PISA programme – the Programme for International School Assessment.[1] This is a massive international exercise that has taken place every three years since its inception in 2000, looking at reading literacy, mathematics and science but with a particular focus on one of these each time. The TIMSS tests[2] that Malcolm Gladwell refers to in *Outliers* (where the success in the test could be predicted by how much effort students put into filling out the lengthy questionnaire that comes with it; those who persisted and completed the questionnaire, it turned out, were the ones who did best in the actual maths, suggesting that it's not more maths we should be teaching but better resilience) is 'dedicated to improving teaching and learning in mathematics and science for students around the world'. As such it is quite an academic test. PISA looks more at the real-world application of what has been learned in the classroom across nearly 90 per cent of the world's economies. For example, in 2006 it was the turn of science to be the special focus under the heading, 'Science Competencies for Tomorrow's World'.[3] The organizers set out to assess not only the quality of classroom teaching as reflected in the performance of 400,000 15-year-olds across 57 countries, but also students' 'awareness of the opportunities that scientific competencies bring as well as the environment that schools offer for science learning'. Whereas it is the countries of the Far East that do consistently well in the TIMSS tests, it was the Western countries that fared better in the PISA tests. (Finland was top – again – and the UK came ninth, just behind Germany but well above average. Don't ask about the US ... .)

What the PISA project does, too, is look behind the headlines and seek to assess the background and attitudes of the students involved. For example, they were able to identify that students from higher socio-economic backgrounds were more likely to 'show a general interest in science', and this was especially the case if a parent was involved in a 'science-related career'. What they also found was that 'streaming' students amplified the effect that their socio-economic background was having; the earlier the streaming process began, the stronger this impact was. What's more, 'Schools that divided students by ability for all subjects tended to have lower student performance on average.' I always used to half joke when I was teaching languages that we 'set' students according to parental income – here is the proof that not only is it so, but also of how debilitating such a vicious cycle is to the young people who need our help most.

What the PISA report makes very clear, and the McKinsey report picks up on with a vengeance, is that the answer to improving the quality of an educational system does not lie in throwing money at it. According to the PISA press release:

> across the OECD area as a whole learning outcomes have generally remained flat, while expenditure on education in OECD countries rose by an average of 39% between 1995 and 2004.
>
> (www.oecd.org/document/22/0,3343,
> en_2649_34487_39713238_1_1_1_1,00.html)

Finland spends a great deal less per head on education than the US and, whereas Finland has come top of the PISA tests three times out of three, the US, well, hasn't. In the opening few lines of the McKinsey report it is pointed out that, using educationally high-performing Singapore as an 'average' (the country that is consistently top of the TIMSS tests), a tiny fraction of children from Africa and the Middle East reach that standard, yet Singapore spends less on educating its primary children than 27 of the 30 countries in the OECD.

So, when it comes to improving education, money isn't the answer, nor is the Holy Grail to be found in reducing class sizes. The McKinsey report describes how improving the teacher-to-child ratio in a bid to raise standards has been a strategy employed by 29 of the 30 OECD members. However, apart from with very young children, there is no evidence *whatsoever* that this makes any difference *whatsoever* to the quality of education the children receive. What each and every one of the 112 studies the McKinsey report looked at on the subject showed was that there was one factor that would 'completely dominate' any reduction in class size anyway, a factor that their report shows to be *the* critical factor in the quality of education systems anywhere in the world, namely – you.

According to the report the top two factors that will determine the quality of any country's educational system are (1) ensuring that country recruits the 'right people' to be teachers – after all, according to a Korean participant interviewed for the report and whose words are taken up as a rallying cry by the authors, 'The quality of an education system cannot exceed the quality of its teachers'; and (2) that these people are then trained to be high quality 'instructors'.

With regards to their first point, the authors point out that the top performing countries employ three main strategies to achieve this. They make the profession a 'highly selective one', recruiting only from the top percentage of any graduate cohort. In South Korea, this is the top five per cent apparently, something that perhaps calls into question the suggested UK policy of letting failed bankers become teachers within six months. That said, the report does say that teaching is the preferred career option of graduates and undergraduates in the UK. What the report doesn't mention is that, of those graduates entering the profession, nearly half drop out before they actually teach a class, with a further 18 per cent dropping out within three years. The report, by the ubiquitous Professor Smithers from Buckingham University, showed that there were more qualified teachers who weren't teaching than were, something that was 'likely to be costing taxpayers tens of millions of pounds a year' according to the *Daily Mail*'s take on the story.[4] Two interesting factors come out of the Smithers report too, that reinforce the McKinsey top two factors. Of the prospective teachers dropping out, it was those with the poorest qualifications to begin with who fared worst. In maths, for example, only 43 per cent have what the report calls a 'good degree' before entering a PGCE course and in science just over 30 per cent of entrants had two A-levels before embarking on an Initial Teacher Training course. As Smithers points out:

> these courses do not wilfully take in the poorly qualified; they are recruiting the best available among the applicants. Raising qualifications depends, therefore, on increasing applications among the well-qualified.
>
> (Smithers and Robinson 2009)

This last point takes us back to the PISA report, as it is something that successful countries do well. Again, it is not a question of throwing money at the problem. McKinsey states that the top performing countries recruit the best potential teachers 'by paying good (but not great) starting compensation' and Smithers concurs when he says that attracting the right people:

> probably will have more to do with the general attractiveness of teaching as a profession in terms of respect, workload, salary and career development rather than short-term incentives such as 'golden hellos'.
>
> (Smithers and Robinson 2009)

If the recruitment of quality people to the job is paramount, then, it is a situation made all the more pressing by the number of teachers who are reaching retirement age. The 2008 *TIMSS Advanced International Report*[5] (from the people who brought you 'TIMSS Classic') looked specifically at 'trends in student achievement in advanced mathematics and physics in the final year of secondary school'. In their final report, the authors expressed general disappointment at what they referred to as 'declines in educational yield, both in the percentages of students taking advanced courses and particularly in their achievement', highlighting the knock-on effect on the economies and global competitiveness of countries who did not have sufficient high calibre people who 'enter and survive the pipeline supplying fields related to mathematics, science, engineering, and technology'. (Of interest here is a report from elsewhere that found that the higher up a country was on a United Nations index of human development, the less interested its 15-year-olds were in school science.[6]) To make matters worse, those that do 'survive the pipeline' were planning careers in business and engineering rather than taking their studies further leading to 'serious teacher shortages in science and technology in the years ahead'. Given the fact that seven out of the top ten most highly paid graduate jobs are science and engineering-based that, perhaps, is no wonder.[7,8] This was coupled with what the report calls 'the most striking feature' it unearthed – that many teachers in the study were approaching retirement age. They conclude ominously that attracting more students into advanced mathematics and physics courses and from there into teaching 'is becoming a compelling necessity'.

So, attracting the right people, keeping them and having more of them coming in than going out is one thing. Training them well is another thing. The second aspect that the Buckingham Univeristy report highlights is that it is teachers who have gone through schools-based training who are more likely to remain in the job, compared to those who have gone through a traditional university-based model of teacher training (with its concomitant doubling in terms of recruitment and interviewing costs). A highly attractive 97 per cent of teachers who had achieved their Qualified Teacher Status through what Smithers calls 'an employment-based route' were still in the classroom after 12 months.

The McKinsey report agrees strongly with what Buckingham University found on this matter and also, when it comes to ongoing teacher development, highlights as examples of good practice things that will come as no surprise to the readers of this book who have their fingers on the pulse of what actually works in their school. Teachers develop best (1) when they work with a good coach, (2) when they have the chance to collaborate and (3) when time and care is spent choosing the best among them to become educational leaders in their own right.

I don't think anyone could argue with such findings when looking at the current paradigm. A teacher, a classroom, a class of children. If this is the way you work then, in the spirit of the way I am asking questions of you in this book, to what extent are you developing as a professional to be the very best professional you can be? Do you demand of your senior management team the very best INSET they can offer you? Do you walk out when it is below par, when you have a 'guess speaker' (that is to say you have to try and work out what they are on about) and demand your money back or do you sit there muttering under your breath as you do your marking? Do you keep yourself up to date with educational research, much of which could or should be related to neuroscience? Do you demand the opportunity – and seize it when it happens – to work collaboratively whenever possible? Do you make the most of every opportunity to both coach and be coached?

But that is all to do with the current way of looking at education. What about, in keeping with the title of this book, the new way of looking at the setting up of the educational system? What about the nature of schools themselves? What about the physical architecture of them? Are you contributing to the debate – and the growing number of examples of good practice – about empowering students to be less reliant on knowledgeable teachers as the source of their learning? Are your students able to, allowed to and encouraged to, use technology to become independent learners in your classroom, not to mention use it as a means of bypassing the class teacher who is not up to scratch, who is part-way through what the McKinsey report refers to as '40 years of poor teaching'? Bear in mind, too, that the report found that students from poorer socio-economic backgrounds are 'twice as likely' to end up with a teacher with less than three years' teaching experience compared to their richer neighbours. This is where Web 2.0 innovations such as Curriki[9] can help, online resources from the best teachers in the world made available to all teachers in the world and all for free.

When I was a tutor, my students were all complaining about the quality of teaching offered by their English teacher who was, by anyone's standards, a remarkably awful teacher. All I could do was to encourage them to do whatever they could to bypass her in order to access the learning they needed in order to pass their GCSE examination. But this was in the early nineties and it was easier said than done. With the advent of the newly wired-up society, the democratization of knowledge and the growing pressure to democratize learning, there is no reason why this could not be achieved today. We will always need great teachers because they inspire us in as many ways as they teach us. But we no longer need to accept poor quality ones. I met a teacher in Northern Ireland once who spent an entire lunchtime telling me how great his colleagues were at teaching but for these awful children who just 'weren't learning'. (My guess that he was the rep for the biggest teaching union proved to be correct, by the way.) This is what I call the 'crap trap', that it's not me doing badly, it's them. But, as we explored earlier, your job isn't to teach them, your job is that they learn. For every handful of teachers telling us why these children just won't learn, there is always one just getting on and doing it, bringing the best out of the same young people and doing it wonderfully. Bill Gates said recently, on the subject of teachers:

> We need to give all teachers the benefits of clear standards, sound curriculum, good training and top instructional tools. But if their students still keep falling behind they are in the wrong line of work and they need to find another job.
>
> (*Fortune*, 18/12/08)

Poor teachers do damage as they fail in the job they are being paid for. But the good ones, they change everything. What's more, the future of the world depends on them. That's why I need a teacher when I've got Google.

Postface

Education isn't everything. For a start, it isn't an elephant.

(Spike Milligan)

Notes

Introduction

1 *Financial Times,* 18/11/06.
2 Lloyd and Mitchinson also suggest that, 'We should teach our children to seek out interestingness'. Amen to that.
3 www.nature.com/nature/journal/v438/n7070/full/438900a.html.
4 *The Economist,* 20/10/07.
5 *Fortune,* 14/05/07. Available at: http://donfick.com/collected-wisdom/old-blog-posts/parents-are-failing-the-education-test.html.

1 Save the world

1 *The Economist,* 24/05/08.
2 *New Scientist,* 17/06/06.
3 *Fortune,* 25/06/00.
4 http://news.bbc.co.uk/2/hi/science/nature/8224923.stm.
5 http://news.bbc.co.uk/2/hi/africa/7752813.stm.
6 http://news.bbc.co.uk/2/hi/americas/8162568.stm.
7 http://news.bbc.co.uk/2/hi/science/nature/1334986.stm.
8 *The Economist.* 08/04/09.
9 http://news.bbc.co.uk/2/hi/americas/8368785.stm.
10 *In Business,* 08/02/07.
11 www.independent.co.uk/environment/the-worlds-rubbish-dump-a-garbage-tip-that-stretches-from-hawaii-to-japan-778016.html.
12 http://ecorner.stanford.edu/authorMaterialInfo.html?mid=1549.

2 The future's coming

1 http://74.125.153.132/search?q=cache:egmjD0Ught4J:www2.goldman sachs.com/ideas/brics/book/99-dreaming.pdf+Goldman+Sachs+Global+Economic+Paper+No:+99.
2 http://business.timesonline.co.uk/tol/business/specials/rich_list/rich_list _2009/article6139333.ece.
3 http://news.bbc.co.uk/2/hi/business/4261354.stm.
4 www.terrapinn.com/2008/ccwza/.
5 *The Economist,* 13/10/07.

6   http://money.cnn.com/magazines/fortune/fortune_archive/2006/03/20/8371802/index.htm.
7   *The Economist*, 11/04/09.
8   But shed no tears, the 2010 list has just revealed his fortune has climbed back up by more than double to £22.45 billion.
9   www.guardian.co.uk/society/2007/jan/04/health.politics.
10 *Wired*, 05/2005.
11 *The Financial Times*, 19/04/08.
12 *The Economist*, 12/07/08.
13 *The Economist*, 14/03/09.
14 www.thersa.org/projects/education/opening-minds.
15 http://curriculum.qcda.gov.uk/key-stages-3-and-4/skills/plts/index.aspx.
16 http://defeatthedebt.com/understanding-the-national-debt/how-much-do-we-owe

3 'The Great Educational Lie'

1   *The Economist*, 07/10/06.
2   www.jamesdysonfoundation.com/contact.asp?formName=student.
3   http://wiifm.independentthinking.co.uk/.
4   *Time*, 06/2006.

4 So, go on then, why do I need a teacher when I've got Google?

1   www.etymonline.com/index.php?term=token.
2   www.etymonline.com/index.php?term=pedagogue.
3   www.indexmundi.com/china/population.html.
4   www.internetworldstats.com/stats.htm.
5   http://dsc.discovery.com/technology/tech-10/internet-languages-top-10.html.
6   http://news.bbc.co.uk/2/hi/technology/8400230.stm.
7   www.culture.gov.uk/what_we_do/broadcasting/5631.aspx.
8   http://en.wikipedia.org/wiki/Exabyte#cite_note-20.
9   www.guardian.co.uk/business/interactive/2009/mar/02/mobile-phones.
10 *New Scientist*, 22/08/09.

5 AQA v AQA

1   www.aqa.org.uk/.
2   http://news.bbc.co.uk/2/hi/uk_news/education/7562835.stm.
3   www.aqa.63336.com/.
4   The AQA answers to which are 'Life has no meaning, it's just the complex result of a sequence of chemical reactions. Assign your own meaning: find out what you love and do it' and 'The egg came first. DNA in the fertilized egg of a chicken-like bird mutated and that egg developed into an embryo that emerged as the first true chicken.'
5   My two favourite examples:

    Q. How can you test to see if someone is a god?
    AQA. You can test to see if someone is a god by saying 'It's a lovely day' to them. If they say 'Yes it is,' they're mortal. If they say 'Thanks,' bow down.

Q. Who is cleverer, a Yorkshireman or a pigeon?
AQA. A typical Yorkshireman has more brainpower than a pigeon.
However, all pigeons have a good sense of direction, and some men
never get out of Yorkshire.

6 Weekly Statistics, Education Parliamentary Monitor, No 271, ISSN 1748–
   7625, 26/06/2006.
7 To find out what your Local Authority spent on supply teachers go to www.
   learningbug.co.uk/SupplyTeacherCostsforEngland/tabid/100/Default.aspx.
8 Based around a multiply-intelligent thinking tool I had developed called
   8Way Thinking of which more in chapter 26.
9 http://en.wikipedia.org/wiki/Flynn_effect.
10 When it comes to advocating technology there is one place I do draw the
   line – PowerPoint, the Devil's OHP. And I'm not alone. Far from making
   us smarter, information design guru Edward R. Tufte claims that it was
   PowerPoint that contributed to the errors that caused the space shuttle disaster.
   In a *Wired* magazine article entitled 'Power Corrupts, PowerPoint Corrupts
   Absolutely', he claims that it 'induced stupidity, turned everyone into bores,
   wasted time and degraded the quality and credibility of communication'
   (www.edwardtufte.com/tufte/powerpoint). The Japanese have a process called
   Pecha-kucha, which means 'chatter' (www.pecha-kucha.org/what). The
   presenter is only allowed 20 PowerPoint slides that can be shown for no
   more than 20 seconds each. This means no presentation will last more than
   six minutes and 40 seconds, but you do want another one an hour later.
11 *Wired*, 05/2007.
12 http://en.wikipedia.org/wiki/Transhumanism.
13 http://en.wikipedia.org/wiki/Technological_singularity.
14 Primary schools were faring much better with integrating this technology.
   According to the report, 'We think that KS3 Consultants might benefit from
   working with KS2 consultants to identify both similarities and differences
   in use so that this can feed into CPD in both areas.' Moss, G. et al. (2007)
   *The Interactive Whiteboards, Pedagogy and Pupil Performance Evaluation: An
   Evaluation of the Schools Whiteboard Expansion (SWE)*, School of Educational Foundations and Policy Studies, Institute of Education, University
   of London at www.dcsf.gov.uk/research/data/uploadfiles/RR816.pdf.
15 *New Scientist*, 16/05/09.
16 *New Scientist*, 8/03/08.
17 www.forbes.com/forbes/2006/0410/084.html.
18 www.cognitiveliberty.org/neuro/ritalin/revving_the_brain.html.
19 *Scientific American*, 10/2009.
20 *New Scientist*, 13/05/06.

6 Your EQ will take you further than your IQ

1 http://en.wikipedia.org/wiki/British_Eugenics_Society.
2 http://en.wikipedia.org/wiki/Nazi_eugenics and http://en.wikipedia.
   org/wiki/Action_T4.
3 http://en.wikipedia.org/wiki/Genetic_Studies_of_Genius.
4 http://en.wikipedia.org/wiki/Luis_Walter_Alvarez.
5 http://en.wikipedia.org/wiki/William_Shockley.

6   *New Scientist*, 10/06/06.
7   *New Scientist*, 16/09/06.
8   *Fortune* magazine, 12/06/2006.

7 Nothing is more dangerous than an idea when it's the only idea you've got

1   www.open2.net/marksteel.
2   http://en.wikipedia.org/wiki/J._P._Guilford.
3   www.columbia.edu/acis/ets/CCREAD/etscc/kant.html.
4   *Wired*, 05/2006.
5   www.etymonline.com/index.php?search=innovate&searchmode=none.

8 It's the brain, stupid

1   The phrase was actually coined by Clinton's lead strategist James Carville who also coined such lines as 'Republicans want smaller government for the same reason crooks want fewer cops: it's easier to get away with murder' and 'Don't get mad. Don't get even. Just get elected, then get even.'
2   http://en.wikiquote.org/wiki/James_Carville.
3   The logical next step from the Decade of the Brain and running from 2010 to 2020.
4   www.dom2009.de/index.html.
5   www.znl-ulm.de.
6   www.guardian.co.uk/education/2003/apr/17/research.highereducation.
7   www.scienceblog.com/community/older/1998/B/199801218.html.
8   *The Financial Times*, 17/11/07.
9   www.newscientist.com/article/mg18925404.300-starve-your-stomach-to-feed-your-brain.html.

9 Neuromyths debunked!

1   www.oecd.org/document/4/0,3343, en_2649_35845581_33829892_1_1_1_1,00.html.
2   http://nobelprize.org/educational_games/medicine/split-brain/background.html.
3   http://jrsm.rsmjournals.com/cgi/content/full/96/6/284#REF46.
4   http://dailyheadlines.uark.edu/12165.htm.
5   This figure seems to vary between 5 and 20, but then 86 per cent of all statistics are made up on the spot.
6   www.oecd.org/dataoecd/39/25/31709587.pdf.
7   www.jsmf.org/.
8   http://en.wikipedia.org/wiki/Observable_universe.
9   *Financial Times*, 29/03/08.
10 www.oecd.org/document/52/0,3343,en_2649_35845581_33830068_1_1_1_1,00.html.

10 Your hands in their brains

1   http://en.wikipedia.org/wiki/General_intelligence_factor.
2   http://en.wikipedia.org/wiki/Flynn_effect.
3   http://en.wikipedia.org/wiki/Arthur_Jensen.

4   Genes and IQ, *New Scientist*, 18/07/09.
5   http://news.bbc.co.uk/2/hi/science/nature/8346715.stm.
6   www.who.int/mental_health/management/depression/definition/en/.

11 Talk to the hand coz the nucleus accumbens ain't listening

1   www.zerotothree.org/site/PageServer?pagename=ter_key_-brainFAQ#changes.
2   http://en.wikipedia.org/wiki/Nucleus_accumbens.
3   http://en.wikipedia.org/wiki/Melatonin.
4   http://news.bbc.co.uk/1/hi/health/8435955.stm.
5   www.independent.co.uk/life-style/health-and-families/health-news/could-you-be-suffering-from-social-jet-lag-473723.html.
6   www.dailymail.co.uk/news/article-1226666/School-trials-10am-start-tired-pupils-lie-in.html.
7   http://en.wikipedia.org/wiki/Tunicate#cite_note-1.
8   www.newhorizons.org/neuro/leiner.htm.
9   *Time Magazine*, 10/05/04
10 www.permanente.net/kaiser/pdf/5062.pdf.
11 www.newstatesman.com/books/2007/04/youth-savage-teenage.

12 Is that an iron bar through your frontal lobes or are you just pleased to see me?

1   www.sciencedaily.com/releases/2008/04/080403183048.htm.
2   www.scienceagogo.com/news/20050904005107data_trunc_sys.shtml.
3   www.greatschools.net/LD/identifying/executive-function-lens-to-view-your-child.gs?content=1017&page=all.
4   www.ncld.org.
5   What they don't need is a stamp on their work with a picture of a tortoise and the damning phrase, 'Getting there' as my dejected daughter showed me she had received once. If you have one of these in your drawer, burn it now!

13 Don't make 'em mad, make 'em think?

1   www.crystalinks.com/reptilianbrain.html.
2   www.hup.harvard.edu/pdf/LINACC_excerpt.pdf.
3   Sequence of information processing for emotions based on the anatomic dialogue between prefrontal cortex and amygdala.

14 Teacher's little helper

1   http://en.wikipedia.org/wiki/Neurotransmitter.
2   http://en.wikipedia.org/wiki/Dopamine.
3   http://en.wikipedia.org/wiki/Melatonin#Circadian_rhythm.
4   *New Scientist*, 06/06/09.

15 The 'f-word'

1   www.huffingtonpost.com/kari-henley/what-are-the-top-10-posit_b_203797.html.
2   http://en.wikipedia.org/wiki/Von_Restorff_effect.

3   Competitive school systems, though, are a far more invidious thing.
4   The BBC heard about what we were planning and summoned us to a meeting at Pebble Mill in Birmingham. They had a vague notion of doing something to mark the Year of the Sea but didn't know what. We shared our ideas and never heard from them again but I do hope you enjoyed *Coast*. Not that I'm bitter … .
5   www.sapere.org.uk.
6   The happiest person, according to research from Warwick University, would be a 'married, self-employed, religiously observant man stroking his cat'.
7   *Scientific American Mind*, 10/2005. Available at: www.scientificamerican.com/article.cfm?id=a-healthy-laugh.
8   *New Scientist*, 24/11/07.
9   *New Scientist*, 16/06/07.
10   *Financial Times*, 18/01/03.
11   http://news.bbc.co.uk/2/hi/uk_news/education/6618431.stm.
12   www.CambridgeWellbeing.org/.

16   It might be touchy feely but it's still the most important thing you do

1   Donahue and Benson 1995, Mecca, Smelser and Vasconcellos 1989, and Mruk 1995, all at http://clearinghouse.missouriwestern.edu/manuscripts/247.php; and James, 2009.
2   www.researchgate.net/publication/26658324_P300_as_an_index_of_implicit_self-esteem.
3   *The Economist*, 13/06/09.
4   www.gresham.ac.uk/event.asp?PageId=45&EventId=439.
5   www.education-consumers.com/oldsite/briefs/Behavioral%20Style%20Study.pdf.
6   http://ehlt.flinders.edu.au/education/DLiT/1999/WEBNOTES/website/develop.htm.
7   http://en.wikipedia.org/wiki/Charles_Cooley; http://en.wikipedia.org/wiki/Looking_glass_self.
8   *New Scientist*, 04/10/08.
9   *The Economist*, 23/12/06.
10   www.youtube.com/watch?v=8iOME-KJZSY.
11   www.poemhunter.com/song/hello-sir/.
12   http://en.wikipedia.org/wiki/Paul_Smith_(fashion_designer).
13   www.guardian.co.uk/sport/2008/oct/26/paul-smith-sport.
14   http://en.wikipedia.org/wiki/Primum_non_nocere.

17   What's the real point of school?

1   http://en.wikipedia.org/wiki/Frederick_Winslow_Taylor.
2   http://en.wikipedia.org/wiki/Child_labor#cite_ref-6.
3   http://en.wikipedia.org/wiki/Factory_Acts#Labour_of_Children.2C_etc.2C_in_Factories_Act_1833.
4   www.21learn.org/activities/staff/jabbott.php.
5   www.21learn.org/index.php.

18   An accidental school system

1   Hansard, House of Commons, Vol 9, 13 July 1807.
2   http://en.wikipedia.org/wiki/John_Amos_Comenius.

3 www.apuritansmind.com/ChristianWalk/McMahonComenius.htm.
4 http://en.wikiquote.org/wiki/John_Amos_Comenius.
5 www.elfin safety.com.
6 http://en.wikipedia.org/wiki/Monitorial_System.
7 http://en.wikipedia.org/wiki/Joseph_Lancaster.
8 http://books.google.com/books?id=eO9Prv4mOGkC&dq=Egmore,+near
   +Madras&printsec=frontcover&source=bl&ots=r21XvUf7xq&sig=YhuyU4
   NomCr24mTbdWFgNu_Qw6U&hl=en&ei=HmUbS4v2LsyGkAXWhsnbA
   w&sa=X&oi=book_result&ct=result&resnum=3&ved=0CBAQ6AEwAg#v=
   onepage&q=&f=false.
9 http://en.wikipedia.org/wiki/David_Stow.
10 *TES*, 03/09/99, research carried out for the NFER.
11 Fouracre (1991), quoted in ibid.
12 *Financial Times*, 04/07/02, research carried out by Ofsted, quoted in ibid.
13 Meet the Alloparents, Interview with Sarah Blaffer Hrdy, *New Scientist*,
   08/04/06.

19 Exams – so whose bright idea was that!?

1 http://en.wikipedia.org/wiki/Han_Zhangdi.
2 www.chinaknowledge.de/History/examination.html.
3 www.encyclopedia.com/doc/1O110-examinations.html.
4 www.cambridgeassessment.org.uk/ca/Spotlight/Detail?tag=150.
5 http://en.wikipedia.org/wiki/Richard_Bentley.
6 http://en.wikipedia.org/wiki/Somalis_in_the_United_Kingdom.
7 http://en.wikipedia.org/wiki/Somali_language.
8 www.guardian.co.uk/books/2001/jul/07/fiction.angeliquechrisafis.
9 *The Times*, 09/01/10.
10 Even Nobel Prize-winning writer Gabriel García Marquez talks about 'My
   personal drama with spelling' (Marquez 2003).

20 Educated is not enough

1 www.findagrave.com/cgi-bin/fg.cgi?page=gr&GSvcid=41816&GRid=12
   149998&.
2 http://en.wikipedia.org/wiki/Josef_Mengele.
3 In an interesting April 2010 for the bank they were up before a US Senate
   investigation for profiting from the housing market collapse and bragging
   about it in e-mails, were being investigated in the US and the UK for
   criminally misleading investors and announced profits for the quarter of
   £2.25 billion.
4 http://trueslant.com/matttaibbi/2009/06/18/the-greatest-non-apology-
   of-all-time/.
5 www.guardian.co.uk/society/2009/dec/09/homelessness-strategy-recession.
6 There have been two occasions where I realized that integrity was a lost
   cause in the UK and that we were becoming a society so shallow we
   would soon beach ourselves upon our own superficiality. The first was
   when I heard that Kenneth Clarke had earned over a million pounds
   promoting tobacco whilst an MP (www.dailymail.co.uk/news/article-
   1127233/Revealed-Ken-Clarke-8217-s-free-trips-F1-opera – courtesy-

tobacco-giant.html); the second was when I heard these excited words on mainstream TV – 'James Hewitt has just edged Bobby Davro out of first place on the high dive.'

21 Is yours a teaching school or a learning school?

1 http://en.wikipedia.org/wiki/Martin_Heidegger.
2 www.learntolearn.ac.uk/cgi-bin/learntolearn/index.pl?start=home/.
3 www.demos.co.uk/files/About_learning.pdf?1240939425.
4 http://curriculum.qcda.gov.uk/key-stages-3-and-4/skills/plts/index.aspx.
5 www.thersa.org/projects/education/opening-minds.
6 www.princes-ti.org.uk.
7 http://publications.teachernet.gov.uk/default.aspx?PageFunction=product details&PageMode=publications&ProductId=DCSF-00499-2009.
8 Resistance by the opposition has meant that the implementation of the review's findings was put on hold until after the election. This was announced in the spring of 2010 but by the time you read this it could be 1950 again.
9 PowerPoint – TLRP Learning How to Learn project: messages for teacher development, school leadership and national strategies by Professor Mary James (Project Director) Institute of Education, University of London.

22 Things that get in the way of the learning that are nothing to do with the teaching

1 www.daylighting.com/hazards.asp
2 http://lhhl/illinois.edu
3 http://wiki.43folders.com/index.php/Working_while_standing.
4 http://hypertextbook.com/facts/2001/JacquelineLing.shtml.
5 Interestingly, I also came across research that found that depressed people were more persistent with a task when slouching, happy people when sitting upright.
6 *The Observer*, 27/02/05.
7 www.independent.co.uk/life-style/health-and-families/health-news/could-you-be-suffering-from-social-jet-lag-473723.html.
8 *New Scientist*, 02/0 9/06.
9 *Wired*, 08/06.
10 http://en.wikipedia.org/wiki/Suspense#Zeigarnik_effect.

23 What do you use when you don't know what to do?

1 www.independentthinking.co.uk/Cool+Stuff/Pre-Starter+Starters/default. aspx.
2 www.independentthinking.co.uk/Cool+Stuff/Thunks/default.aspx.
3 www.guardian.co.uk/commentisfree/2009/aug/16/peter-hyman-educa tion-teaching-exams.
4 http://portal.unesco.org/shs/en/ev.php-URL_ID=12911&URL_DO= DO_TOPIC&URL_SECTION=201.html.
5 http://news.bbc.co.uk/today/hi/today/newsid_8368000/8368176.stm.
6 www.tedxdubai.com.
7 http://news.bbc.co.uk/1/hi/scotland/6330631.stm.
8 www.atozteacherstuff.com/pages/1884.shtml.

9   http://socialscientist.us/nphs/psychIB/psychpdfs/learnedhelplessness.pdf.
10 www.turned-offchild.com/articles/Learned%20Helplessness%20and%20Sch
    ool%20Failure%20-%20Part%201.pdf.
11 www.flyfishingdevon.co.uk/salmon/year2/psy221depression/psy221depr
    ession.htm.
12 www.derby.ac.uk/mhru.
13 http://en.wikipedia.org/wiki/Martin_Seligman.
14 www.telegraph.co.uk/news/uknews/1509016/Pupils-banned-from-putt
    ing-their-hands-up.html.
15 www.teachingthinking.net/.

24 A short word on thinking about thinking

1   http://gse.buffalo.edu/fas/shuell/CEP564/Metacog.htm.
2   http://en.wikipedia.org/wiki/John_H._Flavell.
3   http://en.wikipedia.org/wiki/Neuro-linguistic_programming.
4   VAK is simply a tool in the way that a drill isn't a hole.

25 Remember to succeed

1   *Wired*, 06/2008.
2   www.yenra.com/color-psychology-memory-affect/.
3   www.michaelgruneberg.com/.
4   http://en.wikipedia.org/wiki/Hermann_Ebbinghaus.
5   http://en.wikipedia.org/wiki/SuperMemo and www.wired.com/medtech
    /health/magazine/16–05/ff_wozniak?currentPage=1.

26 How are you smart?

1   Harris, R. (2001) *Rolf Harris: The Autobiography – Can You Tell What It Is
    Yet?* London: Corgi Books.
2   http://en.wikipedia.org/wiki/Rolf_Harris.
3   Rolf Harris is a god and don't let anyone tell you different.
4   Wordsearches – the teacher's general anaesthetic.

27 Muchos pocos hacen un mucho

1   Curse of Being Different, *New Scientist*, 13/01/07. Available at: www.new
    scientist.com/article/mg19325864.800-the-curse-of-being-different.html.
2   Phil Jupitus – www.bbc.co.uk/programmes/b00773b4.
3   Doodle Day – www.independentthinking.co.uk/Cool+Stuff/Articles/
    581.aspx.
4   I have since come across research from Plymouth University showing that
    people who doodled had 29 per cent better recall in lessons than those who
    did not – http://news.bbc.co.uk/1/hi/health/7912671.stm.

28 Your classroom is not just an environment in which you can show how clever you are

1   www.ilxor.com/ILX/ThreadSelectedControllerServlet?boardid=40
    &threadid=33562.

29 Teach less, learn more

1 Bear in mind, too, that according to research from the University of Durham on 20,000 primary children, most homework is, as I have always contested, a waste of time. Available at: http://news.bbc.co.uk/1/hi/education/383843.stm.
2 www.dailymail.co.uk/news/article-1102799/15–000-teachers-sick-EVERY -day-blamed-stress-ministerial-meddling.html.
3 www.ncvs.org/.
4 http://asa.aip.org/web2/asa/abstracts/search.oct09/asa47.html and http://www.firstscience.com/home/news/breaking-news-all-topics/teacher-talk-strains-voices-especially-for-women_73051.html.
5 www.uiowa.edu/~shcvoice/.
6 Although not entirely relevant to our needs here I particularly liked the title of one bit of research from Edge Hill University College in Ormskirk looking at student teacher behaviours with nursery children and entitled, 'You can't shout at them because they just cry' – for more information go to www.informaworld.com/smpp/content~content=a739515004&db=all.
7 *The Economist*, 23/12/06.
8 No such problems for this sign I spotted in a woodwork classroom – 'No messing about'.

30 Enthusiasm and the sort of 7 per cent rule

1 www.time.com/time/health/article/0,8599,1871687,00.html.
2 http://wik.ed.uiuc.edu/index.php/Teacher_Enthusiasm_Research.
3 My colleague Jim Roberson has a way of dealing with students who complain that something is boring. He gives them his board pen. Then he asks for it back. Then he gives them his pen again. Then he asks for it back again … 'Boring!' he then booms in his powerful Bronx accent, 'Passing the pen is boring!'

31 Everyone remembers …

1 http://en.wikipedia.org/wiki/Programme_for_International_Student_Ass essment.
2 http://timss.bc.edu/TIMSS2007/release.html.
3 www.oecd.org/document/2/0,3343,en_32252351_32236191_3971885 0_1_1_1,00.html.
4 www.dailymail.co.uk/news/article-1206477/Half-newly-qualified-teachers -drop-months.html.
5 http://timss.bc.edu/timss_advanced/downloads/TIMSSAdvanced2008-IntlReleaseStatement.pdf.
6 *New Scientist*, 01/12/07.
7 www.payscale.com/best-colleges/degrees.asp.
8 The highest ranking for a 'liberal arts' degree was marketing at number 21. The bottom three were theology, elementary education and, lastly, social work.
9 www.curriki.org.

Bibliography

Abbot, J. and Ryan, T. (2000) *The Unfinished Revolution: Learning, Human Behaviour, Community and Political Paradox*, Stafford: Network Educational Press.

Ambady, N. and Rosenthal, R. (1993) Half a minute: Predicting teacher evaluations from thin slices of nonverbal behavior and physical attractiveness, *Journal of Personality and Social Psychology*, 64(3): 431–41.

Barber, M. and Mourshed, M. (2007) *How the World's Best Performing School Systems Come Out on Top*, McKinsey and Co. Available at: www.mckinsey. com/App_Media/Reports/SSO/Worlds_School_Systems_Final.pdf.

Bell, A. (1807) *An Analysis of the Experiment in Education, made at Egmore, near Madras*, London: Cadell and Davies.

de Bellis, M. D., Keshavan, M. S., Beers, S. R., Hall, J., Frustaci, K., Masalehdan, A., Noll, J. and Boring, A. M. (2001) Sex differences in brain maturation during childhood and adolescence, *Cerebral Cortex*, 11(6): 552–557(6).

Binet, A. (1905) New methods for the diagnosis of the intellectual level of subnormals, *L'Année Psychologique*, 12, 191–244. Available at: http://psych classics.yorku.ca/Binet/binet1.htm.

de Botton, A (2002) *The Art of Travel*, London: Penguin.

Brendgen, M., Wanner, B. and Vitaro, F. (2006) Verbal abuse by the teacher and child adjustment from kindergarten through grade 6, *Pediatrics*, 117(5), May 2006: 1585–98 (doi:10.1542/peds.2005–50). Available at: http:// pediatrics.aappublications.org/cgi/content/full/117/5/1585.

Bringuier, J.-C. (1980) *Conversations with Jean Piaget* (B.M. Gulati, Trans.). Chicago: University of Chicago Press. Available at: http://en.wikipedia. org/wiki/Jean_Piaget.

Brosnan, M., Demetre, J., Hamill, S., Robson, K., Shepherd, H. and Cody, G. (2001) Executive functioning in adults and children with developmental dyslexia, *Neuropsychologia*, 40(12): 2144–2155. Available at: www.science-direct.com/science?_ob=ArticleURLudi=B6T0D-45JY9XJ-1user=10rdoc=1 fmt=orig=searchsort=ddocanchor=&view=csearchStrId=1154555873rerunOri gin=scholar.googleacct=C000050221version=1urlVersion=0userid=10&md5 =c1eeebcae0bddddee5a2996af3cd1c60.

Burt, J. (1963) Is intelligence distributed normally? *The British Journal of Statistical Psychology*, Vol. XVI Part 2.

Carter, R. (1988) *Mapping the Mind*, London: Weidenfield & Nicholson.

Churchill, W. (1930) *My Early Life: A Roving Commission*, London: Eland Publishing. Available at: http://en.wikiquote.org/wiki/Winston_Churchill.

Coats, W. D. and Smidchens, U. (1966) Audience recall as a function of speaker dynamism, *Journal of Educational Psychology*, 57(4), August: 189–91. Available at: http://psycnet.apa.org/journals/edu/57/4/189/.

Collins, M. L. (1978) Effects of enthusiasm training on preservice elementary teachers, *Journal of Teacher Education*, 29: 53–57. Available at: http://jte.sagepub.com/cgi/pdf_extract/29/1/53.

Crystal, D. (ed.) (1987) *The Cambridge Encyclopedia of Language*, Cambridge: Cambridge University Press.

Csíkszentmihályi, M. (1990) *Flow: The Psychology of Optimal Experience*, New York: Harper and Row.

Curran, A. (2008) *The Little Book of Big Stuff About the Brain*, Carmarthen: Crown House.

Dempster, F. N. (1988) The spacing effect: A case study in the failure to apply the results of psychological research, *American Psychologist*, 43(8): 627–34. Available at: http://74.125.153.132/search?q=cache:3B8997xRBBgJ:andrewvs.blogs.com/usu/files/the_spacing_effect.pdf+The+Spacing+Effect:+A+Case+Study+in+the+Failure+to+Apply+the+Results+of+Psychological+Research&cd=8&hl=en&ct=clnk&client=safari.

Duckworth, J. (2009) *The Little Book of Values*, Carmarthen: Crown House.

El-Hai, J. (2005), *The Lobotomist: A Maverick Medical Genius and His Tragic Quest to Rid the World of Mental Illness*, New York: John Wiley and Sons.

Feinstein, S. (2004) *Secrets of the Teenage Brain*, San Diego: The Brain Store.

Findlay, J. (1902) *Principles of Class Teaching*, London: Macmillan and Co.

Forest, J. F. (2005) *The Making of a Terrorist: Recruitment, Training, and Root Causes*, Santa Barbara: Praeger.

Fouracre, S. (1991) *A Case Study of the Transition from Primary to Secondary School*, Stirling University.

Fowler, W. S. (1959) The Origin of the General Certificate, *British Journal of Educational Studies*, 7(2): 140–48.

Fredrickson, B. (2009) *Positivity: Groundbreaking Research Reveals How to Embrace the Hidden Strength of Positive Emotions, Overcome Negativity, and Thrive*, New York: Crown Publishing Group. Available at: www.unc.edu/peplab/home.html.

Freeman, J. (2006) Giftedness in the long term, *Journal for the Education of the Gifted*, 29, 384–403. Available at: http://74.125.153.132/search?q=cache:MgHppn96DVUJ:www.joanfreeman.com/content/JEG%2520Giftedness%2520In%2520the%2520Long%2520Term%252006.pdf+Giftedness+in+the+Long+Term=1&hl=en&ct=clnk&client=safari.

Friedman, T. (2005) *The World is Flat – A Brief History of the Globalised World in the 21st Century*, London: Allen Lane.

Fuster, J. M. (2008) *The Prefrontal Cortex*, Amsterdam: Elsevier.

Gardner, H. (1983) *Frames of Mind*, New York: BasicBooks, Inc.

Gardner, H. (1993) *Multiple Intelligences: The Theory in Practice*, New York: BasicBooks, Inc.

Gatto, J. T. (1992) *Dumbing Us Down*, Canada: New Society Publishers.

Gilbert, I. (2002) *Essential Motivation in the Classroom*, London: Routledge.

Gilbert, I. (2007) *The Little Book of Thunks: 260 Questions to Make Your Brain Go Ouch!*, Carmarthen: Crown House.

Gilbert, I. (2008) *The WIIFM? Report* for QCA that contributed to larger resource. Order online at http://orderline.qcda.gov.uk/bookstore.asp? Action=Book&ProductID=9781847218469.

Gilbert, P. (1984) *Depression: From Psychology to Brain State*, London: Lawrence Erlbaum Associates.

Gill, T. (2007) *No Fear – Growing Up in a Risk Averse Society*, London: Calouste Gulbenkian Society.

Gillard, D. (2007) *Education in England: A Brief History*, Available at: www.educationengland.org.uk/history/.

Gillham, B. A. (1977) The reluctant beneficiaries: The teacher and the public examination system, *British Journal of Educational Studies*, 25(1) (Feb., 1977), pp. 50–62. Available at: www.jstor.org/pss/3120043.

Gladwell, M. (2005) *Blink*, New York: Little, Brown.

Gladwell, M. (2008) *Outliers – The Story of Success*, New York: Little, Brown.

Goddard, H. (1913) *The Kallikak Family: A Study in the Heredity of Feeble-Mindedness*, Quoted at: www.indiana.edu/%7Eintell/goddard.shtml.

Goleman, D. (1995) *Emotional Intelligence*, London: Bloomsbury Group.

Greenfield, S. (2000) *Brain Story*, London: BBC Books.

Harris, D. (2007) *Dropping the Baton*, Carmarthen: Crown House.

Harris, R. (2001) *Rolf Harris: The Autobiography – Can You Tell What It Is Yet?* London: Corgi.

Hatfield, E., Cacioppo, J. and Rapson, R. (1994) *Emotional Contagion*, Cambridge: Cambridge University Press.

Hawks, T. (1999) *Round Ireland with a Fridge*, London: Ebury Press.

Heider, J. (2005) *The Tao of Leadership*, Lake Worth, FL: Humanics Publishing Group.

Holahan, C. K. and Sears, R. R. (1995) *The Gifted Group in Later Maturity*, Stanford, CA: Stanford University Press.

Jackson, N. (2009) *The Little Book of Music for the Classroom*, Carmarthen: Crown House.

James, O. (1998) *Britain on the Couch*, London: Arrow Books.

James, Rochelle, L. (2009) *Correlation Between Adolescent Self-esteem, Religiosity, and Perceived Family Support*, Department of Psychology, Loyola University New Orleans at http://clearinghouse.missouriwestern.edu/manuscripts/247.php.

Jensen, E. (1995) *Super Teaching*, Del Mar, CA: Turning Point Publishing.

Jensen, E. (1996) *Completing the Puzzle: A Research-based Guide to Implementing the New Dramatic Learning Paradigm*, San Diego: The Brain Store.

Jones, S. (1999) Descent with modification, in *Almost Like a Whale*, London: Doubleday.

Juvonen, J. and Wentze, K. (1996) *Social Motivation: Understanding Children's School Adjustment*, Cambridge: Cambridge University Press.

Kalla, T., Downes, J. J. and van den Broek M. (2001) The pre-exposure technique: Enhancing the effects of errorless learning in the acquisition of face-name associations, *Neuropsychological Rehabilitation*, 11(1): 1–16 (19 ref.), Hove: Psychology Press. Available at: http://cat.inist.fr/?aModele=afficheN&cpsidt=893093.

Lapakko, D. (1997) Three cheers for language: A closer examination of a widely cited study of nonverbal communication, *Resource Magazine*. Available at: http://resourcemagazine.co.uk/acatalog/lapakko.pdf.

Lawton, D. (1980) *The Politics of the School Curriculum*, London: Routledge & Kegan Paul.

Layard, R. (2005) *Happiness: Lessons from a New Science*, London: Penguin.

Levenson, R. W., Ekman, P. and Friesen, W. V. (1990) Voluntary facial action generates emotion-specific autonomic nervous system activity, *Psychophysiology*. July 27(4): 363–84. Available at: www.ncbi.nlm.nih.gov/pubmed/2236440?ordinalpos=1&itool=EntrezSystem2.PEntrez.Pubmed.Pubmed_ResultsPanel.Pubmed_SingleItemSupl.Pubmed_Discovery_RA&linkpos=2=relatedarticles&logdbfrom=pubmed.

Levitin, D. (2006) *This is Your Brain on Music*, London: Atlantic Books.

Lewis, C. (1994) *The Unemployables*, Didcot: Management Books.

Linden, D. J. (2008) *Accidental Mind: How Brain Evolution Has Given Us Love, Memory, Dreams, and God*, Cambridge: Harvard University Press.

Lycett, A. (2004) *Dylan Thomas: A New Life*, London: Phoenix Books.

Lyons, J. (2009) *The House of Wisdom: How the Arabs Transformed Western Civilization*, London: Bloomsbury.

McCarthy, P. (2001) *McCarthy's Bar: A Journey of Discovery in Ireland*, London: Sceptre.

McCarty, C., Mason, W., Kosterman, R., Hawkins, J., Lengua, L. and McCauley, E. (2008) Adolescent school failure predicts later depression among girls, *Journal of Adolescent Health*, 43(2): 180–87. Available at: www.ncbi.nlm.nih.gov/pmc/articles/PMC2430389/.

Mcintyre-Brown, A. (2001) *Liverpool: the first 1,000 years*, Liverpool: Capisca.

Maclean, P. D. (1990) *The Triune Brain in Evolution: Role in Paleocerebral Functions*, New York: Plenum.

Marquez, G. C. (2003) *Living to Tell the Tale*, New York: Knopf.

Martin, J. (2006) *The Meaning of the 21st Century*, London: Transworld Publishers.

Mehrabian, A. and Ferris, S. (1967) Inference of attitude from nonverbal communication in two channels, *The Journal of Counseling Psychology*, 31: 248–52.

Moss, G., Jewitt, C., Levaãiç, R., Armstrong, V., Cardini, A. and Castle, F. (2007) *The Interactive Whiteboards, Pedagogy and Pupil Performance Evaluation: An Evaluation of the Schools Whiteboard Expansion (SWE)*, School of Educational Foundations and Policy Studies, Institute of Education, University of London. Available at: www.dcsf.gov.uk/research/data/uploadfiles/RR816.pdf.

National Foundation for Educational Research (NFER) (1997) *Trends in Standards in Literacy and Numeracy in the United Kingdom*, NFER.

Orwell, G. (2000) *Essays*, London: Penguin Classics, New Edn.

Papert, S. (1993) *Mindstorms: Children, Computers, and Powerful Ideas*, New York: Perseus Books.

Peters, T. (1994) *The Tom Peters Seminar, Crazy Times for Crazy Organizations*, New York: Random House.

Peters, T. (2003) *Re-imagine!*, London: Dorling Kindersley.

Prestowitz, C. (2006) *Three Billion New Capitalists: The Great Shift of Wealth and Power to the East*, New York: Basic Books.

Rand, A. (1961) *The Fountainhead*, New York: HarperCollins.

Rich Harris, J. (2007) *No Two Alike: Human Nature and Human Individuality*, New York: W. W. Norton and Company.

Richardson, K. (1999) *The Making of Intelligence*, London: Orion Publishing.

Ridderstråle, J. and Nordström, K. (1999) *Funky Business*, Harlow: Pearson Education.

Ridley, M. (2003) *Nature via Nurture*, London: Harper Perennial.

Robertson, I. (1999) *Mind Sculpture*, London: Bantam Press.

Ryan, W. (2008) *Leadership with a Moral Purpose: Turning Your School Inside Out*, Crown House, Carmathern.

Savage, J. (2007) *Teenage – The Creation of Youth 1875 – 1945*, London: Chatto and Windus.

Sax, L. (2006) *Temperature – Six Degrees of Separation: What Teachers Need to Know about the Emerging Science of Sex Differences*, Educational Horizons.

Schacter, D. L. (1999) The seven sins of memory. Insights from psychology and cognitive neuroscience, *American Psychologist*, 54, 182–203. Available at: www.apa.org/monitor/oct03/sins.html.

Seligman, M. (2003) *Authentic Happiness: Using the New Positive Psychology to Realise Your Potential for Lasting Fulfilment*, London: Nicholas Brealey Publishing.

Siegler, R. S. (1992) The other Alfred Binet, *Developmental Psychology*, 28, 179–90. Available at: www.indiana.edu/%7Eintell/binet.shtml.

Smith, A. (1776) *The Wealth of Nations*.

Smith, J. (2010) *The Lazy Teacher's Handbook*, Carmarthen: Crown House.

Smithers, A. and Robinson, P. (2009) *The Good Teacher Training Guide 2009*, Centre for Education and Employment Research, University of Buckingham.

The Spens Report (1938) *Secondary Education with Special Reference to Grammar Schools and Technical High Schools*, London: HM Stationery Office. Available at: www.dg.dial.pipex.com/documents/docs2/spens03.shtml.

Storr, A. (1989) *Churchill's Black Dog and Other Phenomena of the Human Mind*, London: HarperCollins.

Stray, C. (2001) *The Shift from Oral to Written Examination: Cambridge and Oxford 1700–1900*, London: Taylor and Francis.

Surowiecki, J. (2004) *The Wisdom of Crowds*, New York: Random House.

Taylor, F. (1911) *The Principles of Scientific Management*, New York: Norton & Company.

Wells, N., Evans, G. (2003) 'Nearby Nature, A Buffer of Life Stress among Rural Children' *Environment and Behavior*, 35 (3): 311—330.

White, M. P. (2006) *White Slave: The Autobiography*, London: Orion.

Wichman, F., Sharpe, L. T. and Gegenfurtner, K. R. (2002) The contributions of color to recognition memory for natural scenes, Max-Planck Institut für Biologische Kybernetik and Oxford University, *Journal of Experimental Psychology – Learning, Memory and Cognition*, 28(3).

Zeedyk, M. S., Gallacher, J., Henderson, M., Hope, G., Husband, B. and Lindsay, K. (2003) Negotiating the transition from primary to secondary school. Perceptions of pupils, parents and teachers, *School Psychology International*, 24 (1): 67–79.

Index

A Teen-Age Bill of Rights 69
Abbott, John 101–2
About Learning 121
abstract concepts, memory for 150
Accidental Mind: How Brain Evolution Has Given Us Love, Memory, Dreams, and God 75
Acland, Thomas 113
ADHD 48; and dopamine production 83; executive dysfunction 72; fear and bipolar disorder 178–79; green environment 128
adolescence: brain maturation 64–66; dopamine 83; role of amygdala 77–78, 79–80; sleep deprivation 66–67
Adolescent School Failure Predicts Depression Among Girls 96–97
Africa, call centres 10
Alvarez, Louis 37
Alzheimer's disease 54
Ambady, N. 183
amygdalae 76–78
An Analysis of the Experiment in Education, Made at Egmore, near Madras 107
anchored jobs 11
Any Questions Answered (AQA) 25–26
apologising 80
Aquinas, St Thomas 150
architecture 192
Assessment and Qualifications Alliance (AQA) 25
assessment, PISA project 188–89

attention, attracting 177
attitude 17
attracting attention 177
'Audience recall as a function of speaker dynamism' 184
authority, in classroom 109
autistic spectrum 40–41

background noise 132
baggage 182
Bait al-Hikma 21
Ball, Rouse 113–14
Bandler, Richard 146
bankers 117–18
Barber, Michael 187
Barnes, D. 180
barriers to learning: classroom layout 130–31; eating and drinking 129–30; movement 132–33; noise 132; physical position 130–31; temperature 131–32; time of day 131
Beere, Jackie 123
beginnings and endings of lessons 178
behaviour: genetic modification 29; modelling 80
beliefs, of teachers 126
Bell, Andrew 107, 108–9
Bennett, David A. 54
Binet, Alfred 31–33, 35–36
Binet–Simon test 31–34
bipolar disorder, fear and ADHD 178–79
Bjork, Elizabeth 156–57
Bjork, Robert 156–57

Blink 41
body language 181
boredom 123–24, 185–86
brain: in adolescence 64–66;
    applying knowledge about 47–48;
    EELS 68–69; effects of early
    experience 61–62; engaging as
    whole 51–52; evolution 75; false
    facts 52–56; and gender 175;
    growing 60, 63; maturation
    63–66; neurochemical balance
    79–80; as pleasure-seeking 83;
    potential of 52–53; as single
    entity 51; teachers' knowledge of
    50; understanding of 48–49
Brain Dump 182
brain-enhancing pharmaceuticals 29
brain imaging 51
brain plasticity 52
Brendgen, M. 176
BRIC economies: effects of
    recession 14; predictions 9–10
Britain on the Couch 96
Brizendine, Louann 175
Brosnan, M. 72–73
Bruer, John T. 52, 55
Budd Rowe, Mary 139
Burt, Cyril 35
Bush, George Jnr. 47
Bush, George Snr. 46–47
business: attributes for success 12;
    teams in 39–40

Cacioppo, J. 182, 183
call centres 10
Cambridge University, Well-Being
    Institute 89
Caplan, Arthur 29
Cardus, Neville 181
Carpenter, Karen 94
Carter, Rita 71
cerebellum 67–68
changes, making 167
Chaplin, Charlie 100
Chavez, Hugo 7
Chesterfield, Lord 168
child development, and learning 55
children, as labour 100–101
China 10, 112
chronotypes 131

Churchill, Winston 93–94, 187
Churchill's Black Dog 93–94
Clark, Andy 28
classroom layout, and learning
    130–31
classrooms, as laboratories 164–65
Clinton, Bill 46
Coats, William D. 184
cognitive ability 27
Cohen, Elizabeth 40
collaboration 39
Collins, M. L. 184–85
Comenius, Jan 103–4
Commitment to Learning 19, 20
communication 181–83
community of enquiry 88
competence, and qualifications
    16–17
competency curriculum 122,
    123–24
competing 86–87
concretization 150
control freaks 180
convergent thinking 43
Cooley, Charles 94
Cooper-Hind, Simon 133, 172
copying metacognitive strategies
    146–47
crap trap 192
Crossland, David 13
Csíkszentmihályi, Mihály 83
curiosity 87–88
Curran, Andrew 40, 47, 52, 55, 82,
    84, 127

Daily Mail 123
Darwin, Charles 3, 68
de Bellis, M. D. 110–11
de-motivation 182
deadlines 134
death of competition 39
Decade of the Brain 46–47
decision-making, role of pre-frontal
    cortex (PFC) 71–72
democratization: of knowledge
    22–23, 27; of learning 24, 27,
    163
Demos 121
Dempster, Frank 155–56, 157
Dennis, Felix 13

depression 61–62; and school failure in girls 96–97; and sleep deprivation 66–67
deputy headteachers 173
descent with modification 3
Diffrient, Niels 131
Digital Britain 22
Dijk, Dirk-Jan 67
divergent thinking 43–45
Doodle Day 166
Doomsday Bingo: Asian Development Bank report 5–6; catastrophic global climate change 4; destitute nations slipping into a deepening trap of extreme poverty 5; destruction of life in the oceans 8; exposure from extreme science to new dangers 7; growth of shanty-cities with extreme violence and poverty 5–6; mass famine in ill-organized countries 7; mass recruitment for suicide terrorism 6; nuclear/biological terrorism 6; religious war between Muslims and Christian 6; rivers and aquifers drying up 7; unstoppable global migrations of people 5; unstoppable pandemic of new infectious disease 4–5; weapons of mass destruction becoming inexpensive 5; world war with nuclear and biological weapons 8
dopamine 81–83
'Dreaming with the BRICS: The Path to 2050' 9
drinking, and learning 129–30
Dropping the Baton 110
Duckworth, Julie 179
dumbing up 59, 158, 160, 163
Dunn, Kenneth 128, 129, 131–33
Dunn, Rita 128, 129, 131–33
dyslexia 72–73, 97–98
Dyson, Freeman 44
Dyson, James 18

eating, and learning 129–30
Ebbinghaus, Herman 155–56
education: as distinct from schooling 14; early purpose of 103; not confined to classroom 105–6; point of 99–100; as social control 101
EELS 68–69
'Effects of Enthusiasm Training on Preservice Elementary Teachers' 184–85
8Way Thinking 160–63
80:20 Rule 141
Einstein, Albert 3, 8
11+ 36
emotional contagion 182
Emotional Contagion 182, 183
Emotional Intelligence 39, 77
emotional quotient 39, 41, 77–78
emotions 85–87
empathy 87
empowerment 192
Encyclopaedia Britannica 22, 23
endings and beginnings of lessons 178
engagement 68
enthusiasm 182, 184–85
enthusiasm training 184
entrepreneurship 13
environment: green 128–29; and intelligence 58–59; and learning 55
epigenetics 57
EQ 39, 41, 77–78
Ericsson, Anders 38
ethics 117–19
eugenics 34–37
Eugenics Education Society 34
Evans, Lee 185
evolutionary psychology 48–49
examination system, development 113
examinations, oral and written 114–16
executive function 48; role of pre-frontal cortex (PFC) 72–74
Exeter Experiment 113
expectations 164
expenditure 189
experiences 68

facial expression 181, 183–84
Factory Acts 100–101
failure: being doomed to 18; learning to cope with 140

false facts: critical period of development 53; importance of enriched environments 55; only using 10% of brain 52
fear: ADHD and bipolar disorder 178–79; of adults 179; of getting it wrong 137–38
Feinstein, Sheryl 66, 67, 68, 77
Fellini, Federico 129
Ferris, Susan 181
Findlay, J. J. 110
Finland 189
First, do no harm 98
Fisher, Robert 142
Flavell, John 143
Flow; the Psychology of Optimal Experience 83
fluorescent lights 127–28, 129
Flynn Effect 27, 57–58
Forest, James J. F. 6
Fortune 10, 17, 40
'Four-B' strategy 140–41
frames of reference 179–80
Fredrickson, Barbara 85
Freeman, J. 38
Freeman, Walter 71
Friedman, Thomas 10–11, 14
frogs, boiling 132
Frost, David 17
Fry, Stephen 95
Fu*k it! switch 165
fun 84
fungibility, of jobs 11
Funky Business 39
Fuster, Joaquin, M. 71–72

'g' 57
Gage, Phineas 71
Galton, Francis 34
game of school 42
gaming 27–28
Gandhi, Mohandas 165
Gardner, Howard 120–21, 158
Gates, Bill 12, 20, 193
gender: differentiation 48; and examinations 115
General Education Board (USA) 99–100
general intelligence 57
general practitioners 41

genetic modification 29
Genetic Studies of Genius 37
genetics, and intelligence 58–59
genius 38
George, David 160
gifted and talented, multiple intelligences 160–61
gifted children study (UK) 38
Gilbert, Ian 19–20
Gilbert, Paul 140
Gill, Tim 106
Gillard, D. 103
Gillham, B. A. 112
Gladwell, Malcolm 37, 41, 188
goal setting 144–45
Goddard, Henry 34, 36
Goldman Sachs 117–19
Goldman Sachs Global Economic Paper No: 99 9
Goleman, Daniel 39, 77
Gordon, Myrna 140
Gordon, Robert 140
Grant, Stanley 33
Great Pacific Garbage Patch 8
green environment, benefits 128–29
Grinder, John 146
Gruneberg, Michael 151
guess what's in the teacher's head 42, 45
Guildford, J. P. 43–44

hairy dendritic sprouting 65
hands up to respond 141–42
happiness 88–90
Happiness, Lessons From a New Science 89
Harris, Dave 110
Harris, Rolf 161
Hatfield, E. 182, 183
Hawks, Tony 166
headteachers, brave 172–73
Health and Morals of Apprentices Act 101
Hebbe, Donald 60
Hebbian assemblies 60
Heidegger, Martin 120
Heider, John 170–71
higher education, China 10
HiOP 41
hippocampus 82

Hitler, Adolph 37
Horowitz, Sheldon H. 48, 72
Hot Spot 177, 179
House of Wisdom 21
How the World's Best Performing School Systems Come out on Top 187–88

images, in memory 150
In Business 7, 10, 13
in-out listening 169
independent learners 173
independent learning 26
independent thinking 44
independent thought: stifling 101–2; teaching 106–7
India, economic development 9–10
Industrial Revolution 100–101
Inference of Attitude from Nonverbal Communication in Two Channels 181
Infosys 10
innovation 173
Inside Out Leadership 168
inspiration, from students 168
intelligence: malleability 35; measuring 58; views of 134–35
intelligence testing 31–34, 37
Internet, and access to knowledge 22

James Dyson Foundation 18
James, Mary 126
James, Oliver 96–97
Japan, lost decade 9
Jensen, Arthur 58
Jensen, Eric 110–11, 133, 169, 170–71
jobs: anchored 11; fungible 11; worldwide competition 14
Joint Matriculation Board 113
Jones, Barbara 173
Journal of the Royal Society of Medicine 51
Jupitus, Phill 166
Juvonen, Jaana 19, 94–95

Kalla, T. 151
Kant, Immanuel 44
Keeling, Dave 152

Kitab al-Jabr 21
knowledge: democratization of 22–23, 27; fixed 21
Kurzweil 28

Lambert, Richard 142
Lancaster, Joseph 107, 109
Landscape and Human Health Laboratory, Illinois 128
language rules 175
language, teacher's and child's 179–80
LaoTsu 174
laughter 88–90
Law for the Prevention of Hereditarily Diseased Offspring 36–37
Layard, Richard 89
lazy teachers 173, 180
Lea, Ruth 67
leadership 174
learn to learn 121
learned helplessness 140–41
'Learned Helplessness and School Failure' 140
learning: democratization of 24, 27, 163; and fun 84–85; motivation for 19; and movement 67–68; as neurological connection 60, 63; and positive emotions 85–86; role of dopamine 81–83; styles and strategies 160; and teaching 120
Learning Bug 26
learning how to learn (LHTL) research project 121
Learning How to Learn research 126
learning mix 128
learning practices 121–22
learning schools 121, 168
left brain, right brain theory 50–51
Leighton, Roy 152
lesson planning 165, 167
lessons, beginnings and endings of 178
Levenson, R. W. 183
Levitin, Daniel 38
Lewis, Chris 12–13
Liar, Liar, Your Prefrontal Cortex Is On Fire 71

lighting 127–29
likemindedness 159
limitations, extending to students 159–60
Linden, David J. 75
Linkword 151–52
Lipman, Matthew 88, 135
Little Book of Music in the Classroom 132
Little Book of Thunks 136–37
little things 167
lizards 75–76
looking glass self 94
losing 87
love 69, 186
lying 71

McCabe, Bernice 123
McCarthy, Pete 30
McCarty, C. 97
McCrone, John 51
McKinsey Report 187–88, 190, 191
Maclean, Paul 75–77
Madejski, John 13
Mapping the Mind 71
Martin, James 4, 28–29
mathematics 190–91
maturation, of brain 63–64
meditation 73–74, 79
mega problems, solvability 8
Mehrabian, Albert 181
melatonin 66
memories, of best and worst teachers 187
memory: for abstract concepts 150; association 178; beginnings and endings 178; and VAK 154
memory enhancement 29
memory strategies 148–51; effective registration 153–54; *Linkword* 151–52; review 155–56; RING 152; rote learning 154–55
Mengele, Josef 117, 118
metacognition 143–44
metacognitive knowledge 143–44
metacognitive regulation 144–47
metacognitive strategies 144–47
Mind Sculpture 60
mirror neurons 87

Mittal, Lakshmi 10
mobile phones 23–24
mobility, and learning 132–33
modelling, Neuro-Linguistic Programming (NLP) 146–47
Modern Times 100
monitorial method 107
morality 117–19
Mortimer, John 99
mothers, and self-esteem 95
motivation 19, 124, 182
Mourshed, M. 187
movement, and learning 67–68, 132–33
multiple-chance education 121
multiple intelligences 59, 120, 158, 160–63, 167
Multiple Intelligences: The Theory in Practice 158
Murgatroyd, Christopher 61
muscle memory 155
music 132
myelination 63

National Foundation for Educational Research (NFER) 187–88
nature-nurture interaction 57–61
'Nearby Nature: A Buffer of Life Stress Among Rural Children' 128–29
Neural Connections: Some You Use, Some You Lose 52
neural hijacking 77
neural pruning 60, 63, 65
neural reserve 54
Neuro-Linguistic Programming (NLP) 146–47
neurology *see* brain
neuromyths 52–56
neurotransmitters 81
New Lanark 104
'New Methods for the Diagnosis of the Intellectual Level of Subnormals' 31, 36
New Scientist 23, 28, 47, 48, 51, 54, 61, 164, 178–79
9/11 44
No Fear – Growing Up in a Risk Averse Society 106

No Two Alike: Human Nature and Human Individuality 86–87
Nobel Prize winners 37–38
noise, and learning 132
nonage 44
Nordström, Kjell 39
not teaching 169–70
novelty 86
nucleus accumbens 66
Nuffield Review Higher Education Focus Groups 123

OECD 52, 53, 95, 188–89
Opening Minds 121–22
Orwell, George 175
others, in childhood 94–95
outboard brain 29
outdoor education 105–6
Outliers 188
Outlook 11–12
outsourcing 17
Owen, Robert 104
ownership 167

Papert, Seymour 106
parents, and self-esteem 95
Pareto Principle 141
Parks, Rosa 117
pathos 87
Personal, Learning and Thinking Skills (PLTS) 13, 122
Peters, Tom 14, 16, 99–100, 131
pharmaceuticals, brain-enhancing 29
Philosophy for Children (P4C) 88, 91, 118, 135–39
physical position, and learning 130–31
physics 190–91
Piaget, Jean 62, 134–35
Planin, Robert 59
planning, role of pre-frontal cortex (PFC) 71–72
Plato 84
play 105
PLTS (personal, learning and thinking skills) 13, 122
Politics and the English Language 175
polycognitive curiosity engine 160–63

position, physical, and learning 130–31
positive emotions 85–86
Positivity – Groundbreaking Research Reveals How to Embrace the Hidden Strength of Positive Emotions, Overcome Negativity, land Thrive 85
Possibly Impossible Questions 136–37
pre-frontal cortex (PFC): and amygdalae 78; executive function 72–74; functions 70–72; influence on behaviour 71
Prince Charles 122–23
Principles of Class Teaching 110
problems, as opportunities 8
professional development 191–92
Programme for International School Assessment (PISA) 188–89
Prozac 96–97
pseudostupidity 65
PSHE 89
punishment 107

QCA 19–20
QCA project 123–26
qualifications 14–17
questions 87–88, 136–37

Rabelais 117
Rand, Ayn 118
Rapson, R. 182, 183
Re-imagine! 99–100
reassurance 179
reflection 144
reframing 166
registration, effective 153–54
Repository for Germinal Choice 38
research, learning how to learn (LHTL) 121
response times 139–40
Reul, Hans 61
reward, and dopamine production 82–83
Rich Harris, Judith 86–87
Richardson, Ken 34
Ridderstråle, Jonas 39
Ridley, Matt 57, 58
Ritalin 29

Robertson, Ian 60, 62
Robinson, P. 190
Rockefeller, J. D. 99
Roosevelt, Theodore 100
Rosenthal, R. 183
rote learning 154–55
Round Ireland with a Fridge 166
Rowe, Dorothy 178–79
RSA Competency Curriculum 13
rule-breaking, for success 16
*Rules to be Observed in Planning
    and Fitting Up Schools* 109
Russell, Bertrand 100
Russell, Willy 115
Ryan, Terry 101
Ryan, Will 168

Savage, John 69
Schachter, Daniel 149
school systems: early models 106–9;
    performance 187; structure 103
'School Systems Let Down Our
    Children' 172–73
schooling, as solitary 40
schools: age division 109–11;
    assessing quality 112–13; blocking
    access to information 27; learning
    schools 121; as sociable 40;
    suiting hours to students 67
'Science Competencies for
    Tomorrow's World' 188
Scientific American Mind 64
scientific management 100
sea squirt 67
Secrets of the Teenage Brain 66
Seldon, Anthony 89
self-esteem 19, 91–94; green
    environment 128; and memory
    148
self-worth 95; destruction of 18
Selig, Tina 8
Seligman, Martin 140
sensitive period, for brain
    development 53
serotonin 96–97
Seven Sins of Memory 149
Shockley, William 37–38
shouting 176–77, 179
Siegler, R. S. 33
silence 139

Simon, Theodore (Henri) 31–33
simultaneous language translation
    device 29
Singapore 189
Singhal, Amit 22
single chance education 120
skills-based curriculum 122–23
sleep deprivation 66–67
smartphones 23–24
Smidchens, Ildis 184
smiling 182–84
Smith, Adam 102
Smith, Jim 169, 174
Smith, Paul 97
Smithers, A. 190
social class: and examinations 115;
    and self-esteem 96
social jet lag 131
*Social Motivation: Understanding
    Children's School Adjustment* 19,
    94–95
socio-economic background 188
Somali culture 115
sorry 80
spacing effect 156–57
Spearman, Charles 57
spending 189
*Spens Report – The Report of the
    Consultative Committee on
    Secondary Education with Special
    Reference to Grammar Schools and
    Technical High Schools* 34–35, 36
Sperry, Roger 50–51
Spinoza, 91–92
Spitzer, Manfred 47
Stanford–Binet test 37
STAR 78–79
Storr, Anthony 93–94
Stow, David 110
Stray, Christopher 113–14
streaming 188
stress: dopamine production 82;
    effects on brain 61–62
structure 69
Struggling Teens website 73–74
students: empowering 192;
    involving 173–74
sub-prime mortgages 117–18
sub-vocal speech recognition 29
SuperMemo 156

Super Teaching 133
Superteaching 169
supply teachers 26
Surowiecki, James 159
suspense 86
sweetcorn kids 18
sympathy 87
synaptogenesis 81–82
systems of the mind 86–87

T4 programme 37
Taibbi, Matt 118
talking, limiting teacher's 169–70, 179
Tao of Leadership 170–71
Tao Te Ching 174
Taylor, Frederick W. 100
teacher-child ratio 189
teacher clichés 170
teacher training 191
teachers: alleviating fear 45; beliefs 126; as conduits and bottle necks 180; contributing to debates 192; drop out rates 190; enthusiasm 184; high ego 169; influence of 187; lazy 173, 180; modelling behaviour 80; qualified 109–10; quality of 189–90; recruitment 190, 191; retainment 191; role of 24; and self-esteem 95; stress 174; those remembered 187; understanding and using role of amygdalae 79–80; verbal abuse 176; voices 174–75
teaching: aims of 20; attributes for business success 12–13; and learning 120; reducing obstacles to learning 73
Teaching Assistants 173
teaching strategies 169
Teaching Students Through Their Individual Learning Styles 128
teams, in business 39–40
teamwork, as individual skill 40
technology: access to 27; convergence 28; effect on brain and IQ 27–28; future 28–29
temperature 131–32
Temple, Frederick 113
10,000 hours 38

Terman, Lewis 37
Terman's Termites 37
tests, ways to fail 143
'The Curse of Being Different' 164
The Economist 7, 13, 14, 17, 93
The Female Brain 175
The Fountainhead 118
The Great Educational Lie 16
The Guardian 7, 115
The Impact of Science on Society 100
The Infant System for Developing the Intellectual and Moral Powers of all Children, from One to Seven years of Age 104–5
The Kallikak Family: A Study in the Heredity of Feeble-Mindedness 36
The Lazy Teacher's Handbook 169, 174
The Little Book of Big Stuff About the Brain 47
The Little Book of Values 179
The Making of a Terrorist: Recruitment, Training, and Root Causes 6
The Making of Intelligence 34
The Observer 137
The Pre-Frontal Cortex 71–72
The Principles of Scientific Management 100
The Rose Review 122–23
The Spacing Effect; A Case Study in the Failure to Apply the Results of Psychological Research 155–56
The Teen Brain: Implications for Paediatric Nurses: The Brain Matures: Emotions and Development 77
The Telegraph 173
The Times 116, 172–73
The Tom Peters Seminar 14
The Triune Brain in Evolution: Role in Paleocerebral Functions 76
The Unemployables 12–13
The Unfinished Revolution 101
The Wealth of Nations 102
The World is Flat 10–11
thinking: adapting 3; convergent and divergent 43–45; for students 140
thinking walks 68

Thomas Deacon Academy 106
Thomas, Dylan 160
thought hand grenades 137
*Three Billion New Capitalists: The
  Great Shift of Wealth and Power
  to the East* 10
'three-legged stool' approach 140
Thunks 135–39, 142
Time 20
time of day 131
*TIMSS Advanced International
  Report* 190
TIMSS tests 188
Transfer Centre for Neuroscience
  and Learning 47
transhumanism 28–29
transition generation 8
transition, primary to secondary 110
transorbital lobotomy 71
triune brain theory 75–76

USA 189
Ustinov, Peter 102

VAK 146, 154
verbal abuse 176
Virgil 141
viva voce 114
voices: effects of 176; teachers'
  174–75

wait time 139–40
*Want to Remember Everything
  You'll Ever Learn? Surrender to
  This Algorithm* 156–57
warming up 178
Wellington College 89
Wentze, Kathryn R. 19, 94–95
White, Marco Pierre 44
Wichman, F. 150
Wikipedia 22–23
Wilderspin, Samuel 84–85, 104–5,
  106–7, 109, 110
'Will Designers Brains Divide
  Humanity?' 28
Williams, Robbie 95–96
winning 86–87
Winston, Robert 35
Wired 156–57
working with children 166
*World at Risk: The Report of the
  Commission on the Prevention
  of WMD Proliferation and
  Terrorism* 6
Wozniak, Pietr 156
Wright, Will 27

Zeedyk, M. S. 110
Zeigarnik Effect 132–33
Zippies 11–12